ASIA-PACIFIC
SUSTAINABLE DEVELOPMENT
JOURNAL

United Nations
New York, 2022

ASIA-PACIFIC
SUSTAINABLE DEVELOPMENT JOURNAL

Vol. 29, No. 1, May 2022

United Nations publication
Sales No. E.22.II.F.10
Copyright © United Nations 2022
All rights reserved
Printed in Thailand
ISBN: 9789211208429
e-ISBN: 9789210018364
ISSN (print): 2617-8400
ISSN (online): 2617-8419
ST/ESCAP/3018

Cover design: Nina Loncar

ABOUT ASIA-PACIFIC SUSTAINABLE DEVELOPMENT JOUNRAL

The Asia-Pacific Sustainable Development Journal (APSDJ) is published twice a year by the United Nations Economic and Social Commission for Asia and the Pacific (ESCAP). It is the continuation of ESCAP's Asia Pacific Development Journal (APDJ) with an explicit recognition of sustainable development in line with the United Nations 2030 Agenda for Sustainable Development.

APSDJ welcomes submissions of original contributions on themes and issues related to sustainable development that are policy-oriented and relevant to Asia and the Pacific. Articles should be centred on discussing challenges pertinent to one or more dimensions of sustainable development, policy options and implications and/or policy experiences that may be of benefit to the region. Editorial policy is to maintain a sound balance between theoretical and empirical studies, and to highlight policy relevance.

APSDJ particularly welcomes papers that deal with sustainable development issues using a multidisciplinary approach. Submissions may range from overviews spanning the region or parts of it, to papers with a detailed focus on issues facing individual countries.

APSDJ encourages submissions from researchers residing in countries in special situations, such as small island developing States (SIDS), least developed countries (LDCs) and economies in transition, as well as submissions that deal with challenges of such economies.

APSDJ provides a platform for policymakers to share their experiences. It also offers opportunities to academics and researchers in their early careers to develop their capacity for policy-oriented and applied research.

APSDJ publishes short notes, reflecting experiences in policy and practices, comments, and book reviews – not exceeding 3,000 words – in addition to full length research articles. From time to time, it also publishes special issues on matters of importance to economies in the Asia-Pacific region.

All manuscripts will undergo a rigorous double-blind peer-review process.

Manuscripts should be sent by email to the Managing Editor of the Asia-Pacific Sustainable Development Journal: escap-apsdj@un.org.

For more details, please visit www.unescap.org/publication-series/APSDJ.

ASIA-PACIFIC SUSTAINABLE DEVELOPMENT JOURNAL
Vol. 29, No. 1, May 2022
CONTENTS

Page

Editorial   vii

ESCAP secretariat   Survey: the state of sustainable development in Asia   1
                           and the Pacific

**Special theme: Macroeconomic policies
for inclusive sustainable development**

Valerie Cerra   A framework for inclusive and sustainable growth in   17
                           asia and the pacific

Sally Torbert   Impact of taxes and transfers on inequality in the   43
                           Asia-Pacific region

Peter J. Morgan   Central banks and financial inclusion   67

Thammarak Moenjak   Learning by doing: central bank digital currency in   103
                           Thailand

Invited paper

A. Mukherjee, S. Saha, S. C.   Impact of climate change and variability on food   119
Lellyett and A.K.S. Huda   security in the Asia-Pacific region

Early career researchers

Afnaan Ahmed, S. M. Raihan Uddin   Factors affecting consumer behaviour in mobile 143
and S. M. Rifat Hassan   financial services in Bangladesh

Policymakers' corner

Salehuddin Ahmed   Challenges of monetary policy in a developing   169
                           country

Bambang Brodjonegoro   Mainstreaming the Sustainable Development Goals   179
                           in Indonesia: an experience from the Ministry of
                           Development Planning 2016-2019

Book reviews

Prakash Loungani   *How to Achieve Inclusive Growth,* edited by Valerie   185
                           Cerra, Barry Eichengreen, Asmaa El-Ganainy, and
                           Martin Schindler

Bhim Bhurtel   *Fiscal and Monetary Policies in Developing Countries:* 191
                           State, Citizenship and Transformation, by Rashed Al
                           Mahmud Titumir

EXPLANATORY NOTES

References to dollars ($) are to United States dollars, unless otherwise stated.
References to "tons" are to metric tons, unless otherwise specified.
A solidus (/) between dates (e.g. 1980/81) indicates a financial year, a crop year or an academic year.
Use of a hyphen between dates (e.g. 1980-1985) indicates the full period involved, including the beginning and end years.

The following symbols have been used in the tables throughout the journal:
Two dots (..) indicate that data are not available or are not separately reported.
An em-dash (—) indicates that the amount is nil or negligible.
A hyphen (-) indicates that the item is not applicable.
A point (.) is used to indicate decimals.
A space is used to distinguish thousands and millions.
Totals may not add precisely because of rounding.

The designations employed and the presentation of the material in this publication do not imply the expression of any opinion whatsoever on the part of the Secretariat of the United Nations concerning the legal status of any country, territory, city or area or of its authorities, or concerning the delimitation of its frontiers or boundaries.

Where the designation "country or area" appears, it covers countries, territories, cities or areas.

Bibliographical and other references have, wherever possible, been verified. The United Nations bears no responsibility for the availability or functioning of URLs belonging to outside entities.

The opinions, figures and estimates set forth in this publication are the responsibility of the authors and should not necessarily be considered as reflecting the views or carrying the endorsement of the United Nations. Mention of firm names and commercial products does not imply the endorsement of the United Nations.

EDITORIAL

I am pleased to introduce this year's first issue of the *Asia-Pacific Sustainable Development Journal* (APSDJ, vol. 29, No. 1, May 2022) under reconstituted Editorial and Advisory Boards that capture the regional diversity of the region.

The new Boards have introduced some major changes in editorial policies with regard to the scope and objectives of the *Journal*, reflecting the commitment of ESCAP to the Countries in Special Situations, comprising the least developed countries, landlocked developing countries and small island developing States, to capacity development and to the promotion of policy dialogues.

The *Journal* will welcome original research papers which can inform policymakers about feasible and pragmatic solutions to sustainable development challenges in the Asia-Pacific region. It will also include policy dialogues, submissions by "early career researchers" and book reviews.

The current issue includes a comprehensive survey of sustainable development in the Asia-Pacific region. It shows that the COVID-19 pandemic has affected all aspects of societies and economies. As of early March 2022, there were 252 million cases of COVID-19 in Asia and the Pacific with 2.9 million deaths, representing approximately 57 per cent and 48 per cent, respectively, of official global totals. The pandemic pushed an estimated 85 million people back into extreme poverty, defined as living on $1.90 or less per day. COVID-19 has highlighted inequalities in terms of access to vaccines, diagnostics, therapeutics and medicines, both within and between countries and communities, and has exacerbated the vulnerabilities that have built up over the years. Climate change and environmental destruction have added to a daunting spectrum of hazards emanating from natural and human-made sources. Indeed, the region is the most disaster-prone in the world.

This issue has four original articles on macroeconomic policies for inclusive sustainable development. "A framework for inclusive and sustainable growth in Asia and the Pacific," by Valerie Cerra, lays out a comprehensive and integrated inclusive growth framework and applies it to the Asia-Pacific region to discuss policy options for achieving inclusive and sustainable growth. "The impact of taxes and transfers on inequality in the Asia-Pacific region," by Sally Torbert, reviews studies for 12 countries to assess the impact of fiscal policies, such as targeted direct transfers, education spending and tax policies on inequality. "Central banks and financial inclusion," by Peter Morgan, surveys the policies of central banks and other financial regulators in a number of emerging economies to promote financial inclusion to identify successful experiences and important lessons. In particular, it reviews policies of central banks adopted during the COVID-19 pandemic. "Learning-by-doing: central bank digital currency in Thailand," by Thammarak Moenjak, provides insights into issues relating to the introduction of a central bank digital currency into the economy, as well as how a public institution such as a central bank can go about exploring the use of cutting-edge technologies in public policy for the purposes of financial inclusion.

Two original research papers are included in this issue: "Impact of climate change and variability on food security in the Asia-Pacific region," by Mukherje, Saha, Lellyett and Huda, highlights the effects of climate variability on food production and recommends adaptive climate-smart agricultural measures, from local practices to policy-level initiatives, to help address the 2030 Agenda for Sustainable Development, and future food security in the region; and "Factors affecting consumer behaviour in mobile financial services in Bangladesh," an early career research paper by Ahmed, Uddin and Hassan, identifies the determinants of consumer behaviour of mobile financial services and draws important policy implications for financial inclusion.

The issue contains two policy dialogue papers: one, "Challenges of monetary policy in a developing country" by Salehuddin Ahmed, former Governor of the Central Bank of Bangladesh, discusses relevant and pragmatic policies that are heterogeneous, unconventional and implementable for financial sector stability; and the other, "Mainstreaming the Sustainable Development Goals in Indonesia: an experience from the Ministry of Development Planning 2016–2019" by Bambang Brodjonegoro, former Minister of Finance, former Minister of National Development Planning and former Minister of Research and Technology of Indonesia, discusses that country's experiences in mainstreaming the Sustainable Development Goals in government planning.

The issue also includes two book reviews. Prakash Loungani reviews *How to Achieve Inclusive Growth*, edited by Valerie Cerra, Barry Eichengreen, Asmaa El-Ganainy and Martin Schindler; and Bhim Bhurtel reviews *Fiscal and Monetary Policies in Developing Countries: State, Citizenship and Transformation*, by Rashed Al Mahmud Titumir. The focus of both books complements the special theme of the issue, "Macroeconomic policies for inclusive sustainable development".

Policymakers, academics, researchers and development practitioners will find this issue of the *Journal* extremely useful and interesting.

Armida Salsiah Alisjahbana

Under-Secretary-General of the United Nations and
Executive Secretary of ESCAP

SURVEY: THE STATE OF SUSTAINABLE DEVELOPMENT IN ASIA AND THE PACIFIC

ESCAP secretariat

Introduction

For decades the Asia-Pacific region has been driving global economic growth despite occasional setbacks, such as the collapse of economies in Central Asia immediately following the breakdown of the Soviet Union in 1991 and the 1997–98 Asian financial crisis. Most of the countries in the region have also done well in achieving the Millennium Development Goals (MDGs). In fact, the attainment of the single most critical MDG – halving the global poverty rate – was due to rapid declines in extreme poverty in the region.

The progress has also been reflected in the eligibility of some countries in the region to graduate from the category of least developed countries (LDCs). For example, the small island States, Maldives, Samoa and Vanuatu graduated in 2011, 2014 and 2020, respectively while Solomon Islands is scheduled to graduate in 2024. Bangladesh, the Lao People's Democratic Republic and Nepal were granted a five-year preparatory period leading to graduation by 2026, according to resolution 76/8 of the General Assembly, adopted on 24 November 2021 and Bhutan is due to graduate in 2023.

However, the region has also witnessed a rise in inequality within many countries, with some of the countries having disproportionately more super-rich given their level of per capita income. Ironically, some LDCs are among the countries experiencing the fastest growth in the number of billionaires. The region has also been slow in addressing other inequalities, such as gender disparity, inequities in access to clean water and energy, and digital and rural/urban divides. Many forms of exclusion hinder progress towards achieving the Sustainable Development Goals (SDGs), and multidimensional poverty is up to 10 times higher among people of disadvantaged ethnicities, races or castes.

Asia and the Pacific is the world's most vulnerable region to climate change. In 2020, extreme weather and climate change impacts across the region caused thousands of deaths, displaced millions of people, and cost hundreds of billions of dollars, while wreaking a heavy toll on infrastructure and ecosystems. As documented by the World Meteorological Organization in *The State of the Climate in Asia 2020,* "every part of Asia was affected, from Himalayan peaks to low-lying coastal areas, from densely populated cities to deserts and from the Arctic to the Arabian seas." The intersection of poverty and climate change often impacts the livelihoods of many vulnerable people, especially women, who account for the majority of agriculture sector workers in some regions.

As the region houses several 'factories of the world', it produced 16.75 billion metric tons of carbon dioxide emissions in 2020, a drop of 0.53 billion metric tons from 2019, perhaps due to pandemic-related declines in economic activity. Although in aggregate terms, this was still more than the combined total emissions of all other regions that year, in per capita terms, the region's greenhouse gas emissions are far less than those of many industrial countries, reflecting the region's overall state of development.

Rising inequality and adverse climate change impacts have significantly impaired sustainable development in the region. At the current rate of change, none of the 17 SDGs will be achieved in all five Asia-Pacific subregions. The COVID-19 pandemic dealt further blows to the SDGs, pushing 85 million people into extreme poverty, based on a threshold of $1.90 per day or less. For many vulnerable populations, food security, education and livelihoods have deteriorated during the pandemic.

The present paper provides a comprehensive survey of the state of sustainable development in the region, and it serves to highlight the impact of the COVID-19 pandemic. It is based on the ESCAP flagship publication, *Economic and Social Survey of Asia and the Pacific 2022: Economic Policies for an Inclusive Recovery and Development,* the Commission's 2022 Theme Study, *Reclaiming Our Future: A Common Agenda for Advancing Sustainable Development in Asia and the Pacific* and the ESCAP publication *Asia and the and the Pacific SDG Progress Report 2022: Widening disparities amid COVID-19.*

Uneven progress towards the Sustainable Development Goals

Figure 1 provides a snapshot of SDG progress and illustrates that substantial improvement is still required to achieve most of the goals. While the region has made progress towards several of the goals, further action is needed for the region to achieve its 2030 ambitions. As seen in figure 1, the progress across the 17 SDGs has been uneven and the region is unlikely to achieve any of the SDGs by the target year 2030. Significantly, the region has regressed in climate action (SDG 17) and responsible consumption and production (Goal 12). Nevertheless, the progress on affordable and clean energy (Goal 7) and industry, innovation and infrastructure (Goal 9) has been significant.

Figure 1. Progress towards SDGs in Asia and the Pacific

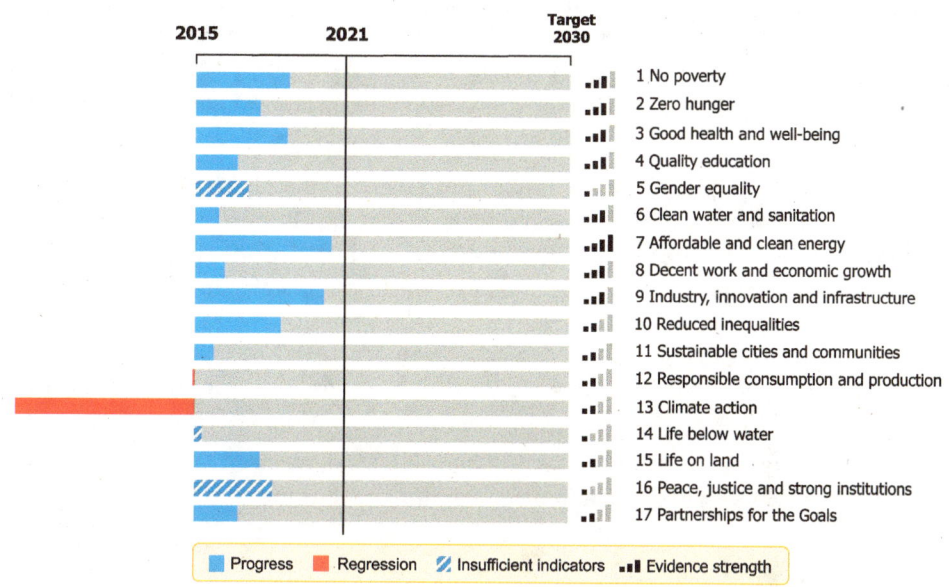

As shown in figure 2, the progress gap for achieving the SDGs grows wider and the prospect of achieving the SDGs now extends decades beyond 2030. In 2017, the estimated year to achieve the SDGs was 2052, and by 2021, the estimated year had increased to 2065. At the current rate of progress in Asia and the Pacific (with 12 per cent of the required progress made as of 2021), the 2030 Agenda for Sustainable Development will only be achieved by 2065, and none of the five subregions will achieve all of the 17 SDGs by 2030. Only East and North-East Asia is on track towards no poverty (Goal 1) and industry, innovation and infrastructure (Goal 9) (figure 3).

Figure 2. Estimated year to achieve the SDGs at the current pace in Asia and the Pacific

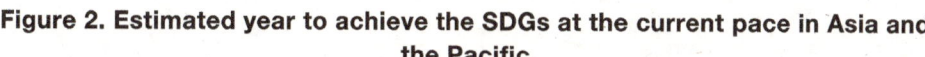

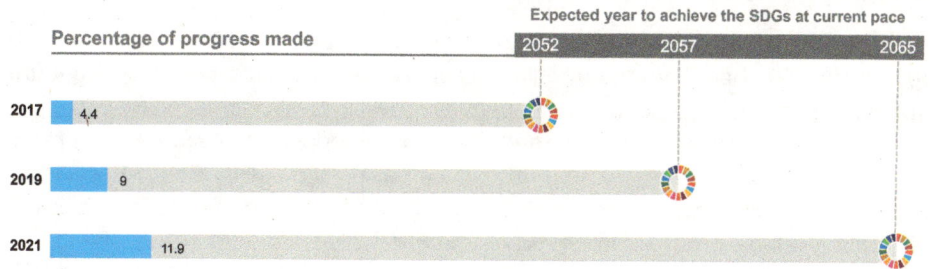

Apart from Goal 1 and Goal 9 in East and North-East Asia, the Asia-Pacific subregions are not on track to achieve the SDGs by 2030. There was some progress towards partnership for the goals (Goal 17) in East and North-East Asia, but not enough to be on track to achieve the goal by 2030. Alarmingly, every Asia-Pacific subregion has regressed on responsible consumption and production (Goal 12) and climate action (Goal 13).

In addition to regression on Goal 12 and Goal 13, the North and Central Asia subregion has regressed on life below water (Goal 14); the Pacific subregion has regressed on clean water and sanitation (Goal 6), reduced inequalities (Goal 10) and sustainable cities and communities (Goal 11); the South-East Asia subregion has regressed on Goal 6, Goal 11 and Goal 14; and the South and South-West Asia subregion has regressed on Goal 11. Negative trends have been found on five goals in South-East Asia and the Pacific, and three subregions are regressing on Goal 11.

Figure 3. Subregional Sustainable Development Goal progress in Asia-Pacific subregions

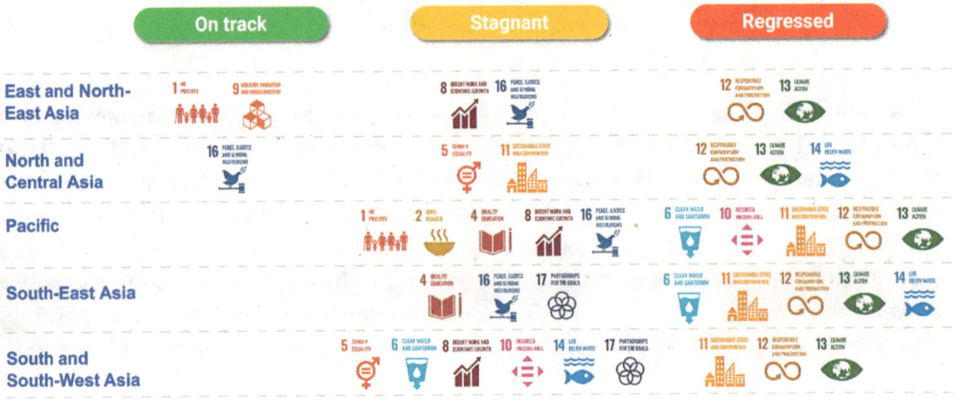

Impacts of the COVID-19 pandemic

According to latest estimates, 85 million people were pushed back into extreme poverty in 2021, based on the threshold of $1.90 per day. When considering higher income thresholds of $3.20 and $5.50 per day, poverty levels increased by 156 million and 160 million, respectively (figure 4). The South and South-West Asia subregion accounts for more than 80 per cent of this increase, followed by South-East Asia at 18 per cent. Thus, the persistence of high levels of poverty induced by the pandemic will erase years of progress in poverty reduction.

Figure 4. Increase in poverty in the Asia-Pacific region in 2021 due to the pandemic

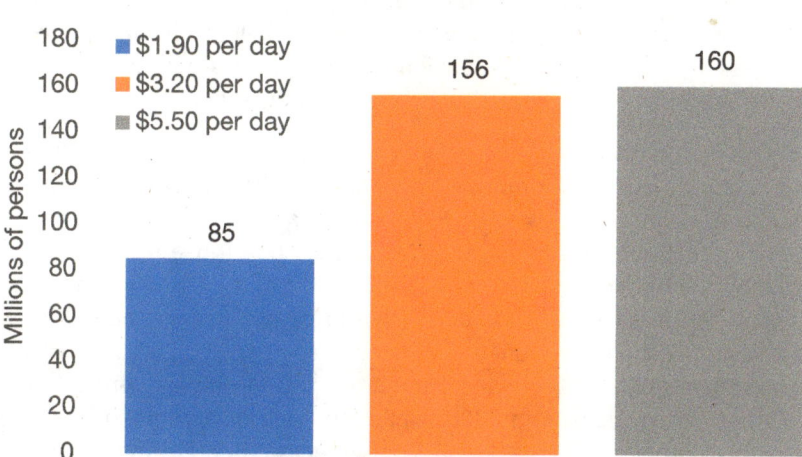

The Asia-Pacific region lost 8.2 per cent of working hours in 2020 relative to the fourth quarter of 2019, which is equivalent to 155 million full-time workers (assuming a 48-hour work week). Even though the situation improved slightly in 2021, working hour losses have continued, and working hours are expected to remain 3.9 per cent below the 2019 benchmark. The two subregions that experienced the highest working hour losses in 2021 are South-East Asia (7.3 per cent) and South and South-West Asia (7.0 per cent).

Employment in the region declined by an estimated 62 million jobs between 2019 and 2020. Regional unemployment increased from 96 million in 2019 to 115 million in 2020, and the unemployment rate (SDG indicator 8.5.2) rose from 4.5 to 5.5 per cent. In 2021, the regional unemployment rate is estimated to have remained at an elevated 5.0 per cent, which is considerably higher than before the crisis. Many more workers have moved into inactivity or have remained on significantly reduced working hours. Among the inactive are many women who lost their jobs or left paid work when household and care responsibilities increased during periods of lockdown.

The rate of employment loss among women in 2020 in the Asia-Pacific region was 3.4 per cent compared to 2.9 per cent for men. Employment of young people shrank by as much as 8.4 per cent compared to 2.3 per cent for adult employment. The number of youth not in employment, education or training has been driven up in some countries of the region (SDG indicator 8.6.1). A heavier impact of the COVID-19 pandemic on the employment of women compared to men and youth compared to adults has been found in nearly all subregions.

Since the onset of the pandemic, informal workers have been the first to suffer adverse impacts due to job insecurity, low skills and lack of social safety nets. Within the region, informal employment to total employment is as high as 95 per cent. Lockdowns had adverse impacts on some 829 million informal workers across the region; subsequently, multidimensional poverty levels doubled, and 71 million children did not have access to online learning during school closures.

Within many countries, women make up a higher proportion of workers in informal employment. Such workers comprise a high share in such sectors as food services, tourism-related services, and wholesale and retail trade, construction, domestic work and labour-intensive segments of manufacturing, such those related to garments. Thus, women are disproportionately affected by job and income losses as all these sectors were the most severely affected by the pandemic. The pandemic led to a decrease in women's employment of 3.8 per cent compared with 2.9 per cent for men in Asia and the Pacific. In 2021, the number of men in employment was projected to have offset the job losses in 2020, while the number of women in employment likely remained below pre-crisis levels. Moreover, women are more likely to leave their jobs to care for families and children during prolonged closures of businesses, schools and care services. The disproportionate effects of the pandemic on women's employment have been called the "she-cession". Youth, on the other hand, faced fewer job prospects, lower pay and fewer opportunities for skill development, all of which will have impacts on their future productivity potential.

There has been a huge learning loss among students at different levels owing to school closures during the pandemic, contributing to a further deterioration of learning outcomes in the Asia-Pacific region. The COVID-19 pandemic has disrupted health services everywhere, including in the region. In 2020, an estimated 8 million children across the region missed routine vaccinations, an increase of approximately 2.5 million from 2019.

Disruptions in health and food systems alongside economic contractions created by the COVID-19 pandemic threatened household food security and diet quality. Surveys conducted in 2020 found that 87 per cent of households in Manila and 66 per cent of households in Jakarta were worried about food in the previous month, an increase of nearly 50 per cent for both countries from 2018 baseline estimates. The surveys found the diets of young children in Indonesia and the Philippines were severely impacted by pandemic-related changes, with reductions of 32 per cent and 68 per cent respectively in the share of children meeting minimum diet diversity. Survey data from Asia and the Pacific substantiated common disruptions to the provision of wasting treatment services during the COVID-19 pandemic.

There was significant increase in violence against women during the pandemic, and violence against women was already highly prevalent in the region before the pandemic. With pre-COVID-19 data ranging from 15 per cent to 64 per cent of women experiencing physical and/or sexual violence at the hands of an intimate partner over their lifetime, Internet searches for "domestic violence signs" and "experiencing sexual violence", increased sharply since the pandemic began.

Pandemic-related closures of borders and restrictions on movement have made it considerably more difficult for people fleeing war and persecution to find safety outside their countries of origin. At the peak of the pandemic in 2020, some 28 countries in the region had closed their borders, and only eight States granted exceptions for people seeking asylum (a number that eventually doubled to 16 by the end of 2020). Country case studies show that the pandemic has disproportionally impacted the livelihoods of refugees. For example, in Malaysia, 80 per cent of refugees reported a loss of income due to the pandemic.

Persons with disabilities experienced difficulties in accessing health care and essential support services, as well as financial hardship and job losses during the pandemic. For example, in Malaysia, 44 per cent of persons with disabilities could not access the services they needed, and 34 per cent wanted more child-friendly and accessible information. Similarly, in the Philippines, major concerns cited by nearly 40,000 survey respondents included the inability to access essential services, specifically education services and learning resources (52 per cent), child development services (51 per cent), habilitation and rehabilitation services (49 per cent), and general health services (43 per cent). In the Philippines, the pandemic affected the employment of 70 per cent of surveyed persons with disabilities. In Viet Nam, 30 per cent of persons with disabilities lost their employment due to the pandemic.

The pandemic also negatively impacted the mental health of older persons. According to preliminary surveys, 42 per cent of older persons felt depressed due to the overall situation related to COVID-19, with more women than men feeling depressed. Isolation, neglect, denial of resources and physical abuse have also been major concerns. Fifty-one per cent of older men and 32 per cent of older women felt that they were at higher risk of emotional abuse as a result of COVID-19 than they were before.

Low social protection coverage in the region has been a major factor for the disproportionate impact of the pandemic on vulnerable people. Only 16 countries in the region have achieved universal coverage with some form of pension. In 20 countries, less than half of all older people receive some form of pension, which means that more than half of the older population is vulnerable to poverty.

Box 1. Potential scarring effects of COVID-19

Globally, long-term damage to potential output from previous pandemics is estimated at close to 3 per cent of gross domestic product (GDP). The impacts of the current pandemic could be larger because of its global scale and complexity. Earning loss for developing countries in the region is estimated at $1.25 trillion or 5.4 per cent of GDP in 2020.

A unique effect of the COVID-19 pandemic is the learning and earning loss from prolonged school closures. Full and partial closure of schools varied across countries in the region with the highest full closure being up to 63 weeks (see figure). The digital divide also meant that those lacking access to the Internet were deprived of learning opportunities as teaching shifted to online formats. Learning losses and earning gaps in developing countries in the Asia-Pacific region were higher for the poorest quintile relative to the richest. The impact of short-term disruptions, such as school closures and postponed or cancelled assessments and qualifications, are likely to have long-term consequences on learning and earning potential.

Pandemic-induced school closures in selected Asia-Pacific countries

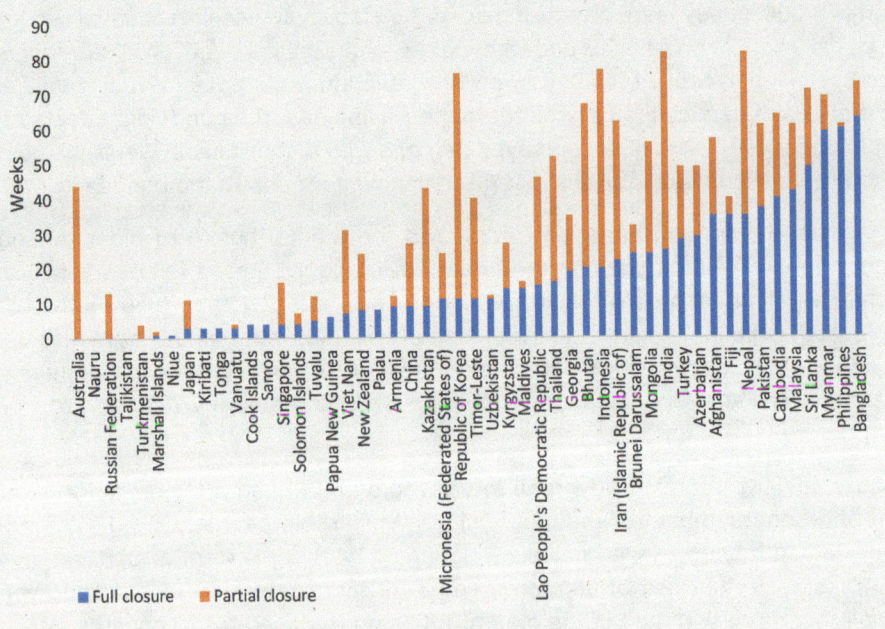

Source: UNESCO global dataset on school closures.

Economic, social and environmental impacts of climate change

While there has been a substantial decline in loss of life from disasters in the past decade, ESCAP estimated that since 1970, natural hazards in the region affected 6.9 billion people and killed more than 2 million. In terms of forecasted climate change impacts, ESCAP estimated total annual average losses from multiple hazards under the worst-case scenario (representative concentration pathway (RCP) 8.5) to be approximately $1.4 trillion.

In 2020 floods and storms affected approximately 50 million people in Asia and resulted in more than 5,000 fatalities. This is below the annual average of the past two decades (158 million people affected and approximately 15,500 fatalities) due to the success of early warning systems in many countries in Asia.

Tropical cyclones, floods and droughts induced an estimated average annual loss of several hundred billion dollars, according to ESCAP. Losses were estimated at approximately $238 billion in China, $87 billion in India and $83 billion in Japan. Relative to gross domestic product (GDP), the average annual loss is expected to be as high as 7.9 per cent ($7.5 billion) for Tajikistan, 5.9 per cent ($ 24.5 billion) for Cambodia and 5.8 per cent ($17.9 billion) for the Lao People's Democratic Republic. The highest average annual losses are associated with drought.

In 2020, intense cyclones, monsoon rains and floods hit highly exposed and densely populated areas in South Asia and East Asia and led to the displacement of millions of people in China, Bangladesh, India, Japan, Pakistan, Nepal and Viet Nam. Cyclone Amphan, one of the strongest cyclones ever recorded, hit the Sundarbans region between India and Bangladesh in May 2020, displacing 2.4 million people in India and 2.5 million people in Bangladesh.

Progress on food security and nutrition has also slowed down. In 2020, an estimated 48.8 million people in South-East Asia, 305.7 million in South Asia and 42.3 million in West Asia were undernourished. Asia accounts for more than half of the global total. The true impacts of COVID-19 on food security and nutrition are yet to be established, but compared with 2019, the number of undernourished people in 2020 increased by 6 per cent in South-East Asia and West Asia, and by 20 per cent in South Asia. Climate-related disasters compounded the problem.

Data show that areas with high rates of multidimensional poverty are also areas with high exposure to climate related natural as well as biological hazards. The overlaps of poverty with extremely high exposure to natural and biological hazards lead to cascading risks and cyclical and intergenerational poverty, which can negatively affect the achievement of the SDGs.

An analysis by ESCAP shows that populations with lower scores on the Human Development Index are at increased risks from multiple natural and biological hazards under moderate (RCP4.5) and severe (RCP8.5) climate change scenarios. The poor populations at greatest risk under RCP8.5 live in Bangladesh, India and Nepal in South and South-West Asia; the Lao People's Democratic Republic, Myanmar and the Philippines in South-East Asia; Kyrgyzstan and Tajikistan in North and Central Asia; China in East and North-East Asia; and Papua New Guinea in the Pacific. The top five countries at the greatest increased risk between 2020 and 2040 are Pakistan, Afghanistan, Bhutan, Myanmar and Cambodia.

Rural women in Asia and the Pacific play a large role in rural economies and are, therefore, disproportionately impacted by climate change. In some countries, such as the Lao People's Democratic Republic, nearly 64 per cent of employed women are engaged in agriculture. Similarly, in Nepal and Bangladesh, the shares of women in agriculture employment are 60 and 50 per cent, respectively. Women in agriculture, forestry and fishing are also more likely than women in non-agricultural sectors to engage in the informal sector (for example, the rate is 1.6 times higher in Brunei Darussalam).

Changing weather patterns will also affect access to drinking water, and firewood for cooking may also become limited. This is likely to increase women's burden and time spent on unpaid work. For example, women and girls in 67 per cent of households in Viet Nam are responsible for water collection. A large share of women live in households that primarily use wood for cooking, up to 72 per cent in Cambodia and 59 per cent in Myanmar.

Climate change and extreme weather conditions are also adversely affecting the environment and biodiversity. Glacier retreat and the dwindling of freshwater resources have major repercussions for water security and ecosystems in Asia, and the decline of coral reefs will negatively affect food security. Mangroves in Bangladesh, exposed to tropical storms, decreased by 19 per cent from 1992 to 2019. Forest cover declined in Myanmar (26 per cent), Cambodia (24 per cent) and the Democratic People's Republic of Korea (12 per cent). The frequency and intensity of dust storms are increasing due to land-use and land-cover changes and climate-related factors particularly in regions such as Central Asia.

Rising inequality

Even if reducing extreme poverty is considered as a measure of success, inequalities of opportunities and outcomes have remained persistent and have even risen in many economies in Asia and the Pacific. Income inequality increased in the region between the 1990s and 2010s when it was generally decreasing in other parts of the world (figure 5a). More recent estimates show that income inequality has increased for about 85 per cent of the region's population since 2000 (figure 5b). The income share of the top 10 per cent of people was close to 50 per cent of the total while the bottom 10 per cent account for only 0.2 per cent of that share (figure 5c).

Figure 5. Persistent and rising inequality in Asia and the Pacific

(a) Changes to Gini index between the early 1990s and early 2010s, by region

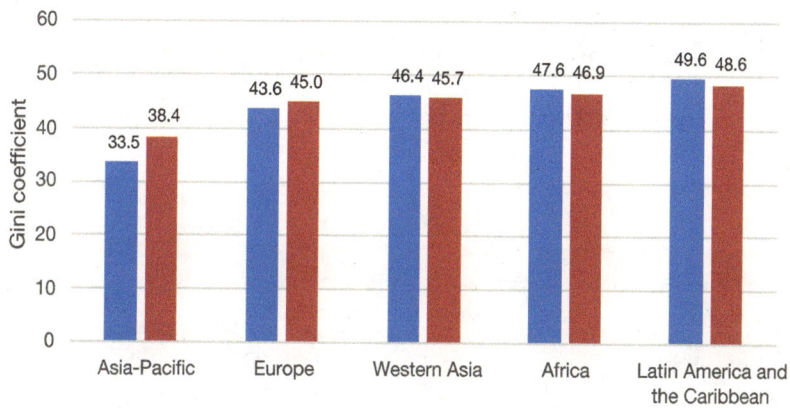

(b) Gini index in Asia-Pacific subregions between the early 2000s and 2020 or latest available year

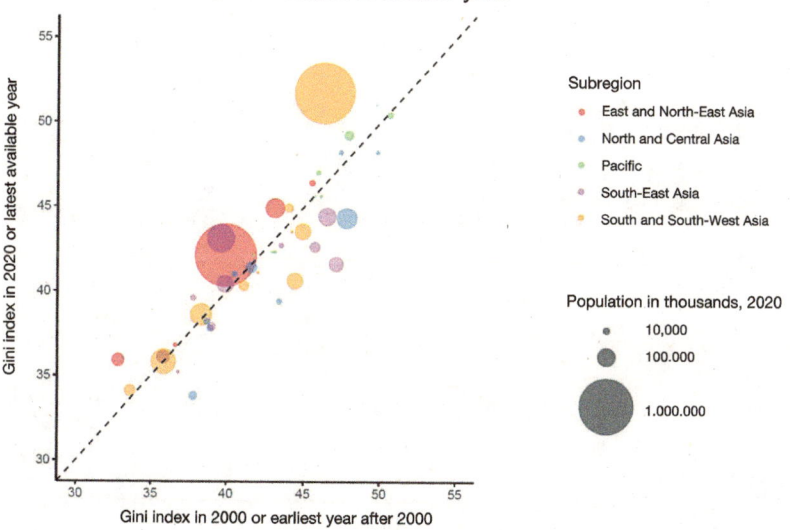

Source: The Standardized World Income Inequality Database, available at www.wider.unu.edu/database/world-income-inequality-database-wiid (accessed on 23 June 2021); and 2019 Revision of World Population Prospects, available at https://population.un.org/wpp/ (accessed on 23 June 2021).

Note: The dotted line is at a 45 degree slope.

(c) Pre-tax income share by income group in Asia, selected years

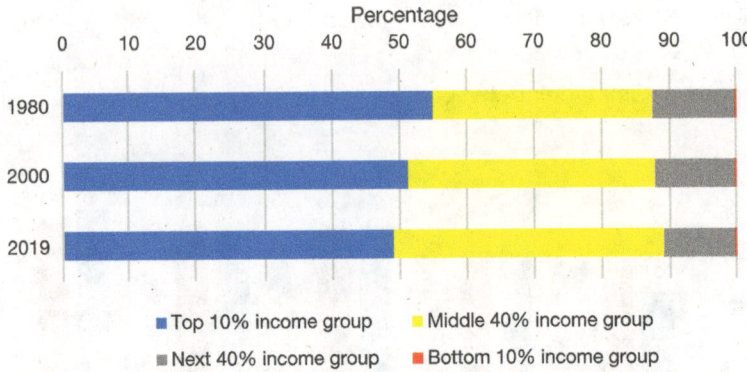

Source: World Inequality Database, available at https://wid.world/data/ (accessed on 7 June 2021).

Intergenerational mobility has declined in the Asia-Pacific region for cohorts born between 1940 and 1980 (figure 6), indicating widening inequalities in opportunities.

Figure 6. Mobility education in Asia and the Pacific, 1940–1980 birth cohorts

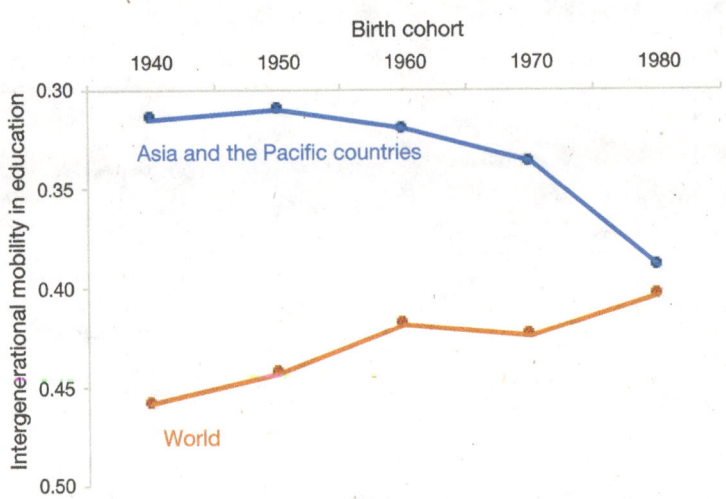

Source: World Bank (2018). Global Database on Intergenerational Mobility (accessed on 28 May 2021).

Note: The vertical axis shows intergenerational persistence, but in reverse order. Hence, if a line goes up, it means improved intergenerational mobility; if it goes down, it means worsened intergenerational mobility. The median value is taken to estimate intergenerational persistence/mobility for the Asia-Pacific region and the world.

Using household survey data of 27 countries in the region, ESCAP developed an index of inequality of access to opportunities and barriers in eight areas: basic water and sanitation (WASH); child nutrition; education; sexual and reproductive health care; violence against women; energy; financial inclusion; and Internet use. Inequality in both access to opportunities and barriers is measured by the Dissimilarity Index (D-Index). The results reveal a mixed picture of fairly equal access to approximately half of these basic services, but the rest show inequalities and marginalization.

Inequality of opportunity is high in use of the Internet, access to financial services and tertiary education where attendance is unequal in several countries in South and South West Asia and in South-East Asia. Inequality is also high in the use of clean fuels, an area that links health with environmental quality. It is the most unequally distributed opportunity in approximately half of the 27 countries in the analysis.

The level of inequality in the use of clean fuels is highest in Papua New Guinea, Bangladesh, the Lao People's Democratic Republic and Kiribati, and lowest in Kazakhstan, Maldives and Armenia. Papua New Guinea, Afghanistan, Timor-Leste, the Lao People's Democratic Republic and Kiribati stand out with above average inequality in many development areas.

Using classification and regression tree (CART) analysis, ESCAP identified population groups with the lowest access to basic opportunities (e.g. education and skilled birth attendance) or with the highest prevalence of barriers (e.g. stunting and violence against women) based on their shared circumstances. The groups left furthest behind are not the same across different development areas or countries. For example, while women are more frequently found in the furthest behind groups in education completion, men are worse off in some countries. Generally, living in a household in the bottom 40 per cent of the wealth distribution is strongly associated with vulnerabilities across development areas. Most frequently, people in the most vulnerable conditions experience material poverty combined with other factors, such as living in rural areas, age and sex.

However, in some cases, such as access to financial services and the likelihood of overweight or wasting, a greater disadvantage is formed by the interaction of other circumstances, such as rural/urban residence, sex or age. For instance, urban children with no siblings (or just one sibling) are more likely to be overweight, irrespective of their family's wealth.

Uneven and K-shaped recovery

After experiencing a contraction in 2020 owing to the COVID-19 pandemic, developing countries in Asia and the Pacific recovered strongly in the first half of 2021, thanks to robust external demand for the region's exports and sustained monetary and fiscal support (figure 7). Despite setbacks caused by the Delta variant of COVID-19, developing countries in the Asia-Pacific region recovered from a contraction in economic activity of 0.3 per cent in 2020 to an estimated expansion of 7.1 per cent in 2021.

Figure 7. Year-on-year change in gross domestic product in developing countries, by Asia-Pacific subregion, 2019–2021

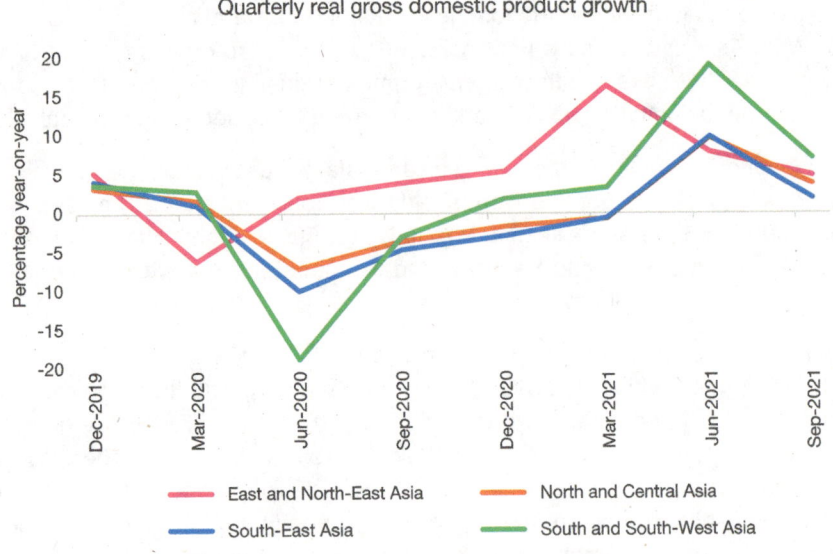

Quarterly real gross domestic product growth

Source: Based on CEIC Data. Available at www.ceicdata.com/en (accessed on 4 March 2022).

Note: Subregional aggregates are the weighted average, based on 28 economies in Asia and the Pacific for which quarterly data on gross domestic product are available.

However, despite strong rebounds in the growth of output in developing Asia-Pacific countries in 2021, output was still approximately 2 per cent below the pre-pandemic trend as of the end of 2021. The recovery has been uneven across subregions and across different sectors. On the one hand, the manufacturing sector benefited from the rising global demand for goods from the region and has seen sustained growth since mid-2020. On the other hand, mobility restrictions and border closures had a severe impact on the transportation and hospitality sectors. Despite improvement in both sectors, they have yet to return to their pre-COVID-19 levels. The tourism sector has yet to recover due to a host of factors. By the end of 2021, approximately 65 per cent of borders were still closed. Tourist arrivals in Asia and the Pacific are

92 per cent below pre-pandemic levels, although improvements were seen in the last months of 2021.

Formal employment seems to have partially recovered in 2021, as losses in working hours declined. For Asia and the Pacific in 2021 estimated working hour loses declined to 4 per cent compared with 8.2 per cent in 2020, indicating some adjustments to pandemic-related restrictions. This translates into 71 million full-time job losses in 2021 compared with 145 million in the previous year.

The divergence in employment recovery is also seen in more rapid recovery in sectors such as information and communications technology, wholesale and retail segment and manufacturing. Contact-intensive sectors, such as accommodation and food services, have not seen a substantial improvement.

Given inequality, disparity and exclusion in the region, the recovery is K-shaped both between and within countries. Such a recovery will worsen pre-COVID-19 vulnerabilities in a region that was already behind on all SDGs before the pandemic.

Between countries, different recovery trajectories, unequal vaccine access and differences in stimulus measures are observed. Within countries, vast differences in recovery among sectors and opportunity gaps among sections of society are contributing to increased poverty and inequalities, and undermining progress towards achieving the SDG, in particular the goal of ending extreme poverty and the pledge of the 2030 Agenda of to leave no one behind. It highlights that an integral part of strategies for rebuilding must be equitable access and opportunities.

Regional cooperation

Regional cooperation will play a critical role in averting a K-shaped recovery. Regional cooperation is needed to reopen economies safely and restore travel, trade and value chains while adequately addressing sustainability and climate change. Regional cooperation also should support people-centred development pathways, through strengthening health-care systems and public health emergency preparedness and tackling long-standing weaknesses of social protection systems. Regional cooperation should strive to foster to new forms of cooperation in finance, especially digital finance, to improve access to financial resources in less developed countries. The pandemic has demonstrated the need to refocus economic cooperation on inclusion, sustainability and resilience. Regional cooperation on digital connectivity for the 2030 Agenda is critical to enabling equitable digitalization in the region to strengthen resilience to external shocks. Physical and digital connectivity can both enable and be enabled by regional cooperation.

SPECIAL THEME: MACROECONOMIC POLICIES FOR INCLUSIVE SUSTAINABLE DEVELOPMENT

Special theme: Macroeconomic policies for inclusive sustainable development

A FRAMEWORK FOR INCLUSIVE AND SUSTAINABLE GROWTH IN ASIA AND THE PACIFIC

Valerie Cerra

International Monetary Fund[1]
Email: vcerra@imf.org

The Asia-Pacific region faces extraordinary challenges due to economic and social disparities, made worse by the COVID-19 pandemic and rising vulnerabilities caused by climate change. Addressing these challenges will require a holistic and unified plan of action for combatting these economic and social disparities. The present paper serves to outline a comprehensive and integrated inclusive growth framework and apply it to the Asia-Pacific region. It also contains a discussion of policy options for achieving inclusive and sustainable growth.

Keywords: inclusive growth, growth, inequality, poverty, well-being, policy framework, sustainable development

JEL classification: I30, O40

---

1 The views expressed herein are those of the author and should not be attributed to the IMF, its Executive Board, or its management.

I. INTRODUCTION

Economic growth has powered improvements in average living standards. Since 1990 alone, extreme poverty declined by more than a billion people globally, mainly due to strong growth in China, India and other populous Asian countries. Likewise, economic growth is correlated with other outcomes. Globally, it has contributed to a dramatic rise in educational attainment and literacy, vast improvements in health, and a strong increase in the share of the world living in a democracy.

Yet, stark inequality across Asia and the Pacific and within countries of the region creates vast differences in living conditions and millions remain in poverty. Growth has been distributed unevenly, creating large income differences between countries. Gross domestic product (GDP) per capita on average from 2010 to 2019 ranges from more than $80,000 in Singapore and Macao, China, to less than $3,000 in several Pacific Island and Central Asian countries, expressed in comparable international prices.

Within country inequality has an increasing impact on economic well-being. National growth is not enough to ensure the improvement of individual welfare. Within-country inequality has risen in many advanced economies and several large emerging market economics (notably China, India, Indonesia and the Russian Federation) between the 1990s and 2010s.

The COVID-19 pandemic exposed and amplified existing inequalities. It impacted low-income people more than those at the upper end of the distribution, as they were more vulnerable to losing their jobs and had less access to high quality medical care. In addition, because their jobs required more person-to-person contact, low-income people were more at risk of exposure to the virus. The COVID-19 pandemic was expected to push an additional 89 million people in Asia and the Pacific into extreme poverty (ESCAP, 2021).

The pandemic also threatens economic and social scarring. Lower-income countries and vulnerable populations risk falling further behind (Cerra, Fatas and Saxena, 2021). The pandemic has intensified pre-existing gaps in the labour market and in education. Employment losses have been larger for women, youth and low-skilled workers (Alon and others, 2020). Likewise, developing countries have had longer school closures during the pandemic compared with advanced countries and they typically have substantial digital divides (Agarwal, 2022; ESCAP, 2021). Previous epidemics led to a rise in inequality and a decline in the medium term in per capita income, investment and consumption in Asia and the Pacific (ESCAP, 2021).

Looking to the future, technological advances, globalization and climate change pose additional challenges and risks for improving inclusive growth. The impact of technological progress and automation on employment and wages is more uncertain than ever. Continued technological advancements in communications combined with differences in opportunities across countries are likely to maintain incentives for further globalization, including in financial flows, trade and migration. Over the coming decades, climate change is expected to cause large weather shocks, alter agriculture and increase pressures that drive migration. Climate-linked disasters in the Asia and Pacific region could significantly increase its Gini coefficient and under-5 mortality rate, reduce education rates (ESCAP, 2019) and cause losses of about 2.5 per cent of GDP (ESCAP, 2020).

The remainder of the present paper provides policy perspectives for addressing these challenges and improving inclusive growth. Section II serves to outline the design of an overarching inclusive growth policy framework, considers the trade-offs between growth and inclusion, and discusses how to integrate the policy framework into decision-making processes. Section III elaborates on each component of the inclusive growth framework, summarizing the key issues and policy options for Asia and the Pacific. Section IV concludes the paper.

II. DESIGNING AN INCLUSIVE GROWTH FRAMEWORK

2.1 The inclusive growth framework

Economic well-being, social inclusion and environmental sustainability are interdependent and fundamental to sustainable and inclusive development. In 2015, United Nations member States adopted the 17 Sustainable Development Goals as a call to action to end poverty and hunger and reduce a wide range of deprivations and disparities while spurring economic growth and safeguarding the natural environment. Given that inclusive, green and sustainable growth is multidimensional, a whole of society approach will be required for progress.

In this paper, inclusive growth refers to strong economic growth that is inclusive and sustainable. Economic growth refers to increases in the production of goods and services that are valued by people, providing the means for a better standard of living. Growth is often measured as changes in GDP for practical purposes, but economic welfare can include alternative measures that address the shortcomings of GDP (IMF, 2020). Inclusion refers to broadly sharing the improvements in living standards among all groups in society, providing access to basic services, ensuring participation in economic life and empowerment in social and political life through strong governance and public sector accountability. Sustainability means that the current path of consumption and social welfare can be sustained into the future to the benefit of both current and future generations. This requires avoiding boom-bust policies and maintaining environmental sustainability.

An inclusive growth framework provides a systematic way to analyse the economic interlinkages and to design the appropriate policy responses for inclusive and sustainable development. It can describe the elements and outline how they are connected (figure 1). The framework draws on the standard economic paradigm of a production function that combines inputs from both the private sector and the Government to generate economic activity and to determine its distribution.

Figure 1. Inclusive growth framework

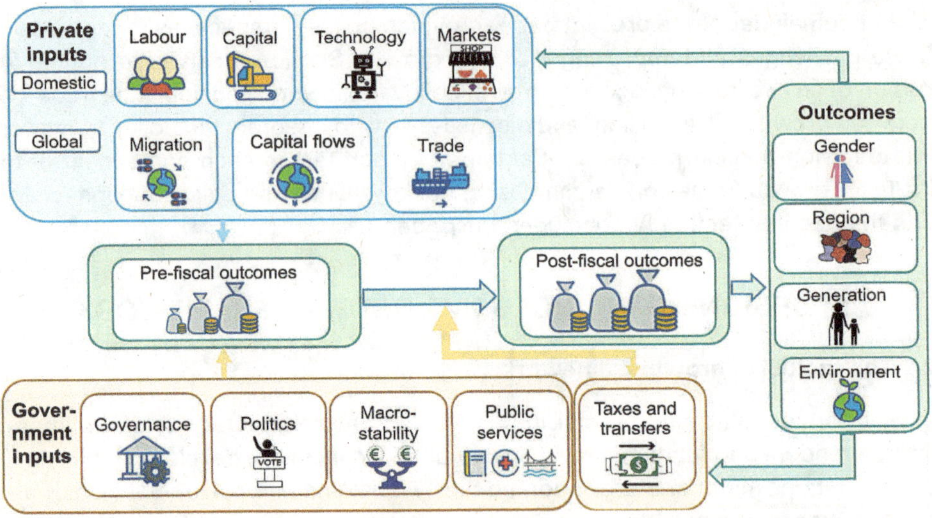

Source: Author's illustration.

A large share of growth and inequality is determined by private sector activities and by policies that affect the private sector. Private sector firms produce goods and services and individuals earn income on their inputs of labour, capital and technological innovation. These inputs can be derived from domestic sources or through globalization, which contributes to the supply of labour, capital and technology through migration, capital flows and technology transfers across borders. In addition, the private sector responds to price signals and incentives to ensure that goods and services are produced and sold in markets. Inclusive growth requires fair and competitive marketplaces with level playing fields – domestically and through international trade – to ensure appropriate prices and opportunities for all to contribute and to reap the output of production. At the stage of production, Governments shape the functioning of the market and the incentives that firms and individuals face in their employment, investment and innovation decisions.

The Government contributes inputs and establishes the right conditions for growth and for inclusion. Government initiatives for developing and distributing vaccines and health services more generally have been critical during the pandemic. The Government delivers an array of public services, including public education and infrastructure. In some sectors, especially those characterized as natural monopolies, the Government engages directly in production. Government policies and provision of public services that increase access to health, education and finance affect the "pre-distribution" phase, impacting the stocks of human and physical capital that feed into the production process. The Government uses macroeconomic tools such as fiscal and monetary stabilization to smooth economic fluctuations and avoid disruptive recessions and crises. Beyond that, the institutions of the State need to provide legal protections and a governance framework to establish the "rules of the game". The political system establishes opportunities for citizens to voice their views on social goals and advocate for inclusive and sustainable reforms and hold political leaders accountable for making decisions in the best interest of the country. After production and the distribution of market income, the Government uses tax and spending instruments to redistribute income to increase the welfare of the very poorest and reduce income disparities according to the weights that the society places on equality. Usually, the market or pre-fiscal outcomes tend to be more unequally distributed than outcomes after government redistribution through taxes and transfers.

The sharing of economic benefits can be analysed beyond just an aggregate measure of inequality. Inclusivity can be considered along a variety of dimensions, such as gender, age and other personal attributes, as well as across regions in a country. Comparing the outcomes of the young and the old is important, as in some countries these groups tend to be more vulnerable to poverty. Furthermore, there is an intertemporal aspect of inclusion: economic benefits, including from resource wealth, need to be shared across current and future generations. Therefore, inclusive growth must be sustainable, and sustainability requires addressing the potential detrimental impact of climate change on future generations.

Finally, there is a feedback loop from the distribution of outcomes to private and public sector inputs. The distribution of outcomes affects future production through labour supply, savings and entrepreneurship, including through the impact on the next generation. Outcomes feed into future government inputs and policies through the political system.

Ultimately, each element of the framework is linked to the rest. The framework illustrates each component and its main function and channels of interaction. But inclusive growth is macroeconomic in nature, and thus all components of the framework are fully interdependent. The framework is also dynamic. Outcomes create endowments of wealth and capital that affect subsequent inputs to production. Outcomes and factor payments create differential opportunities and rewards that translate into political action for policy reform. Changes in governance or in policies affect outcomes, but they also affect incentives in private production. Thus, in establishing an agenda for reform, it is important to start from a holistic view of the framework.

2.2 Trade-offs between growth and inclusion

One obvious policy question is whether a society needs to sacrifice growth to achieve more inclusion. Or more generally, is there a trade-off between growth and inclusion? There are complex linkages between growth and inclusion, with causation going in both directions and several channels mediating the relationship (Cerra, Lama and Loayza, 2021). On the one hand, higher growth can create more job opportunities as well as providing resources for redistribution, lowering poverty and inequality. On the other hand, depending on the source of growth, some sectors may grow faster than others, or the returns to capital and skilled labour might be higher than the returns to unskilled labour, leading to higher inequality. Empirical evidence shows that economic growth leads robustly to poverty reduction but has an ambiguous impact on inequality.[2] In the opposite direction of causation, policies that result in moderate inequality based on rewards for saving, investing, studying, innovating and taking risks can generate higher growth. Conversely, inequality that is too high may produce poverty traps, crime and social conflict, which could impair growth.

Must societies tolerate inequality to spur growth? The evidence suggests that it is important to distinguish between equality of outcomes and equality of opportunities. Policies that provide incentives for saving, investing and innovating may lead to higher growth and result in moderate inequality. However, expanding access to opportunities – such as through access to health care, education, social protection and finance – can raise growth and improve equality at the same time.

2.3 Integrating inclusive growth into policymaking

Adopting an inclusive growth framework into the policy cycle involves several steps, as outlined below.

Diagnosis: The first step is to diagnose the facts of growth, inclusion and sustainability. This can include measures of poverty and inequality and gaps in a variety of outcomes and opportunities, as well as comparing the country's performance

---

[2] Analysing the dynamics of the extreme poverty rate (at the poverty line of $1.90 per day in purchasing power parity) in 135 countries from 1974 to 2018, Bergstrom (2020) finds that 90 per cent of the variation of poverty rates can be explained by changes in GDP per capita. Even so, the poverty reduction elasticity of growth (percentage decline in poverty due to percentage increase in growth) depends on inequality. Growth that is more inclusive (inequality reducing) has a greater impact on poverty reduction than growth accompanied by rising inequality.

to peers and international benchmarks using indicators of several international organizations.

Prioritization: Few countries are likely to do well on all aspects of inclusive growth. Policymakers need to prioritize the goals and targets of their inclusive growth strategy. In developing the overarching objectives and strategy of the reform, it is critical to consider the main concerns of the society and the interests of stakeholders and their capacity to support or block reform.

Policy analysis and implementation: Specific policies must be devised and implemented by ministries and agencies responsible for each policy area. This would be underpinned by analysis of the expected impact, the political and practical feasibility, and the country's specific circumstances. Insights can be gained from economic literature and comparable country experiences, but inevitably some judgment of the country's specific circumstances will be required in designing the right policy mix.

Monitoring and evaluation: As the strategy is implemented, results must be monitored and evaluated. This information would feed back into adjustments to the strategy as experience develops.

III. AN INCLUSIVE GROWTH FRAMEWORK FOR ASIA AND THE PACIFIC

3.1 Labour, capital and technology

The inclusive growth framework described above can be applied to assess policy options for Asia and the Pacific. Trends in poverty and inequality often depend more on changes in the market or pre-tax distribution than on changes in redistribution. Production of output and services provides income for those providing labour, capital (or finance) and technology. The Government nonetheless has a role in shaping outcomes in the private sector through public policies and regulation.

Labour income represents the largest share of the economic pie and, for most people, constitutes most if not all of their income. An inclusive labour market provides opportunities to people of working age to participate in high quality, paid employment to meet basic needs (El-Ganainy and others, 2021). It rewards workers based on producing outputs, rather than personal attributes unrelated to their productivity. An inclusive labour market provides mechanisms to insure against shocks and protect against exploitation. It is flexible in providing working arrangements for workers with family care responsibilities and avoids barriers to access. A labour market that is supportive of inclusive growth reallocates workers quickly and effectively between jobs as the economy adjusts to macroeconomic shocks and provide incentives and opportunities for improving skills to adjust to technological change. In developing and emerging market economies, informal work and domestic work constitute a high share of total employment. For instance, informality accounts for at least half of the labour force in Asian regions, and nearly 90 per cent in South Asia (figure 2). Informal jobs usually lack the benefits and protections of formal work. Even in the formal sector, there are different employment arrangements, with workers receiving only part-time or temporary contracts.

Figure 2. Share of informal employment, 2019

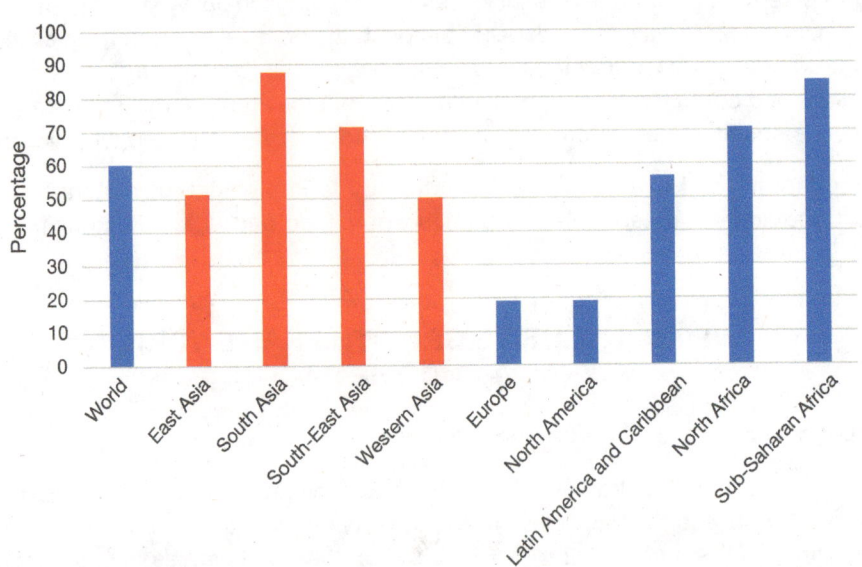

Source: United Nations SDG Indicators database.

Inclusive labour markets can be supported through private and public initiatives. Private firms, employers' associations, and labour unions play a role in promoting an inclusive labour market and workplace. Even without legal requirements or regulation, private entities can create mutually beneficial agreements and solutions on benefits, working conditions, family leave and programmes for enhancing skills. The Government can use tax, legal and regulatory powers to set standards and provide supporting programmes. Important labour market policies include unemployment insurance, minimum wage, employment protection legislation and active labour market policies.

The conversion of savings into investment adds to capital and spurs economic growth. Financial development and inclusion ensure people have access to savings vehicles and can borrow to invest in physical and human capital. A well-functioning financial system helps to mobilize and pool savings and allocates savings into productive investment projects, monitors investments, diversifies risk and facilitates the exchange of information and goods and services (Levine, 2005).

Financial inclusion has many benefits for households and firms. Financial institutions can provide funding for education and allow talented but financially constrained individuals to become entrepreneurs. It allows existing firms to scale up operations to efficient levels. Using financial institutions for savings can reduce theft and reinforce women's economic empowerment. Insurance products can help households to manage financial risks. Financial inclusion is considerably higher in advanced economies than in emerging market economies and developing countries, with five countries in Asia accounting for approximately 40 per cent of the global unbanked population (figure 3).

Figure 3. Adults without a bank account, percentage of global total, 2017

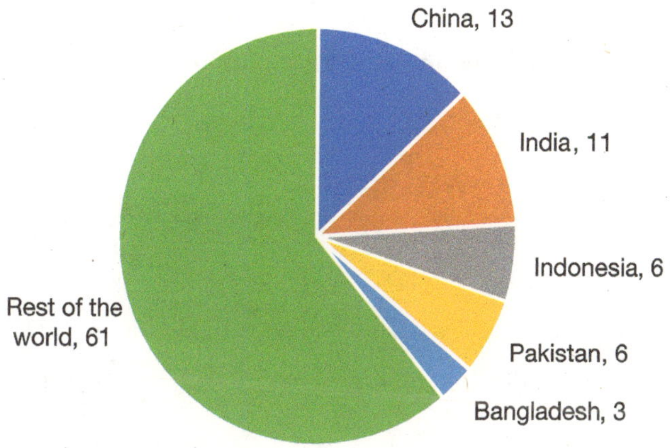

Source: Global Findex database.

Financial inclusion can be promoted by addressing informational asymmetries and other frictions. This includes facilitating access to financial services such as credit bureaus and collateral registries and enhancing financial literacy, and through technologies such as peer-to-peer lending, mobile banking and microcredit (Barajas and others, 2020). But increasing the use of formal finance, particularly access to credit, needs to be balanced with maintaining financial stability through appropriate laws and regulation.

Technological progress is the principal force behind rising global prosperity, but it risks major disruption. Technological advancement over the past few decades has reflected rapid progress in information and communications systems, among other factors. It has been a key driver of global prosperity, which has helped many people to rise out of poverty. However, technology has been more complementary to high-skilled labour, leading to a wage premium for skilled over unskilled labour and contributing to inequality. Average wages in many countries, including Indonesia, Japan and the Republic of Korea, have fallen far short of the technology-driven rise in productivity (figure 4). Contributing factors include a relative decline in investment goods prices (IMF, 2017), the impact of automation (Acemoglu and Restrepo, 2018), and increases in monopoly and monopsony power (Eeckhout, 2021). Looking ahead, there is fear that technology, including artificial intelligence, will be a disruptive force and could take away even more human jobs (Korinek, Schindler and Stiglitz, 2021). Technological progress has the potential to deprive many developing countries of their key comparative advantage (cheap labour) while excluding them from participating in some of the gains provided by new technologies and leading to premature deindustrialization.

Figure 4. Productivity and earnings growth in selected countries

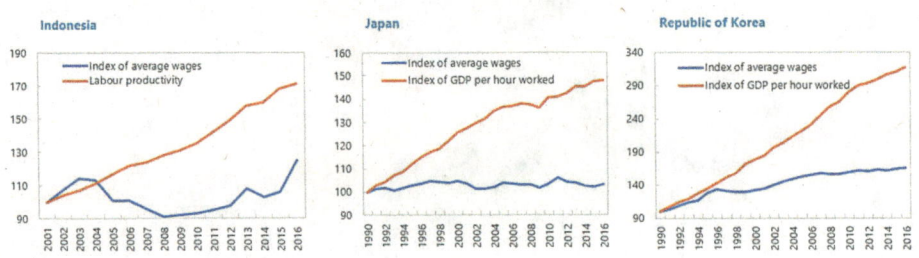

Source: Organisation for Economic Co-Operation and Development (OECD), Bureau of Labour Statistics for Japan and the Republic of Korea; Tadjoeddin and Chowdhury (2018) for Indonesia; and authors' calculations.

Notes: Data for Japan and the Republic of Korea are measured using purchasing power parities for private consumption, so the series may differ from national sources.

GDP, gross domestic product.

Factors of production do not operate in isolation; they are organized into firms that compete in markets for goods and services. Since 2000, there has been a rise in market concentration and corporate market power (Aghion, Cherif and Hasanov, 2021). Moreover, while some types of technology may be non-rival in use (thus, in theory they can facilitate broad-based growth), in practice technology is generated by innovation activity that is excludable and may permit supernormal returns for some time. Innovation and competition are two key aspects of the market structure that impact inclusive growth.

3.2 Globalization

Global integration related to trade and cross-border capital and labour flows is likely to continue. A large part of the income of any individual is determined by her/his country of residence, and disparities across countries are wide. There is a strong incentive for people in lower income countries to benefit from the global economy by migrating to higher income countries which may offer higher returns on investments, and lower income countries can tap into global savings through financial market integration. In addition, countries tend to specialize in different products and services, and opening the economy to international trade can enable countries to benefit from lower cost imports and to find additional foreign markets for domestic goods. International trade, capital flows (including foreign direct investment), and migration are the open economy counterparts to the labour market, capital/finance, technology and markets/business environment.

The preponderance of empirical evidence suggests that trade is beneficial to inclusive growth. As in other regions, countries in Asia and the Pacific that increased trade as a share of GDP between 1950 to 2014 experienced a sharply higher rate of economic growth (figure 5). Studies using a variety of research methodologies find that trade openness has a positive relationship with growth, productivity and innovation, and leads to lower poverty and reduced prices (Bacchetta and others, 2021). Economic theory predicts that trade openness raises the demand for a country's abundant factor and its associated factor returns (Stolper and Samuelson, 1941); therefore, the theory predicts a decline in inequality in developing countries due to rising wages of unskilled labour (where unskilled labour is the abundant factor). Simulation studies find mixed results of trade: Artuc, Porto and Rijkers (2020) find that the richest quintile of households gains more than the poorest from tariff reductions in 37 of 54 developing countries (while the poorest quintile gains more than the richest in 17 countries), but Fajgelbaum and Khandelwal (2016) find that trade typically favours the poor. Panel regressions using actual historical data show that trade openness was associated with lower inequality in emerging and developing countries and has no significant aggregate relationship with the Gini coefficient in advanced countries (Beaton, Cebotari and Komaromi, 2017; Jaumotte, Lall and Papageorgiou, 2013). Event studies of liberalization episodes, mainly reflecting emerging market countries, corroborates the beneficial impact of trade. In addition to boosting growth, investment and foreign direct investment, trade liberalization prevented the steep rise in inequality experienced by countries that remained relatively closed to international trade (Beaton, Cebotari and Komaromi, 2017). Cerdeiro and Komaromi (2020) exploit the exogenous geographic characteristics of countries to estimate the causal effect of trade on inequality; they find the positive impact of trade on income is highest for the poorest income deciles, and trade openness that is one percentage point higher is associated with 0.2–0.6 points lower net Gini coefficient. In addition, open economies have lower rates of informality and higher levels of gender equality, including smaller gender wage gaps (Black and Brainerd, 2004; Klein, Moser and Urban, 2010). Firms that engage in international trade employ substantially more women than non-exporting firms (World Bank and World Trade Organization, 2020). Bacchetta and others (2021) provide a survey of the empirical findings between trade and inclusive growth.

Figure 5. Trade and growth in Asia and the Pacific, 1950–2014

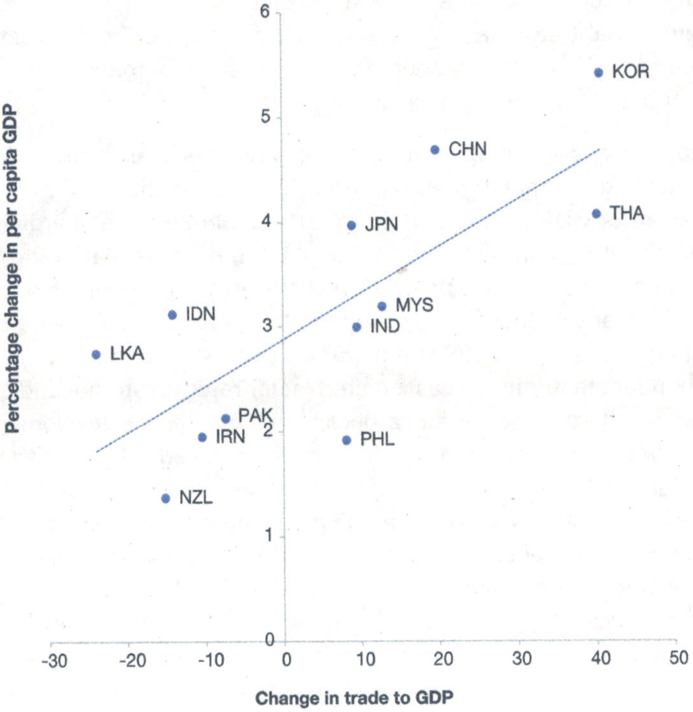

Source: World Bank and author's calculations.

Notes: CHN, China; GDP, gross domestic product; IDN, Indonesia; IND, India; IRN, Iran (Islamic Republic of); JPN, Japan; KOR, Republic of Korea; LKA, Sri Lanka; MYS, Malaysia; NZL, New Zealand; PAK,; PHL, Pakistan; THA, Thailand.

While theory and evidence point to gains from trade at the aggregate level, policy intervention is needed to help those who lose out. The economic impact of trade depends on country circumstances and the specifics of the trade policies, implying that trade, like any other force of structural transformation, can have an adverse impact on some individuals or communities (UNCTAD, 2019). Trade policies can be designed to minimize adverse distributional effects, such as gradually phasing in trade liberalization, contributing to export promotion and trade facilitation, including helping firms to meet health and regulatory standards required by destination countries. Governments can use complementary policies, including social assistance programmes, providing information, job search support, education and retraining. They can promote firm entry and job creation by maintaining a strong business environment and ensuring an inclusive labour market.

Financial integration allows developing countries to tap foreign savings for domestic investment, thereby speeding up the rate of capital accumulation and growth. However, there are pitfalls. While the evidence confirms that financial integration has a positive relationship with growth, it tends to be associated with higher inequality (Eichengreen and others, 2021). Short-term capital flows may contribute to macroeconomic volatility and crises. Foreign direct investment inflows raise gross capital formation, but associated technology transfers may advantage skilled labour over unskilled labour, leading to higher wage inequality.

A broad policy package is needed to limit the risks associated with financial integration. These include macroeconomic adjustment and stabilization, and micro- and macroprudential policies to improve the resilience of the financial sector, capital flow management policies to influence the level and composition of flows, and redistributive policies and social safety nets to mitigate adverse effects.

3.3 Government

Governments can foster inclusive growth in a variety of ways. Governments establish the institutions and governing conditions of the economy, use policy instruments to promote economic stability and directly impact the distribution of income through tax policies and spending and transfers, especially in key public services such as health and education. Understanding the appropriate tools for improving inclusive growth is not enough. Public policies must be implemented within a given national or local system of unequal political power.

The quality of a State's governance shapes its effectiveness in spurring inclusive development. Governance includes the institutional frameworks and practices of the public sector, mechanisms and quality of oversight of key institutions such as the central bank, oversight of the financial system, regulation of the private sector to address market failures and the rule of law, including protection of property rights

(Ivanyna and Salerno, 2021). Avoiding corruption is an important component of governance. Corruption can have a sizeable macroeconomic impact. Some studies find for example that bribes account for as much as 2 per cent of global GDP. A significant share of firms, as much as 9 per cent in South Asia, report corruption as a top concern about the business environment (figure 6). Corruption and poor governance can breed lack of trust in the Government and undermine support for reform. This is especially critical when the Government wants to introduce a reform that has potentially large benefits over a long horizon, but entails some short-term costs. If citizens are suspicious of public officials, they may not tolerate reforms with short-term costs because they will not trust that the reforms will deliver long-term benefits.

Figure 6. Percentage of firms choosing corruption as top business environment obstacle

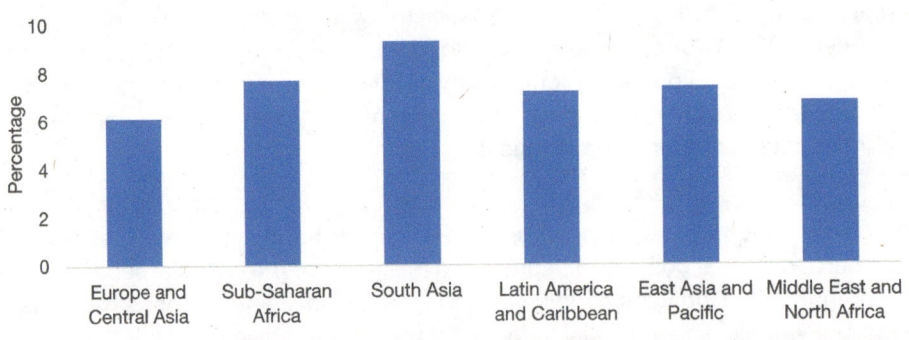

Source: World Bank Enterprise Surveys, average 2009–2019.

Strengthening governance involves enhancing the capacity and efficiency of public sector operations. It entails reducing the opportunities for corruption, increasing its cost and likelihood of detection, such as through a regulatory framework with fewer discretionary decisions and greater transparency in government processes. Cross-border agreements are important for combatting corruption and tax evasion. For example, anti-money laundering measures and agreements to share financial data with home country tax authorities can combat illicit activity while tax agreements between countries can reduce legal tax avoidance.

The political economy defines the relationship between the State and its citizens. It determines the amount of redistribution through the tax and transfer system and shapes the pre-distribution economic structure through policies on access to education, health and finance. The relationship between the political system and inclusive growth is complex and much depends on history, laws and customs, social trust and ethnic cleavages, among other factors. Support for redistribution is typically higher in democracies and during periods of economic insecurity and among sociodemographic groups that have been disadvantaged (Dutzler, Johnson and Muthoora, 2021). Evidence suggests that inclusive political institutions are correlated with inclusive economic institutions and broad-based growth.

Direct government intervention policies affect the distribution of income and prevalence of poverty. Fiscal policy is a powerful tool to reduce inequality through redistribution. In advanced economies, direct taxes and transfers reduce income inequality by about one third on average. Given higher administrative capacity, advanced countries are able to implement more fiscal redistribution (and therefore reduce inequality more) than developing countries. Transfers have had a greater impact than taxes on reducing income inequality. In developing countries, fiscal policy reduces the poverty rate by 2.25 per cent on average with nearly all of the impact coming from transfers rather than taxes. Even so, the impact of fiscal policy on inclusive growth needs to jointly account for the revenue and expenditure side. For example, even if taxes alone result in little direct reduction in poverty and inequality, they provide resources for transfers and spending that can improve the lives of the poor. So, efforts to mobilize domestic revenue can be impactful for inclusive growth.

Taxation serves to raise revenue to finance government spending priorities, but it can also be a tool for redistribution. Tax policy design balances principles of efficiency, equity and practicality, and it is influenced by political economy considerations (Abdelkader and de Mooij, 2020). Digging deeper, some tax policies require a trade-off between reducing inequality and increasing growth. Progressive income taxes can reduce inequality, but high marginal tax rates could discourage work and investment. The value added tax is less damaging to growth but may be regressive given that it is a tax on consumption and the poor typically consume a higher share of their income. Tax policies that improve efficiency and equity at the same time include broadening the tax base, especially by eliminating loopholes and exemptions, simplifying the tax code and taking other measures to fight corruption and tax evasion, and taxing profits that arise from excess market power.

Government expenditure promotes inclusive growth through the provision of public services and infrastructure and typically achieves more redistribution than does taxation. Education and health are among the most critical components of public expenditure for eliminating poverty and improving inclusive growth. Countries need to spend effectively to provide access and quality in education and health care services. Empirical evidence shows social spending as a share of GDP has been strongly associated with reductions in inequality (Zouhar and others, 2021). Other public spending to raise equitable growth includes public infrastructure to bolster private investment and improve productivity, measures to improve labour-force participation and budget support for research and development. Conversely, some types of universal subsidies are bad for both growth and equity. One important example is energy subsidies, which are large in some countries. Energy subsidies tend to disproportionately benefit the rich and promote the overuse of energy, which is detrimental to the environment.

Macroeconomic volatility and shocks have considerable impacts on growth, the distribution of income and wealth, and other dimensions of inclusive growth.[3] For example, more individuals become unemployed during recessions and crises, or experience a cut in their wages or work hours. Indeed, countries that have high volatility of GDP per capita also have high volatility of unemployment and poverty (Davoodi, Montiel and Ter-Martirosyan, 2021). Inequality, poverty and other aspects of inclusive growth, in turn, can be sources of macroeconomic volatility and trigger or amplify shocks.

Economic crises and political instability generate scarring in both advanced and developing economies. A recession leads to a fall in economic activity below the economy's previous trend, and usually the lost output is never fully recuperated (Cerra and Saxena, 2008). Economic volatility and scarring increase inequality within countries (Davoodi, Montiel and Ter-Martirosyan, 2021). In Asia and the Pacific, adverse economic and natural shocks have resulted in lower incomes, higher inequality and unemployment, slower accumulation of physical and human capital, and weaker environmental performance (ESCAP, 2021). Output scarring, or hysteresis, can be reduced by fiscal and monetary expansions during recessions and flexible exchange rate regimes (Cerra, Panizza and Saxena, 2013; ESCAP, 2021). Thus, countercyclical macroeconomic policies can not only reduce volatility but also improve inclusive growth.

The COVID-19 pandemic illustrates the importance of a strong macroeconomic policy response. For example, the United States of America and other advanced economies provided massive macroeconomic support to firms and households in terms of both the health response and income support. Recent forecasts from the International Monetary Fund show the GDPs of advanced economies bouncing back to their pre-pandemic trends. Many emerging and developing countries, however, have

---

[3] Many studies define macroeconomic volatility as the standard deviation of real GDP and others as the frequency and/or depth of recessions and crises. Some other studies focus on the volatility of nominal GDP and inflation below a low threshold (i.e. 5 per cent) in order to explore the role of monetary policy (Romer and Romer, 1999).

not had the macroeconomic space to respond as vigorously and are consequently projected to have substantially lower levels of GDP in the next several years relative to pre-pandemic forecasts (figure 7). The pandemic and the policy response led to projected increases in public debt levels for all country groups. For example, in emerging and middle-income Asian economies, the pandemic led to an increase in projected gross government debt by between 5 and 10 per cent of GDP. This reduced the fiscal space for dealing with future challenges and increased the risk of public debt distress.

Figure 7. Effect of the pandemic on gross domestic product and general government gross debt

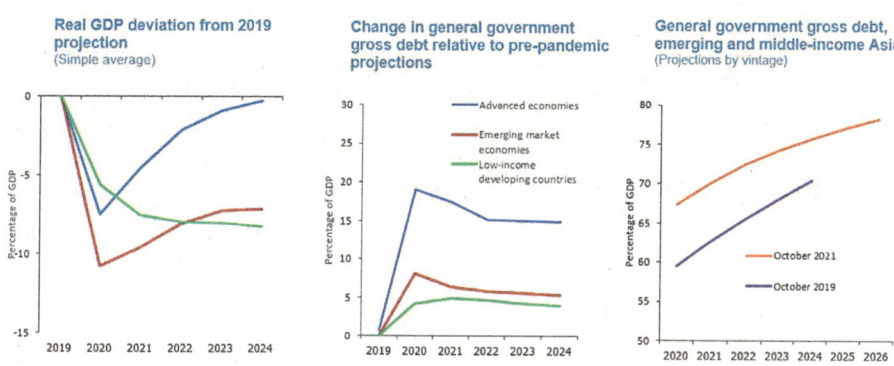

Source: International Monetary Fund (IMF), World Economic Outlook database; and IMF staff estimates.

Notes: All quantities are converted into 2019 prices using the projected evolution of the GDP deflator.

GDP, gross domestic product.

Output scarring also thwarts development. According to traditional growth theory, poor countries should catch up to the per capital income levels of rich countries because each dollar of investment should generate a higher return in poor countries that have little capital to start with. The historical evidence, however, does not support the theory of convergence. Output scarring provides an explanation (Cerra and Saxena, 2017). All countries experience negative shocks with persistent impacts, but recessions are larger and more frequent in poor countries than in rich countries, and they keep pushing poor countries back, preventing them from catching up.

3.4 Outcomes

Opportunities and outcomes are not equally distributed to all groups in society for a variety of economic, historical and cultural reasons. Disparities vary from country to country, but opportunities and outcomes depend on gender, race, ethnicity, age, sexual orientation, religion, language and other attributes. There are often large disparities between regions within a country. Inequality across generations arises from natural resource depletion, climate change and other forms of environmental damage that have detrimental effects on future generations.

Despite progress in narrowing the gaps, gender disparities persist. Across a spectrum of labour market indicators, outcomes for women lag behind those for men (Fernandez and others, 2021). Notably, labour force participation of women remains significantly below that of men and wages and earnings are far from parity. These gender disadvantages translate into higher inequality and poverty for women. For example, median gender pay gaps average more than 10 per cent in advanced and emerging economies and are as high as 40 per cent in Pakistan (figure 8). In addition to the labour market outcomes, women face other obstacles, such as legal barriers to property ownership, low rates of political empowerment, higher rates of infanticide and domestic violence.

Figure 8. Factor-weighted gender pay gaps using hourly wages, average of 2015–2019

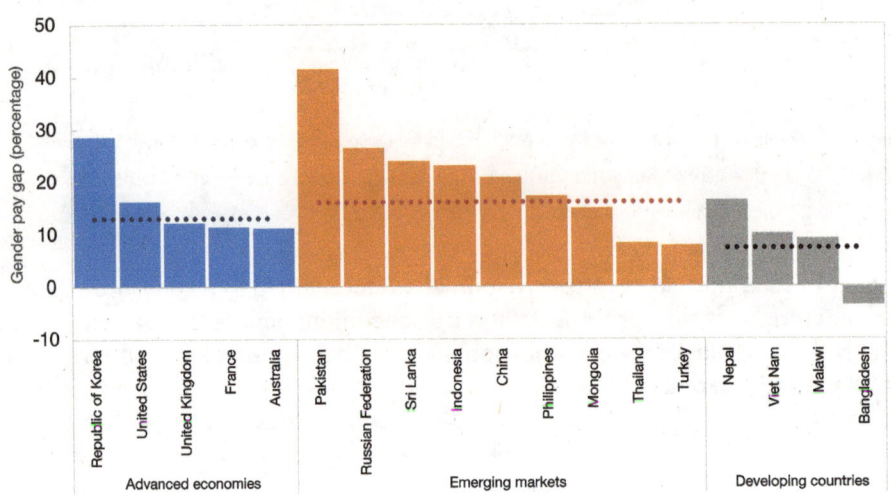

Source: International Labour Organization (ILO) and authors' calculations.

Note: Country groupings are based on the International Monetary Fund (IMF) World Economic Outlook classification. Averages are calculated based on countries shown in each group.

Given the pervasive nature of gender disparities, a panoply of policies is required to break barriers and foster gender equity. This starts with changing laws that discriminate against women working and owning property, and encouraging women's participating in economic life. Governments can enact and enforce laws to protect against violence and child marriage. The Government can use fiscal instruments to provide sufficient spending on education and health and to eliminate discriminatory and higher marginal taxes on second earners. Many countries are adopting gender budgeting, a practice in which fiscal measures are assessed based on the impact they have on gender inequality. An array of labour market policies, such as childcare support, parental leave and flexible working arrangements, can encourage women to enter the labour force.

The youth are often among the most vulnerable demographic groups. They have significantly worse labour market outcomes than other groups in many countries. Strategies to foster youth integration into the labour market need to be broad based (Badual, Isakova and Ter-Martirosyan, 2021). They would include ensuring good quality education from the primary level all the way up to tertiary education, vocational training and apprenticeships. They would also include policies to foster flexible labour markets with social safety nets to protect workers and active labour market policies to support employment along with measures to foster private sector development and entrepreneurship.

In some countries, the poverty rates for people over 65 years of age are much higher than for the overall population. Older people often rely on income and health care support from public systems that are under increasing strain due to demographic and other trends. In countries with comprehensive and mature systems of social protection and ageing populations, policies should maintain a good balance between financial sustainability and pension adequacy. In many developing countries with large informal sectors, the policy objective is to broaden coverage and increase formalization, including through minimum social pensions. For example, only about half the population of pensionable age receives a pension in Asia and the Pacific, and only about a quarter in South Asia (figure 9).

Figure 9. Pension coverage for older persons

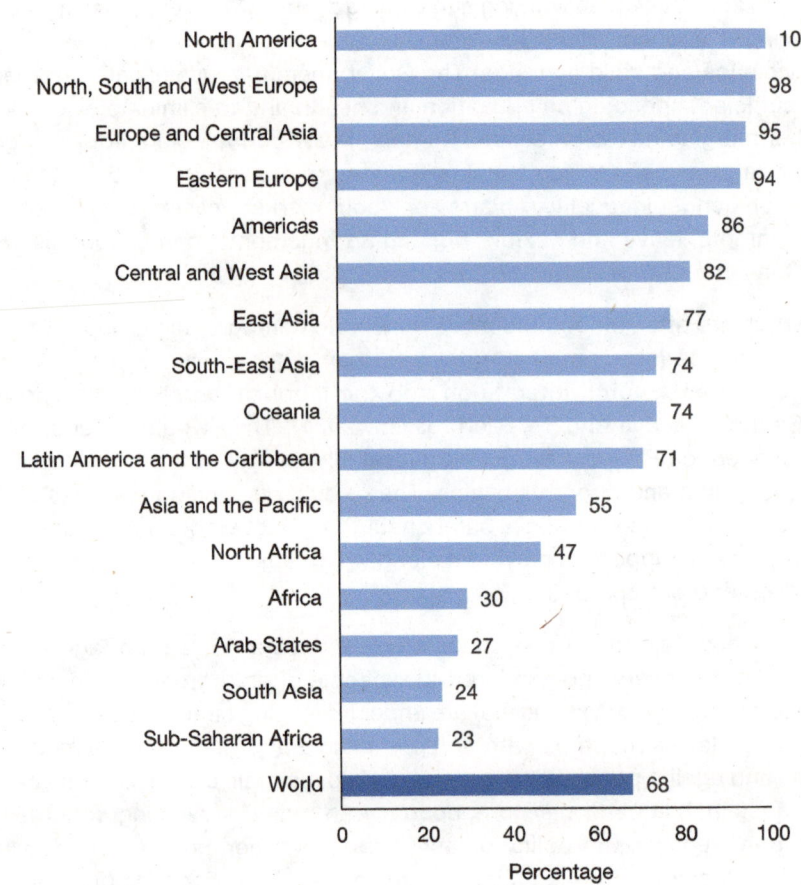

Source: ILO, World Social Protection database, based on Social Security Inquiry; ILOSTAT; OECD Social Benefit Recipients database; and national sources.

Note: Proportion of older persons receiving a pension: ratio of persons above statutory retirement age receiving an old-age pension to the persons above statutory retirement age. Regional and global estimates weighted by population of retirement age.

Different regions within countries face significant disparities in economic performance and living standards, contributing to overall inequality. Options for reducing regional disparities include policies focused on raising growth and business opportunities in lagging regions; integrating or better connecting leading and lagging regions; and improving the ability of people in lagging regions to relocate to leading regions (Floerkemeier, Spatafora and Venables, 2021). Some countries and regions are highly dependent on income from natural resources, which often fuels conflict and corruption (Pouokam, 2021). Strong political governance is especially important to avoid fragility. In addition, Governments need to invest resource windfalls in human capital and infrastructure and adopt appropriate fiscal frameworks to share the benefits of resource wealth across generations.

3.5 Climate

Climate change is arguably the most significant threat to the sustainability of growth and the well-being of future generations. Climate change brings about substantial socioeconomic damages. These depend on country circumstances, but they are generally larger for the poor, as they have fewer resources to adapt, are more dependent on agriculture and tend to live in areas that are already exposed to more adverse climate conditions (Bhattacharya and others, 2021). Some of the most severe impacts are expected in South Asia.

Governments need to employ a broad policy package to enable the green transition. Putting a price on carbon helps to address the externality of the use of fossil fuel while raising needed revenue for development. This can be complemented with offsetting any impact on the poor and affected workers, businesses and regions through transfers and social spending. Carbon pricing can be reinforced with sector-specific policies, including regulations, energy efficiency standards and feebates. It is critical to eliminate fossil fuel subsidies, which degrade the environment, deprive the Government of revenue and generally benefit the rich. Other policies include aligning financial sector policies with climate objectives, providing incentives for green investment and innovation, and promoting international cooperation, including mobilizing financial resources for lower-income countries. Even with strong global mitigation efforts, adaptation is necessary for many countries to cope with climate change. The key policies are information and investment policies to reduce the exposure to climate shocks and macroeconomic policies to smooth and facilitate the structural transformation. Mitigation and adaptation policies such as land restoration and sustainable agriculture can help poor subsistence farmers. Mitigation can provide important co-benefits. For example, switching to cleaner sources of energy in transport can help to reduce air pollution, which is a major source of health problems and death, especially in developing countries. According to Parry, Mylonas and Vernon (2017), annually increasing the tax per ton of coal by 150 rupees ($2.25) from 2017 to 2030 could avoid over 270,000 air pollution deaths, raise revenue of 1 per cent of GDP in 2030, reduce carbon dioxide emissions by 12 per cent and generate net economic benefits of approximately 1 per cent of GDP.

IV. CONCLUSION

Given the multidimensional linkages, a comprehensive policy approach should be employed to improve inclusive growth. The challenge is to engineer higher growth and inclusion in tandem. An equitable distribution of income from market activities depends on the Government to ensure a fair and competitive market for goods, deepen financial inclusion and promote inclusive labour markets, both domestically and as the country integrates its economy with the rest of the world. The Government also has a role in providing complementary infrastructure and education and health services, as well as creating strong institutions and maintaining macroeconomic stability. In addition, the Government can use tax and spending tools and other policy instruments to provide social protection for the poor and vulnerable, redistribute income and address economic and social disparities, in accordance with the society's preferences. Finally, policies need to focus not only on the immediate situation, but also on ensuring economic and environmental sustainability over time to safeguard the well-being of current and future generations.

ACKNOWLEDGEMENTS

The views expressed herein are those of the author and should not be attributed to the IMF, its Executive Board, or its management.

NOTE ON CONTRIBUTORS

Valerie Cerra is an Assistant Director in the Fiscal Affairs Department of the IMF and has previously been involved in policy advice, lending and capacity development in several other IMF departments. She has published in leading economics journals on economic scarring, inclusive growth and international macroeconomics.

REFERENCES

Abdelkader, Khaled, and Ruud de Mooij (2020). Tax Policy and Inclusive Growth. IMF Working Paper, No. 20/271.

Acemoglu, Daron, and Pascual Restrepo (2018). The Race between Man and Machine: Implications of Technology for Growth, Factor Shares, and Employment. *American Economic Review,* vol. 108, No. 6, pp. 1488–1542.

Agarwal, Ruchir (2022). Pandemic Scars may be Twice as Deep for Students in Developing Countries. IMF Blog, 2 February 2022.

Aghion, Philippe, Reda Cherif, and Fuad Hasanov (2021). Competition, Innovation, and Inclusive Growth. IMF Working Paper, No. 21/80.

Alon, Titan, and others (2020). This Time It's Different: The Role of Women's Employment in a Pandemic Recession. CEPR Discussion Paper, No. 15149.

Artuc, Erhan, Guido Porto, and Bob Rijkers (2020). "Inequality and trade: Simulation evidence for 54 developing nations" Vox EU blog, 6 January. Available at https://voxeu.org/article/inequality-and-trade-simulation-evidence-54-developing-nations.

Bacchetta, Marc, and others (2021). Trade and Inclusive Growth. IMF Working Paper, No. 21/74.

Badual, Benedite, Asel Isakova, and Anna Ter-Martirosyan (2021). Generational Aspects of Inclusive Growth. IMF Working Paper, No. 21/72.

Barajas, Adolfo, Thorsten Beck, Mohamed Belhaj and Sami Ben Naceur (2020). Financial Inclusion: What Have We Learned So Far? What Do We Have to Learn? IMF Working Paper, No. 20/157.

Beaton, Kim, Aliona Cebotari and Andras Komaromi (2017). Revisiting the Link between Trade, Growth and Inequality: Lessons for Latin America and the Caribbean. IMF Working Paper, No. 17/46.

Bergstrom, Katy (2020). The Role of Inequality for Poverty Reduction. Policy Research Working Paper, No. 9409. Washington, D.C.: World Bank.

Bhattacharya, Amar, Maksym Ivanyna, William Oman and Nicholas Stern (2021). Climate Action to Unlock the Inclusive Growth Story of the 21st Century. IMF Working Paper, No. 21/147.

Black, Sandra, and Elizabeth Brainerd (2004). Importing Equality? The Impact of Globalization on Gender Discrimination. *Industrial and Labor Relations Review,* vol. 57, No. 4, pp. 540–559.

Cerdeiro, Diego, and Andras Komaromi (2021). Trade and income in the long run: Are there really gains, and are they widely shared? *Review of International Economics,* vol 29, Issue 4, pp. 703–731.

Cerra, Valerie, Antonio Fatas and Sweta C. Saxena (2021). Fighting the Scarring Effects of COVID-19. *Industrial and Corporate Change,* vol. 30, No. 2, pp. 459–466.

_____ (forthcoming). Hysteresis and Business Cycles, *Journal of Economic Literature.* Available at: www.aeaweb.org/articles?id=10.1257/jel.20211584&from=f.

Cerra, Valerie, Ruy Lama and Norman Loayza (2021). Links Between Growth, Inequality, and Poverty: A Survey. IMF Working Paper, No. 21/68.

Cerra, Valerie, Ugo Panizza and Sweta C. Saxena (2013). International Evidence on Recovery from Recessions. *Contemporary Economic Policy,* vol. 31, No. 2, pp. 424–439.

Cerra, Valerie, and Sweta C. Saxena (2008). Growth Dynamics: The Myth of Economic Recovery. *American Economic Review,* vol. 98, No. 1, pp. 439–457.

_____ (2017). Booms, Crises, and Recoveries: A New Paradigm of the Business Cycle and its Policy Implications. IMF Working Paper, No. 17/250.

Davoodi, Hamid, Peter Montiel and Anna Ter-Martirosyan (2021). Macroeconomic Stability and Inclusive Growth. IMF Working Paper, No. 21/81.

Dutzler, Barbara, Simon Johnson and Priscilla Muthoora (2021). The Political Economy of Inclusive Growth: A Review. IMF Working Paper, No. 21/82.

Eeckhout, Jan (2021). *The Profit Paradox: How Thriving Firms Threaten the Future of Work.* Princeton University Press.

Eichengreen, Barry, Balazs Csonto, Asmaa El-Ganainy and Zsoka Koczan (2021). Financial Globalization and Inequality: Capital Flows as a Two-Edged Sword. IMF Working Paper, No. 21/4.

El-Ganainy, Asmaa, Ekkehard Ernst, Rossana Merola, Richard Rogerson and Martin Schindler (2021). Inclusivity in the Labor Market. IMF Working Paper, No. 21/141.

Fajgelbaum, Pablo, and Amit Khandelwal (2016). Measuring the Unequal Gains from Trade. *The Quarterly Journal of Economics,* vol. 131, Issue 3, pp. 1113–1180.

Fernandez, Raquel, Asel Isakova, Francesco Luna and Barbara Rambousek (2021). Gender Equality and Inclusive Growth. IMF Working Paper, No. 21/59.

Floerkemeier, Holger, Nikola Spatafora and Anthony Venables (2021). Regional Disparities, Growth, and Inclusiveness. IMF Working Paper, No. 21/38.

International Monetary Fund (IMF) (2017). Understanding the Downward Trends in Labor Income Shares. In *World Economic Outlook: April 2017: Gaining Momentum?* Washington, D.C.

_____ (2020). Measuring Economic Welfare: What and How? Policy Paper, No. 2020/028. Washington, D.C.

Ivanyna, Maksym, and Andrea Salerno (2021). Governance for Inclusive Growth. IMF Working Paper, No. 21/98.

Jaumotte, Florence, Subir Lall and Chris Papageorgiou (2013). Rising Income Inequality: Technology, or Trade and Financial Globalization? *IMF Economic Review,* vol. 61, No. 2, pp. 271–309.

Klein, Michael, Christoph Moser and Dieter Urban (2010). The Contribution of Trade to Wage Inequality: The Role of Skill, Gender, and Nationality. Working Paper No. 15985. National Bureau of Economic Research.

Korinek, Anton, Martin Schindler and Joseph E. Stiglitz (2021). Technological Progress, Artificial Intelligence, and Inclusive Growth. IMF Working Paper, No. 21/166.

Levine, Ross (2005). Finance and Growth: Theory and Evidence. In *Handbook of Economic Growth,* Philippe Aghion and Steven Durlauf, eds. Amsterdam: Elsevier Science, 1st ed., vol. 1, chap. 12, pp. 865–934.

Parry, Ian, Victor Mylonas and Nate Vernon (2017). Reforming Energy Policy in India: Assessing the Options. IMF Working Paper, No. 17/103.

Pouokam, Nathalie (2021). Sharing Resource Wealth Inclusively Within and Across Generations. IMF Working Paper, No. 21/97.

Romer, Christina, and David Romer (1999). Monetary Policy and the Well-Being of the Poor. *Federal Reserve Bank of Kansas City Economic Review,* 1st Quarter, pp. 21–49.

Stolper, W.F., and P.A. Samuelson (1941). Protection and Real Wages. *The Review of Economic Studies,* vol. 9, No. 1, pp. 58–73.

United Nations, Economic and Social Commission for Asia and the Pacific (ESCAP) (2019). Economic and Social Survey of Asia and the Pacific.

_____ (2020). Economic and Social Survey of Asia and the Pacific.

_____ (2021). Economic and Social Survey of Asia and the Pacific.

United Nations Conference on Trade and Development (UNCTAD) (2019). Trade Policies and Their Impact on Inequalities. TC/B/66/4.

World Bank and World Trade Organization (2020). Women and Trade: The Role of Trade in Promoting Gender Equality. Washington, D.C.: World Bank; Geneva: World Trade Organization.

Zouhar, Younes, Jon Jellema, Nora Lustig and Mohamed Trabelsi (2021). Public Expenditure and Inclusive Growth – A Survey. IMF Working Paper, No. 21/83.

Special theme: Macroeconomic policies for inclusive sustainable development

IMPACT OF TAXES AND TRANSFERS ON INEQUALITY IN THE ASIA-PACIFIC REGION

Sally Torbert

Senior Programme Officer, International Budget Partnership
Email: storbert@gmail.com

Governments that aim to adjust their fiscal policies to reduce inequality can look to several analytical tools that are being produced in Asia-Pacific countries, including commitment to equity studies and public expenditure reviews. The present paper contains a review of studies for 12 Asia-Pacific countries. Consistent with previous research on the impact of fiscal policies on inequality, the findings of the review show that policies such as targeted direct transfers, education spending and tax policies that favour direct instead of indirect taxes are most effective at inequality reduction.

Keywords: fiscal policy, inequality, redistribution, taxes, transfers

JEL classification: D63, E63, 023

I. INTRODUCTION

As countries rebound from the economic shock of COVID-19, many Governments will face constrained fiscal space or move into a period of fiscal adjustment in coming years. In the Asia-Pacific region, the fiscal policy decisions that Governments will make in the coming years are even more critical given the risks of exacerbating existing trends toward inequality. Alongside remarkable economic growth, over the past two decades income inequality had been rising in many Asia-Pacific countries (Jian and Lee, 2018). After the COVID-19 crisis, this trend is likely to accelerate further without significant government interventions. Lessons from previous pandemics and economic shocks have shown that they can widen inequality, and countries with lower health and social protection expenditures faced larger and longer setbacks in their efforts to achieve economic growth, poverty reduction and reduced inequality (ESCAP, 2021).

Fiscal policy decisions can effectively support an inclusive recovery. Reforms to address increasing constraints on fiscal space can be adjusted to promote greater spending on policies that have proven to be effective at reducing poverty and inequality in other countries while minimizing spending on policies that have lesser impact or that may even increase inequality.

Many Governments in the Asia-Pacific region already have access to reports that analyse the impact of fiscal policies on inequality, or they may learn from analyses that have been done in other countries. To identify how government fiscal policy choices can impact inequality, the present paper provides a review of fiscal policies in 12 Asia-Pacific countries as assessed using the Commitment to Equity (CEQ) methodology and public expenditure reviews (PERs).

At the national level, CEQ assessments use a common methodological framework developed by the CEQ Institute[1] to analyse the distributional impact of taxes and transfers. Government fiscal data and household income data reported in national household surveys are used to estimate the impact of fiscal policies on income redistribution and poverty reduction. This approach covers only part of the fiscal system. It excludes some sector expenditures, such as public administration, public safety and transportation, that have diffused benefits which are difficult to attribute to households, as well as some revenues, such as the corporate income tax, where the incidence by household cannot be determined.

---

[1] Led by Nora Lustig since 2008, CEQ Institute is an initiative of the Center for Inter-American Policy and Research and the Department of Economics, Tulane University, the Center for Global Development, and the Inter-American Dialogue. For more details visit www.commitmentoequity.org.

To compliment the analysis of the distributional impact of government taxation and transfer policies in the CEQ assessment, the review in the present paper includes key findings from public expenditure reviews (PERs) and systematic country diagnostics (SCDs) in several of the selected countries (table 1). The World Bank and other institutions conduct PERs, which are non-standard assessments of government budgets that may include an analysis of efficiency and effectiveness of fiscal policies, expenditure trends in sectors and equity analysis (Freinkman and Skhirtladze, 2015). World Bank investment planning in countries is underpinned by SCDs, which are analytical reviews of country progress and opportunities for sustainable and inclusive growth. Comparing the findings of PERs, SCDs and CEQ assessments can identify elements of fiscal policies that have successfully reduced inequality and poverty, factors that limit the impact and effectiveness of redistribution and poverty reduction, and policies that may inadvertently widen disparities or poverty gaps.

Table 1. Countries covered in review of commitment to equity assessment, public expenditure review and systematic country diagnostics

Country	Commitment to equity assessments (Year of fiscal/survey data)	Public expenditure review (Year of publication)	Systematic country diagnostics (Year of publication)
Armenia	2011	2014	
Cambodia		2010, 2019	
China	2013		2017
Georgia	2013	2015, 2017	
Indonesia	2012	2020	
Iran (Islamic Republic of)	2011–2012		
Mongolia	2016	2018	
Philippines		2018, 2020	2019
Russian Federation	2010		2016
Sri Lanka	2009		2016
Turkey	2016		2016
Viet Nam	2014	2017	2014

The presesnt paper has the following three sections: evidence on fiscal policy choices that impact poverty and inequality; evidence from the reviewed studies on transfer and tax policies in Asia and the Pacific; and conclusions and policy recommendations.

II. FISCAL POLICY CHOICES THAT IMPACT INEQUALITY

Government policy decisions can have a range of intended and unintended impacts on inequality. Fiscal policy decisions on taxes and transfers, which are the focus of CEQ assessments, have the most observable impact on household incomes in a given year. However, the CEQ methodology does not assess whether these policies are desirable based on different goals for fiscal policies, which can include macroeconomic stability, growth and poverty reduction (Lustig, 2017). Spending decisions to invest in physical and human capital also benefit future generations and may impact the distribution of income over time (Lustig, 2018, p. lxiv). Public investments in agriculture, transportation, electrification, telecommunications and other sectors can have significant impacts on long-term growth and poverty reduction, but may have variable impacts on inequality, depending on the quality of spending, how projects are financed and which groups access and benefit from these public resources the most (Calderón and Servén, 2014; Seneviratne and Sun, 2013). Government regulations and policies can also influence inequality in terms of access to finance, labour markets and industrial production factors, such as research and development or trade terms (Blanchard and Rodrik, 2021).

Previous research on the relative impact of fiscal policies on inequality and poverty has shown that different types of policies tend to have either progressive or regressive impacts on household incomes, but the impact varies depending on the country context and policy design. Several studies have analysed the impact of different policies on inequality in the Asia-Pacific region, and the findings of these studies are summarized below.

Evidence around the impact of government transfer programmes shows that direct transfers such as social safety nets and cash transfer programmes tend to be effective at reducing inequality. Social safety nets can be an effective driver for reducing inequality when programmes are well targeted toward the poor (Claus, Martinez-Vazquez and Vulovic, 2012), and conditional cash transfers have been found in some cases to reduce inequality by raising school enrolment and improving health outcomes (Zouhar and others, 2021). Pension programmes can lead to reductions in inequality (Abdel-Kader and Mooij, 2020), but an analysis of pension programmes in 20 countries also found that many are not well targeted toward the poor (Chu, Davoodi and Gupta, 2004). Government subsidies, which act as indirect transfers to households, have been shown to be less effective at reducing poverty and there is some evidence that energy subsidies tend to benefit upper-income households (Claus, Martinez-Vazquez and Vulovic, 2012).

Government spending on education and health, which can be seen as in-kind transfers to households, tends to be progressive. For health spending, rural/urban disparities can lead to fewer benefits for low-income groups, but spending on primary care tends to be more progressive (Abdel-Kader and Mooij, 2020; Claus, Martinez-Vazquez and Vulovic, 2012). Education spending tends to be more progressive at the primary level and sometimes at the secondary level, depending on enrolment rates at different education levels (Abdel-Kader and Mooij, 2020; Claus, Martinez-Vazquez and Vulovic, 2012; Jian and Lee, 2018).

For tax policies, direct taxes such as income tax tend to have a greater impact on reducing inequality than indirect taxes such as value added tax (VAT) and excise tax. Personal income tax can have a greater impact on inequality when tax rates are progressive and the tax base is broader with fewer exclusions (Abdel-Kader and Mooij, 2020; Jian and Lee, 2018). Corporate income tax can be progressive for domestic business owners, and it can help governments to collect taxes from foreign-owed firms (Jian and Lee, 2018), however there is some evidence from Asia-Pacific counties that corporate taxes can increase inequality when there are tax concessions and subsidies for some firms (Claus, Martinez-Vazquez and Vulovic, 2012). Property taxes based on house prices can be progressive, but the incidence can vary depending on how many owners pay taxes and whether tax costs are passed on to renters, which can make the tax more regressive (Abdel-Kader and Mooij, 2020; Claus, Martinez-Vazquez and Vulovic, 2012). Social security contributions, which can be considered a tax in pension systems that are government funded instead of pay-as-you-go, can have a regressive incidence in systems where contributions are capped, however, when they are only levied on smaller formal employment sectors, the incidence can be progressive (Claus, Martinez-Vazquez and Vulovic, 2012).

In general, VAT is assumed to be regressive, but this can vary depending on whether it is paid only by the formal sector with higher incomes, and there can be exceptions for basic goods as opposed to luxury goods. Excise tax, like other taxes on goods and services, is generally considered regressive, but can be progressive when levied on luxury goods such as cars and perfumes rather than more broadly consumed items such as kerosene for cooking and tobacco (Abdel-Kader and Mooij, 2020; Claus, Martinez-Vazquez and Vulovic, 2012).

Evidence from previous studies on the impact of taxes and transfers is useful for analysing the impact of each policy individually. The CEQ methodology provides additional evidence about the combined impact of taxes and transfers on households.

In particular, it looks at the marginal contribution of each policy within the fiscal system, which accounts for the potential interaction between different taxes and spending programmes. The analysis captures situations when a nominally progressive tax could potentially fund regressive expenditures that increase inequality or revenue from a regressive tax is used to fund programmes and transfers that ultimately reduce inequality (Inchauste and Lustig, 2017).

III. EVIDENCE FROM 12 ASIA-PACIFIC COUNTRIES

Of the 12 Asia-Pacific countries covered in the present paper, nine have CEQ assessments that quantify the impact of spending policies on inequality. The assessments show the impact of the combined fiscal system on inequality by comparing market incomes, or the distribution of household incomes before taxes and transfers, to final income after considering the impact of all measured taxes and transfers. The difference between these two measures shows the estimated change in the Gini index from the assessed fiscal policy interventions. The methodology also allows for different measurements of the impact of fiscal policies on inequality based on the way that contributory pension systems are structured that show different results when pension income is assessed as a government transfer or as deferred income.[2]

These studies show that the redistributive impact of taxes and transfers in a country is related to three aspects of the fiscal system: the overall size of the tax or transfer; the distribution of the transfer across households, whether progressive or regressive; and the composition of fiscal policies in the government budget. For example, a higher-income country with a larger budget will typically have more fiscal space to deploy expenditures on transfers, and tax policies will also have a broader impact (Inchauste and Lustig, 2017, p. 4).

Looking at the combined effect of all measured taxes and transfers in the nine CEQ assessments, all fiscal systems reduce inequality (table 2). Countries with higher incomes per capita also tend to redistribute a greater amount of income, with Turkey, the Russian Federation, and the Islamic Republic of Iran having both the highest gross national income (GNI) per capita during the CEQ assessment year, and also showing the largest measured impact of the fiscal systems on inequality. However, other countries with lower incomes per capita, such as Georgia and Armenia, show relatively large impacts from their fiscal systems, suggesting that other factors may account for the impact of their fiscal systems.

---

[2] See annex for additional details about the methodology.

Table 2. Impact of fiscal policy on inequality in nine Asia-Pacific countries

Country	CEQ assessment year	GNI per capita, PPP	Pension as deferred income			Pension as transfer		
			Market income plus pensions	Final income	Gini index change	Market income	Final income	Gini index change
Armenia	2011	8 310	29.42	25.22	*-4.20*	35.73	25.22	*-10.52*
China	2013	11 780	*Not published in the report*			55.58	46.45	*-9.14*
Georgia	2013	10 420	*Not applicable for the fiscal system*			50.74	38.30	*-12.44*
Indonesia	2012	9 440	39.83	37.05	*-2.78*	39.44	36.98	*-2.46*
Iran (Islamic Republic of)	2011	18 010	43.20	36.50	*-6.70*	44.66	36.50	*-8.16*
Mongolia	2016	9 850	*Not published in the report*			41.83	35.07	*-6.76*
Russian Federation	2010	23 460	37.88	29.89	*-7.99*	49.21	29.89	*-19.33*
Sri Lanka	2009	7 470	34.37	31.01	*-3.36*	*Not applicable for the fiscal system*		
Turkey	2016	26 230	47.10	36.64	*-10.47*	50.83	36.64	*-14.20*

Source: CEQ standard indicators (CEQ Institute, 2021).

Note: Market income comprises pre-tax wages, salaries, income earned from capital assets (rent, interest or dividends) and private transfers; Final income is market income, less payments for taxes and incidence of indirect taxes, plus direct transfers, indirect subsidies and the value of in-kind transfers (education and health care). Values are shown as Gini index on a score of 0 to 100 percentage points. Data on GNI per capita, PPP, is reported for the CEQ assessment year in current international dollars (World Bank, 2022).

Abbreviations: CEQ, Commitment to Equity; GNI, gross national income; PPP, purchasing power parity.

For some countries, the measured impact of fiscal policies on inequality varies widely depending on whether pensions are assessed as deferred income or as government transfers. Four CEQ assessments considered pensions using both methodologies, as the pension systems are both funded from general revenues and through social security contributions: Armenia, Indonesia, the Russian Federation and Turkey. In Armenia and the Russian Federation, where pensions are a large share of social spending and have broad coverage, the difference between the two measures is significant. For example, the fiscal system in the Russian Federation reduces inequality by 19 percentage points, the highest in the sample, when spending on pensions is assessed as a transfer, but only eight points when pensions are assessed as deferred income. This is due to the large amount of spending on contributory pensions – which also accounts for the majority of spending that impacts inequality within the CEQ assessment.

3.1 Impact of transfers

This section provides a review of the evidence in CEQ assessments, PERs and SCDs on the impact of transfer programmes on inequality in selected Asia-Pacific countries. Evidence shows that direct transfers, especially targeted social safety net programmes, can have a substantial impact on reducing inequality. Less spending, however, is directed toward effective social safety net programmes than toward pension programmes. Relative to the amount of spending on subsidies, the impact on inequality was limited. Education spending, measured as in-kind transfers to households with eligible children, also functions to reduce inequality in all countries, while spending on health has more mixed results.

Direct transfer programmes, as quantified in CEQ assessments, have the largest marginal contribution to the reduction of inequality of any measured policy intervention (figure 1). The largest reductions of inequality as a result of direct transfers are seen in countries with large pension programmes, such as the Russian Federation, Georgia and Armenia, however, for the Russian Federation and Armenia, this impact decreases when pensions are assessed as deferred income rather than as government transfers. Given that contributory pensions in both countries are funded through a mix of social security contributions and general revenues, the impact of these pensions systems is likely somewhere between these two results.

Figure 1. Direct transfer spending compared to marginal contribution in reducing inequality

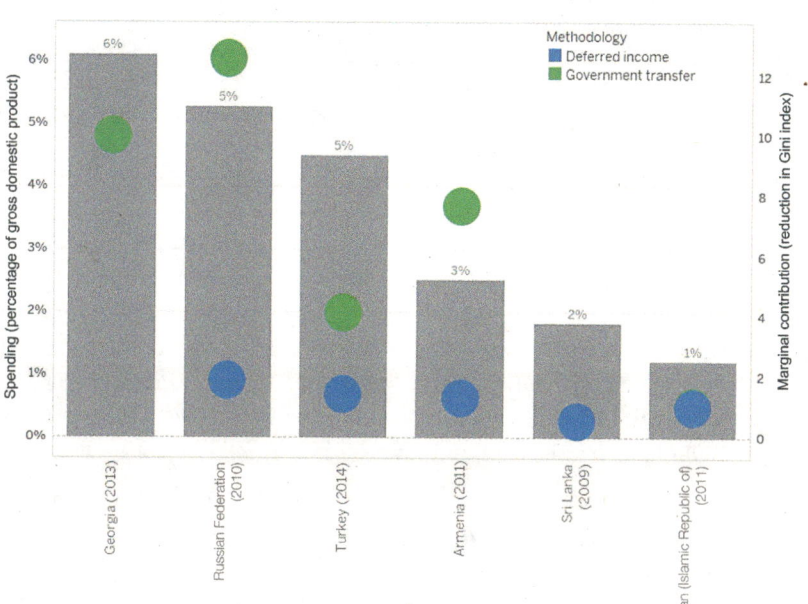

Source: CEQ standard indicators (https://commitmentoequity.org/datacenter/), November 2021 update.

Note: Marginal contribution values show the difference in the Gini index, on a scale of 0 to 100 percentage points, with and without the intervention; positive values show a reduction in inequality. Indonesia was excluded for data inconsistencies.

Old-age pension programmes with broad coverage can effectively reduce inequality, even when pensions are not explicitly targeted to lower-income groups. In Armenia in 2011, contributory pensions were the largest budget line (20 per cent of the State budget and 68 per cent of social protection spending) and accounted for more than half of the observed reduction in inequality in the overall fiscal system. Despite being universal without any targeting by income, pensions were the most effective policy instrument at reducing poverty due to broad coverage, despite the relatively small size of the transfers to each recipient (Younger and Khachatryan, 2017). In 2013, Georgia had a universal, non-contributory old-age pension system that had a significant impact on reducing poverty and inequality. The programme amounted to 42 per cent of total public spending and was entirely financed out of general revenues. Pensions were not explicitly targeted toward the poor, however 55 per cent of transfers were made to poor beneficiaries (Cancho and Bondarenko,

2017; World Bank, 2015). However, for all three countries, pensions programmes are expensive and may face sustainability issues. Reforms to limit benefits or improve targeting may be challenging given the public support for these benefits.

Social safety net policies targeted toward the poor account for a smaller share of spending on direct transfers. For example, the flagship poverty reduction programme in Sri Lanka, Samurdhi, saw declining funding between 2001 and 2012. The CEQ assessment estimated that if funding had not declined, poverty rates could have been 10 per cent lower at the time of the study. Despite the large potential impact on poverty, the small size of the transfers to each family and issues with targeting result in spending on these programmes having a relatively minimal impact on inequality (Arunatilake, Inchauste and Lustig, 2017). In Indonesia, spending on the Family Hope Programme amounts to only 0.02 per cent of gross domestic product (GDP), and the programme has a relatively modest impact on inequality commensurate with the size of the allocation. Along with other direct cash benefits in Indonesia, the programme faces challenges with targeting in that only a quarter of expenditures go to recipients below the national poverty line (Inchauste and Lustig, 2017, chap. 5).

Targeting of social safety net programmes is a challenge also seen in Armenia and the Islamic Republic of Iran. Whether either too robust or too lax, targeting can reduce the potential impact of a policy on inequality. In Armenia, the Family Benefit Programme for poor families is considered one of the better-targeted poverty programmes in the world due to means-tested targeting with criteria that exclude higher income groups. However, some poor households are also excluded, and it is estimated to reach only 22 per cent of households with incomes under $2.50 a day. As a result, the limited expenditures on this programme have only a minor impact on inequality (Younger and Khachatryan, 2017). In the Islamic Republic of Iran, the Government implements a targeted subsidy programme, which is a lump-sum transfer programme that replaced energy and bread subsidies after a reform in 2010. Initially introduced as a universal programme to help transition the country from subsidies, the Government has since aimed to target the transfer to the lower 80 per cent of income earners, but it has only succeeded in excluding a few wealthy individuals. Spending on this programme is therefore significant, with a larger fiscal footprint than the subsidies it replaced. Because of this spending, the programme has a significant impact on poverty, but it is less effective at reducing inequality than other programmes in the country (Enami, Lustig and Taqdiri, 2019).

Subsidies seen in the reviewed countries have limited impacts on inequality. This is the case even for subsidy programmes that are explicitly targeted to low-income households, as seen in Sri Lanka for fuel, fertilizer, water, electricity and transport. The total cost of these subsidies is six times the cost of the flagship poverty reduction programme. While these subsidies have an equalizing impact overall, higher income families also benefit from this spending. Approximately 20 per cent of spending benefited families in the top 20 per cent by income. A significant share (more than 30 per cent) of poor populations do not have access to these subsidized services, including piped water and electricity (Arunatilake, Inchauste and Lustig, 2017). Similar constraints are seen for energy subsidies in Indonesia. Before the fuel subsidy programmes were reformed in 2015–2016, spending on fuel subsidies also had a minimal impact on inequality, but a larger role in poverty reduction. In 2009, these subsidies amounted to 0.16 per cent of GDP. However, the impact of fuel subsidies on reducing inequality was about the same as spending on direct transfers, even though the subsidy budget was 10 times larger. When the Government implemented significant fuel subsidy reforms in late 2014 and early 2015, subsidy expenditures were reallocated to programmes such as the Family Hope Programme that are more effectively targeted at the poor, and the 2020 PER highlighted that these policy changes had a larger impact on reducing inequality (World Bank, 2020).

Figure 2. Impact of in-kind education and health spending on inequality

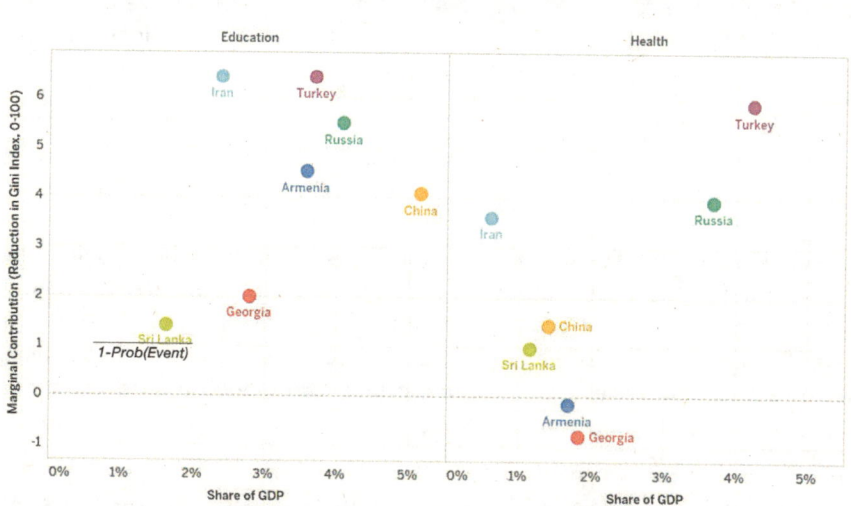

Source: CEQ standard indicators (https://commitmentoequity.org/datacenter/), November 2021 update.

Note: Marginal contribution values show the difference in the Gini index, on a scale of 0 to 100 percentage points, with and without the intervention; positive values show a reduction in inequality. Indonesia was excluded for data inconsistencies.

Total education spending in all countries with CEQ assessments is progressive, with significant reductions in inequality, where the impacts on inequality are broadly correlated with the amount of public spending in the sector (figure 2). Health spending had a more variable impact, with notable cases in Georgia and Armenia where health spending results in a decrease in inequality.

In-kind spending on education is one of the largest factors reducing inequality in Indonesia, Georgia and Sri Lanka. In Indonesia, for example, while education shows the largest marginal contribution to reducing income inequality (1.9 Gini index points), the sector also accounts for a large share of public spending and 70 per cent of social spending. Interestingly, despite unregulated user fees for families to access public education services, which are also a significant cost for many families, these fees do not serve to increase inequality as the incidence of the burden of the fees is progressive. Enrolment rates for students are high for primary school but decline for lower-income students in lower-to-upper secondary school. This equates to the impact of spending in primary and lower-secondary education transfers having a much greater impact on inequality than higher levels of schooling. Indonesia is the only country in the sample where spending on tertiary education slightly increases inequality, due to the concentration of students that come from wealthy families. For other countries, while tertiary education spending is less progressive than spending on lower education levels, the net effect of spending still reduces inequality.

Even if education spending is progressive and reduces both inequality and poverty, incidence analysis cannot capture the effectiveness of these programmes. For example, in Armenia public spending on education both lowers inequality and reduces poverty, with education spending in primary and middle school being the most progressive spending for education (Younger and Khachatryan, 2017). However, the Armenia PER notes that education spending in rural areas is inefficient, where "mini-schools" produce the worst educational outcomes (World Bank, 2014). In Turkey, spending on tertiary education does not have as much impact on reducing inequality as primary or secondary education spending, however, the 2016 SCD notes that improving the quality of education at these levels is important for meeting the needs of the job market and promoting long-term growth and labour competitiveness (World Bank, 2016).

The relative importance of education and health spending compared to other fiscal policies that address inequality may be influenced by the question of efficiency. The measured fiscal incidence for in-kind spending on different government services may be higher than the actual benefits received by households, given that the quality of services is varied, and many countries have issues of wasted spending. For example, the World Health Organization estimates that as much as 20 to 40 per cent of health spending is lost due to inefficiencies (Zouhar and others, 2021).

Other types of spending, for example on roads and agriculture, can also be important for poverty reduction even as the impact on inequality is harder to estimate.

In Cambodia, growth in the agriculture sector was a driver of rural development and poverty reduction between 2006–2012. As the agriculture sector accounted for 26.6 per cent of GDP and 41.5 per cent of employment in 2015, growth in this sector had a significant impact on the national poverty headcount. Public investments in the sector were only part of the reason why the sector experienced growth – high international prices, improved technologies and crop diversification were also contributing factors (World Bank, 2019a).

3.2 Tax policies and inequality

For the countries measured by the CEQ methodology the tax systems overall do not have as much of an impact on income inequality as spending policies. This is consistent with findings from other developing countries, especially where tax as a share of GDP is lower than advanced economies (Claus, Martinez-Vazquez and Vulovic, 2012; Zouhar and others, 2021). Data from the nine countries with CEQ assessments show that revenues from indirect taxes tend to be larger than direct taxes, with only Indonesia, the Islamic Republic of Iran, the Russian Federation and Turkey collecting a greater share of revenue from direct taxes. In contrast, Armenia, China, Georgia and Mongolia all collect more than 60 per cent of their total revenues from indirect taxes.

Figure 3. Impact of direct and indirect taxes on inequality

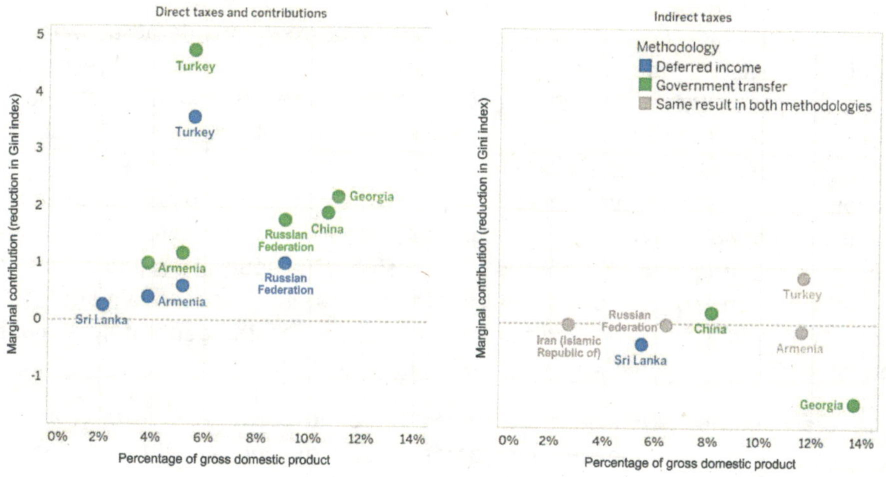

Source: CEQ standard indicators (https://commitmentoequity.org/datacenter/) for the November 2021 update.

Note: Marginal contribution shows the change in the Gini index from market to final income on a scale of 0 to 100 percentage points. Indonesia was excluded for data inconsistencies.

Consistent with previous studies on the incidence of taxes on different income groups, the CEQ assessments find that the relative contribution of indirect taxes increases inequality in Armenia, Georgia, Indonesia, the Islamic Republic of Iran, the Russian Federation and Sri Lanka . In China, while indirect taxes remain regressive, the overall fiscal system adjusts the net effect of the tax to reduce inequality. Conversely, direct taxes reduce inequality in all countries except Indonesia, where direct taxes are nearly neutral to inequality in part because only 0.5 per cent of households pay personal income tax and are too few to be captured in the household survey. As a generally observed trend, the impact on inequality increases with the amount of revenue collected from direct taxes (figure 3).

The most common direct taxes in the reviewed countries are personal income taxes and social security contributions. Personal income tax structures are usually progressive, except for flat taxes in Georgia and Mongolia. Despite the potential for social security contributions to be regressive where there are limits on contributions, the net effect for countries with contributions, such as Armenia, China, the Russian Federation and Sri Lanka, is to reduce inequality. Even so, personal income tax tends to have a greater impact on reducing inequality than social security contributions. In Armenia, tax reforms were introduced in 2013 to eliminate the social security tax and replace it with personal income tax while also eliminating personal tax deductions, which could improve the progressivity of the Armenian tax system.

For indirect taxes, the VAT in Sri Lanka in 2009–2010 and Georgia in 2013 both had a significant impact to increase inequality. In Sri Lanka, VAT rates (0, 12 and 20 per cent) depended on whether the good or service was considered a luxury. The effective rate of VAT was lower than the official tax rates, it generated revenues of 3.4 per cent of GDP and its marginal contribution increased inequality by 0.63 Gini index points. Similarly, in Georgia, a standard 18 per cent tax is added to all sales of goods and services and imported goods, although there are some exemptions. Tax collections from VAT amount to 10.6 per cent of GDP, which also resulted in an increase in inequality by 1.03 Gini index points. In Indonesia, while overall indirect taxes increase inequality, the VAT is progressive and reduces inequality. Instead, the excise tax on tobacco is the most significant factor in the inequality of indirect taxes – which is a common finding across all countries the separately evaluated tobacco excises, including Armenia, Sri Lanka and Turkey.

Several countries reviewed in the present paper have low revenue-to-GDP ratios compared to other countries in their income groups, making tax reforms to increase collections an important prerequisite before expanding equitable or redistributive policies. Many countries may initially expand taxes on revenues that are easier to collect. For example, in contrast to corporate taxes that may be hard to collect where Governments cannot identify retained corporate earnings, taxes from excises are easier to collect because they are levied on a few large businesses, and import tariffs can be collected as goods transit the country's border (Abdel-Kader and Mooij, 2020). Yet excise taxes were found in the CEQ assessments to be highly regressive and to increase inequality for most countries.

Due to the risk that increased tax collection, in particular VAT and excise tax, will result in higher inequality and poverty rates, one option is for countries to package tax increases alongside cash transfer programmes to mitigate the impact on the poor. In the Philippines, a 2016 tax reform that increased corporate income tax, excise tax and VAT rates was assessed as likely to increase poverty rates due to higher prices on goods that are often consumed in greater amounts in low-income groups, such as sweetened beverages and petroleum products. To offset the impact of these taxes, the reform was accompanied by a new unconditional cash transfer programme that was launched in 2018 (World Bank, 2019b).

As Governments look to increase tax revenues to fund social spending, many countries are also working to strengthen tax systems by improving the collection of existing taxes. For example, in Cambodia, revenue collections across all taxes increased from 12.7 per cent of GDP in 2012 to 16.1 per cent in 2016 through reforms that strengthened taxpayer registration and services, including online tax payments, better tax auditing, more qualified tax collectors and a revised information technology system (World Bank, 2019a). In Indonesia, tax reforms on tax administration and tax policy, including a tax amnesty programme to expand the tax base and electronic invoices and e-filing of taxes are estimated to have increased revenues by 0.6 per cent of GDP in 2018 (World Bank, 2020). In Armenia, the Government identified reducing tax exemptions for the VAT as an avenue to improve tax revenues (World Bank, 2014). As Governments make efforts to increase collections, often by strengthen VAT collections, these efforts can unwittingly increase taxes on the poor, as well as increase inequality in the tax system. Reviewing the incidence of taxes as Governments implement reforms can help them to identify whether strengthening collections for different taxes can have unintended consequences for income redistribution.

IV. CONCLUSIONS AND POLICY RECOMMENDATIONS

In the Asia-Pacific countries reviewed in the present paper, fiscal policies contributed to reductions in inequality, although the relative impact of tax and spending policies varied both with their size and their distribution across the population. Direct transfer programmes, especially pensions, were the most significant factors in the redistributive effect of fiscal policy systems. The impact of these programmes varies based on the size of the programme, however, so Governments that look to expand social protection programmes and social safety nets will also need to identify the most effective ways to expand fiscal space.

Across the reviewed countries, the structure of tax policies was a contributory factor but not a deciding factor in the magnitude of redistribution in the overall fiscal system. For that reason, Governments may pursue tax policies with other goals in mind, including balancing other priorities for the tax system, such as price distortions and externalities. Tax compliance in developing countries raises challenges for Governments, especially in economies with high rates of informal employment and underdeveloped capital markets, and therefore investments to strengthen tax administration may yield higher revenues. Tax reforms can also be pursued when they are combined and justified by proposals to use revenues towards more progressive and redistributive spending, such as health and education programmes.

Examining the impact of existing fiscal policies on inequality is important to help to prioritize and recalibrate current spending, but Governments can work to reduce inequality by identifying gaps in the social protection system that may have been exposed by the COVID-19 pandemic. For example, informal workers and women with care responsibilities may not have been covered in formal unemployment or other benefit programmes.

Countries that already have sizable social spending can often improve its impact by shifting spending from programmes that are less progressive toward programmes that are better targeted towards poor and marginalized groups. For example, the Targeted Subsidy Programme in the Islamic Republic of Iran is a sizable budget items that has limited targeting toward poorer groups, and shifting a portion of the spending toward more targeted policies can increase the distributive effect of social spending. Countries that already have effective targeting mechanisms can link those targeting systems to additional programmes. This was seen in Armenia, where a successful means-based targeting mechanism used in the Family Benefits Programme was expanded for health benefits in 2014. In the Philippines, the targeting system for a conditional cash programme, the National Household Targeting System for Poverty Reduction, is expanding to improve targeting for other programmes.

Fiscal distribution analyses, such as the ones conducted using the CEQ methodology, can be helpful tools for Governments to review their existing mix of policies and prioritize expanding taxes and spending that promote greater redistribution. These studies can also be complemented by additional analysis to understand the long-term impacts of spending on inequality. For example, expanding access to education for low-income groups may result in raising earning potential and returns to labour that generate benefits and redistribute income within a society beyond the impact of the in-kind transfers assessed in the CEQ approach. Countries can consider a mix of policies that increase the redistributive impact of spending in a given fiscal year, balanced with investment decisions that promote more equitable societies over time.

Annex: Methodology and data sources

The paper contains a review of the findings of CEQ assessments, which use fiscal incidence analysis to examine the combined impact of taxes and transfers on the distribution of income for a given fiscal system at one point in time. The methodology for CEQ assessments is described in the *Commitment to Equity Handbook* (2018)[3] as well as annex 1A.1 of chapter 1 of *The Distributional Impact of Taxes and Transfers: Evidence from Eight Developing Countries* (2017). The present annex provides an overview the CEQ methodology and provides definitions for key concepts and data used in the paper.

The CEQ methodology combines household survey data alongside disaggregated government budget data on spending and revenues to estimate how much income redistribution and poverty reduction is accomplished through fiscal policies. The CEQ methodology and the paper use the Gini coefficient as the main measure of inequality. A measure of the distribution of income across a population, the Gini coefficient expressed as a percentage (Gini index) ranges from perfect equality (0 per cent), to perfect inequality (100 per cent).

The CEQ approach looks at all available data on taxes and transfers, analysing the combined impact of the entire fiscal system. Using household survey data, a CEQ assessment maps taxes and transfers to individuals and households, either based on information provided with survey data or estimates of the incidence of taxes and transfers across income and demographic groups. The actual amount of taxes and transfers, especially for direct transfers and direct taxes, that are identified in household survey data often differs from what is in official budget data, meaning that researchers must use a set of assumptions to scale public revenue and spending data to match the incidence of taxes and transfers observed in households. This is also true for indirect taxes and indirect transfers, which cannot easily be mapped to individual households and therefore are mapped to individual households based on the estimated actual incidence, rather than statutory incidence. The CEQ methodology encourages researchers to give precedence to data on taxes and transfers found in household surveys, unless there are valid and documented reasons to believe that certain transfers or taxes are underreported in survey data compared to administrative data. Benefits to individuals and households from in-kind education and health spending are based on per-beneficiary costs from administrative data, while the actual benefits to households may vary depending on their own estimation of the value of these free or subsidized services.

---

[3] The most recent version of the CEQ Handbook was published in 2018, but some of the CEQ assessments reviewed in this paper use the earlier 2013 methodology that was published as a working paper. See table 1 for the version of the CEQ methodology used in each study.

As the CEQ methodology looks at types of government expenditures and revenues that can be mapped to individuals and households, this approach excludes some types of spending and taxes where the benefits are more diffuse and cannot be attributed to individuals or households. Types of spending that are excluded from this analysis include defence and public safety spending, and spending on roads, communications and other infrastructure spending. Revenue sources that are excluded include non-tax revenues, as well as corporate taxes and sometimes property taxes, depending on their incidence. As a result, the CEQ assessment only covers a portion of government expenditures and revenues, usually around half of public spending. In addition, because the analysis relies on public data on government spending and revenues, it may not cover some types of off-budget spending that could impact household incomes.[4]

CEQ assessments look at fiscal distribution by looking at the impact of direct and indirect taxes and transfers on individuals and households by different income concepts. Four income concepts are used in the CEQ methodology:

- Market income, which is also known as original income before taxes and transfers;

- Disposable income, which is market income less direct taxes and with the addition of direct transfers;

- Consumable income, which is disposable income less indirect taxes and with the addition of indirect subsidies;

- Final income, which is consumable income plus the estimated value of in-kind transfers for education and health, less any user fees associated with these services.

---

[4] One exception is the Mongolia CEQ assessment, which does look at off-budget spending for electricity, heating, and housing (mortgage interest) subsidies.

Definitions of income concepts

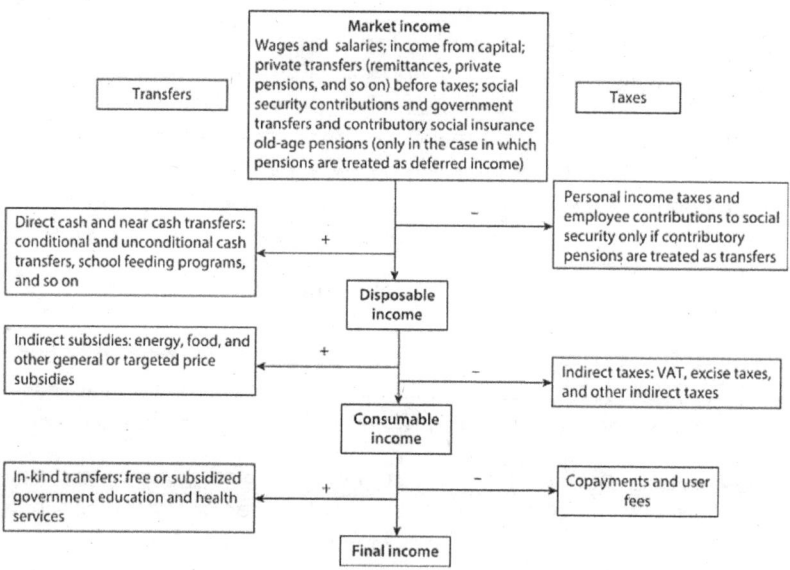

Source: Gabriela Inchauste and Nora Lustig (2017). *The Distributional Impact of Taxes and Transfers: Evidence from eight developing countries*. Washington, D.C.: World Bank, figure 1A.1.

Within this framework, social insurance contributory pensions present a methodological challenge in terms of whether to calculate the income received from these pensions as government transfers or as deferred income. Some contributory pension systems as are pay-as-you-go, where benefits received in retirement are tied to contributions into the pension system made throughout working-age years. In this case, these contributory pensions are not assessed as a transfer, but instead as deferred income, where income from contributory pensions is assessed as part of a household or individual's market income and contributions into the pension system are assessed as savings. However, some contributory pension programmes are not clearly tied to individual contributions or are funded from general government revenues. In these cases, an argument can be made to treat contributory pensions as a government transfer, and contributions into the system as a tax. Across the literature for fiscal incidence analysis, there is no consensus on which method is more appropriate, therefore the CEQ methodology encourages researchers to present results from both methods for countries where there are contributory pension programmes.

The impact of taxes and transfers on equity and poverty within a given fiscal system is calculated within the CEQ methodology by generating estimates of inequality and poverty rates at each of the income concepts (market, consumable, disposable, final). The CEQ method of measuring fiscal redistribution allows for the impact of multiple taxes and transfers to result in the reranking of individuals and households within the income distribution when moving from market to final income. The reranking is important for determining whether a fiscal intervention is equalizing, given the interaction with other interventions within a fiscal system, as it can result in progressive policies being equalizing or regressive policies being equalizing – a situation that is known as Lambert's conundrum.[5]

To measure the impact of an individual policy on equality within a given fiscal system, the CEQ methodology calculates the *marginal contribution* for each fiscal intervention that is assessed. The marginal contribution is the difference between the inequality of a fiscal system (for example, as measured as a calculated Gini index) without a given intervention compared to the inequality with the intervention.

In the figures presented the paper, the impact of the marginal contribution is also compared to the amount of spending on each transfer or revenue collected from each tax. The data used to make the comparisons are taken from the CEQ database (Tabs 4 and 27) by mapping related taxes and transfers to the marginal contribution (market to final income), based on the categories below:

Marginal contribution	Taxes and transfers
Direct taxes and contributions	Total direct taxes
Indirect taxes (without indirect effect)	Total indirect taxes
Value added tax (without indirect effect)	Value added tax
Contributions to pensions	Social security contributions
Other Contributions	Other direct taxes

---

[5] The CEQ Handbook references the work of Peter Lambert on the question of whether knowing the progressivity or regressivity of a certain fiscal intervention is enough to know whether it is equalizing or equalizing within a given fiscal system of multiple interventions. Lambert shows that this is not the case, even without reranking, if taxes are regressive when compared to original income, but not regressive in comparison to post-benefit incomes. This situation results in a case where a fiscal system is more equalizing with the addition of a regressive tax than it would be without it, even without counting the impact of progressive transfers. See Peter Lambert (2001). *The Distribution and Redistribution of Income,* 3rd ed.: Manchester University Press.

Marginal contribution	Taxes and transfers
Direct transfers	Direct transfers
Contributory pensions	Contributory pensions
Indirect subsidies (without indirect effect)	Subsidies
Education	Education
Health	Health

NOTE ON CONTRIBUTORS

Sally Torbert is a Senior Programme Officer with the International Budget Partnership based in Tbilisi, Georgia. She holds degrees from Princeton University and the Fletcher School of Law and Diplomacy.

REFERENCES

Abdel-Kader, Khaled, and Ruud A. Mooij (2020). Tax Policy and Inclusive Growth. IMF Working Paper, No. 20/271.

Arunatilake, Nisha, Gabriela Inchauste and Nora Lustig (2017). The Incidence of Taxes and Spending in Sri Lanka. Commitment to Equity (CEQ) Working Paper Series, No. 63. Tulane University, Department of Economics.

Blanchard, Olivier, and Dani Rodrik, eds. (2021). *Combating Inequality.* Cambridge, Mass: MIT Press.

Calderón, César, and Luis Servén (2014). Infrastructure, Growth, and Inequality: An Overview. Policy Research Working Paper, No. 7034. Washington, D.C.: World Bank.

Cancho, Cesar, and Elena Bondarenko (2017). The Distributional Impact of Fiscal Policy in Georgia. CEQ Working Paper, No. 42.

CEQ Institute (2021). CEQ Data Center on Fiscal Redistribution. Available at https://commitmentoequity.org/datacenter/.

Chu, Ke Young, Hamid Davoodi and Sanjeev Gupta (2004). Income Distribution and Tax and Government Social-Spending Policies in Developing Countries. In *Inequality Growth and Poverty in an Era of Liberalization and Globalization,* Giovanni Andrea Cornia, ed. Oxford University Press.

Claus, Iris, Jorge Martinez-Vazquez and Violeta Vulovic (2012). Government Fiscal Policies and Redistribution in Asian Countries. ADB Economics Working Paper Series, No. 310.

Enami, Ali, Nora Lustig and Alireza Taqdiri (2019). Fiscal Policy, Inequality, and Poverty in Iran: Assessing the Impact and Effectiveness of Taxes and Transfers. *Middle East Development Journal,* vol. 11, Issue 1, pp. 49–74.

Freinkman, Lev M., and Sophiko Skhirtladze (2015). Taking the stock of PERs: Emerging patterns and examples of good practice. Washington, D.C.: World Bank.

Inchauste, Gabriela, and Nora Lustig (2017). *The Distributional Impact of Taxes and Transfers: Evidence from eight developing countries.* Washington, D.C.: World Bank.

Jian, Zheng, and Daniel Jeongdae Lee (2018). Prospects for Progressive Tax Policies in Asia and the Pacific. In *Tax Policy for Sustainable Development in Asia and the Pacific.* Tientip Subhanij, Shuvojit Banerjee, and Zheng Jian, eds. Bangkok: United Nations Economic and Social Commission for Asia and the Pacific (ESCAP).

Lustig, Nora (2017). Fiscal Policy, Income Redistribution and Poverty Reduction in Low and Middle Income Countries. Tulane University: CEQ Institute.

Lustig, Nora (2018). *Commitment to Equity Handbook.* Brookings Institution Press.

Seneviratne, Dulani, and Yan Sun (2013). Infrastructure and Income Distribution in ASEAN-5: What Are the Links? IMF Working Paper, No. 13/41.

United Nations, Economic and Social Commission for Asia and the Pacific (ESCAP) (2021). *Economic and Social Survey of Asia and the Pacific 2021: Towards post-COVID-19 resilient economies.* Bangkok: United Nations.

World Bank (2014). *Republic of Armenia Public Expenditure Review: Expanding the Fiscal Envelope.* Washington, D.C.

World Bank (2015). *Georgia Public Expenditure Review: Selected Fiscal Issues.* Washington, D.C.

World Bank (2016). *Turkey's Future Transitions: Republic of Turkey Systematic Country Diagnostic.* Washington, D.C.

World Bank (2019a). *Improving the Effectiveness of Public Finance: Cambodia Public Expenditure Review.* Washington, D.C.

World Bank (2019b). *Systematic Country Diagnostic of the Philippines: Realizing the Filipino Dream for 2040.* Washington, D.C.

World Bank (2020). *Indonesia Public Expenditure Review: Spending for Better Results.* Washington, D.C.

World Bank (2022). GNI per Capita, PPP (Current International $). Available at https://data.worldbank.org/indicator/NY.GNP.PCAP.PP.CD.

Younger, Stephen D., and Artsvi Khachatryan (2017). Fiscal Incidence in Armenia. Commitment to Equity (CEQ) Working Paper Series, No. 43.

Zouhar, Younes, Jon Jellema, Nora Lustig and Mohamed Trabelsi (2021). Public Expenditure and Inclusive Growth – A Survey. IMF Working Paper, No. 21/083.

Special theme: Macroeconomic policies for inclusive sustainable development

CENTRAL BANKS AND FINANCIAL INCLUSION

Peter J. Morgan

Senior Consulting Economist and Advisor to the Dean
Asian Development Bank Institute
Email: pmorgan@adbi.org

Central banks can address barriers to financial inclusion in multiple ways, including regulations regarding banks and non-bank institutions, identity and know-your-client (KYC) rules, support for innovative financial products, and support for innovative financial technology (fintech). At the same time, central banks must weigh the trade-offs between financial inclusion, financial innovation and financial stability. The present paper contains a survey the policies of central banks and other financial regulators in a number of emerging Asian economies to promote financial inclusion. It serves to identify successful experiences and important lessons, and it provides a review of policies central banks adopted during the COVID-19 pandemic.

Keywords: financial inclusion, central banks, financial regulation, payments systems, small and medium-sized enterprises, financial education, fintech

JEL classification: G21, G28, I22, O16

I. INTRODUCTION

Financial inclusion is receiving increasing attention as having the potential to contribute to economic and financial development while at the same time fostering more inclusive growth and greater income equality. Leaders of the Group of 20 (G20) countries have approved the Financial Inclusion Action Plan and established the Global Partnership for Financial Inclusion[1] to promote the financial access agenda. The Finance Ministers' Process, a forum for members of Asia-Pacific Economic Cooperation (APEC), addresses regional financial issues, including financial inclusion.[2] In the Association of Southeast Asian Nations (ASEAN), financial inclusion is a key objective of the Framework on Equitable Economic Development. Development organizations have been responsive, too. Many individual Asian economies have adopted strategies on financial inclusion as an important part of their overall strategies to achieve inclusive growth.

However, there is still much to achieve. One key indicator of household access to finance is the percentage of adults who have an account at a formal financial institution such as a bank, credit union, cooperative, post office, microfinance institution or mobile money provider. According to the World Bank Global Findex database for 2017, the worldwide average for this measure is 69 per cent, and while the total number of adults without a formal financial account remains high at approximately 1.7 billion, it has declined substantially from 2.7 billion in 2011. In Asia, China has the world's largest unbanked population (225 million or 20 per cent of adult population), followed by India (190 million or 20 per cent), Pakistan (100 million or 82 per cent) and Indonesia (95 million or 52 per cent). These four countries alone account for over one third of the unbanked globally (Demirgüç-Kunt and others, 2018).

The development of financial technology, fintech (i.e. a new generation of electronically delivered financial services), shows great potential to enhance financial inclusion by lowering costs and increasing efficiency. The COVID-19 pandemic accelerated the trend of adopting fintech services because face-to-face contact was more difficult and riskier. At the same time, fintech introduces new risks for consumers, especially those in disadvantaged groups with lower levels of financial sophistication.

The present paper contains a survey of a number of central banks and other regulators in emerging Asian countries to identify and assess their policies aimed at promoting financial inclusion. The countries examined are Bangladesh, India,

---

1 See www.gpfi.org/.

2 The annual forum was held most recently in May 2021 (See www.adb.org/news/events/11th-asia-pacific-financial-inclusion-forum).

Indonesia, the Philippines, Sri Lanka and Thailand. It includes a review of policies adopted to counter the effects of the COVID-19 pandemic. It also covers financial education programmes, financial regulatory frameworks and consumer protection programmes. The aim of the present paper is to identify successful experiences and important lessons that can be adopted by other emerging economies.

II. DEFINITIONS OF FINANCIAL INCLUSION

Financial inclusion broadly refers to the degree of access to financial services for households and firms, especially poorer households and micro-, small and medium-sized enterprises (MSMEs). However, as the sampling of definitions below shows, there are important variations in usage and nuance.

"Inclusive financial systems provide individuals and firms with greater access to resources to meet their financial needs, such as saving for retirement, investing in education, capitalizing on business opportunities, and confronting shocks" (World Bank, 2014, p. xi).

"...the process of promoting affordable, timely and adequate access to a wide range of regulated financial products and services and broadening their use by all segments of society through the implementation of tailored existing and innovative approaches including financial awareness and education with a view to promote financial well-being as well as economic and social inclusion" (Atkinson and Messy, 2013, p. 11).

"...four commonly used lenses through which financial inclusion can be defined, in order of complexity: access...quality...usage... welfare" (AFI, 2010, p. 6).

Notably, the word "access" does not mean just any kind of access, but implies access at reasonable cost and with accompanying safeguards, such as adequate regulation of firms supplying financial services and laws and institutions for protecting consumers against inappropriate products, deceptive practices and aggressive collection practices. Of course, it is difficult to define reasonable cost in cases where amounts involved are small and where there are information asymmetries. Therefore, one key question is the extent to which the Government should subsidize such services or otherwise intervene in the market. This perspective highlights the need for adequate financial education, as consumers cannot take advantage of access to financial services if they do not understand them. The rapid development of fintech points to the need for digital financial literacy.

Access to financial services has a multitude of dimensions reflecting the range of possible financial services from payments and savings accounts to credit, insurance, pensions and securities markets. The relevant services vary for individuals and for firms. Another important dimension is actual usage of such products and services. Campaigns to increase the number of bank accounts cannot be regarded as successful if those accounts are used rarely or never.

III. RATIONALE FOR FINANCIAL INCLUSION

There are several arguments in favour of greater financial inclusion. Poor households are often severely cash constrained, so innovations that increase the efficiency of their cash management and allow them to smooth consumption can have significant impacts on welfare. Relying on cash-based transactions imposes many costs and risks. In some cases, transactions entail carrying relatively large amounts of cash over long distances, raising issues of safety. Also, many studies find that the marginal return to capital in MSMEs is large when capital is scarce, which suggests that they could reap sizeable returns from greater financial access (Demirgüç-Kunt and Klapper, 2013). This is particularly important in Asia due to the large contribution of MSMEs to total employment and output. Greater financial inclusion can also contribute to reducing income inequality by raising the incomes of the poorest income groups disproportionately (Beck, Demirgüç-Kunt and Levine, 2007). Financial inclusion may also contribute to financial stability by increasing the diversity of bank assets and by increasing the stable funding base of bank deposits. Greater financial access could support shifts by Governments toward cash transfer programmes rather than wasteful subsidies, and the greater transparency associated with electronic funds transfers could help reduce corruption, money laundering and terrorism financing. The benefits of greater financial access proved to be a very important benefit during the COVID-19 pandemic.

IV. STATUS OF FINANCIAL INCLUSION IN ASIA

Households

The most commonly used measure of financial access is the share of adults over age 15 who have an account at a formal financial institution. Financial access of households tends to rise with per capita gross domestic product (GDP), as would be expected, but there is still huge variation across countries for which data are available (figure 1). The magnitude of variation implies that other factors besides income play important roles, including overall financial development and regulatory, institutional, social and geographic factors. For example, Bangladesh has much higher deposit penetration than Nepal or Afghanistan, even though per capita income levels are similar. India lies well above the trend line due to its successful campaign for bank deposits, while the Philippines and Viet Nam are considerably below it. More importantly, perhaps, the majority of Asian economies have deposit penetration of less than 50 per cent.

Figure 1. Relation of per capita gross domestic product to deposit penetration for adults, 2017

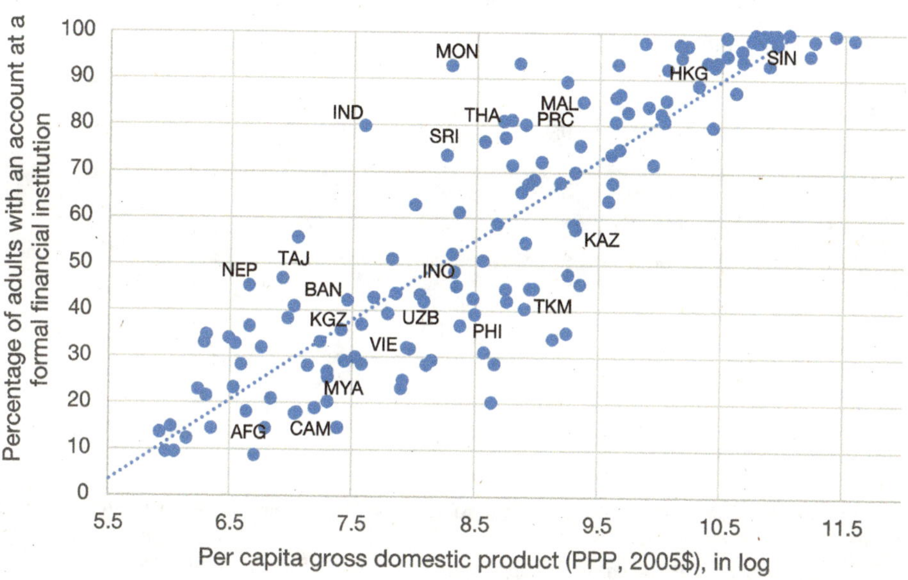

Source: World Bank Global Findex Survey, www.worldbank.org/en/programs/globalfindex.

Abbreviations: AFG, Afghanistan; BAN, Bangladesh; HKG, Hong Kong, China; IND, India; INO, Indonesia; KAZ, Kazakhstan; KGZ, Kyrgyzstan; MAL, Malaysia; MON, Mongolia; MYA, Myanmar; NEP, Nepal; PHI, Philippines; PPP, purchasing power parity; PRC, China; SIN, Singapore; SRI, Sri Lanka; TAJ, Tajikistan; THA, Thailand; TKM, Turkmenistan; UZB, Uzbekistan; VIE, Viet Nam.

Firms

Figure 2 shows a fairly strong positive relationship between per capita GDP and the share of small firms with a line of credit, but the pattern among emerging Asian economies shows a high degree of variation. Compared to the availability of data on household access to finance, data are available for considerably fewer countries on the share of small firms with line of credit. Notably, the borrowing share of small firms is more than 30 per cent in very few Asian countries.

Figure 2. Share of small firms with line of credit

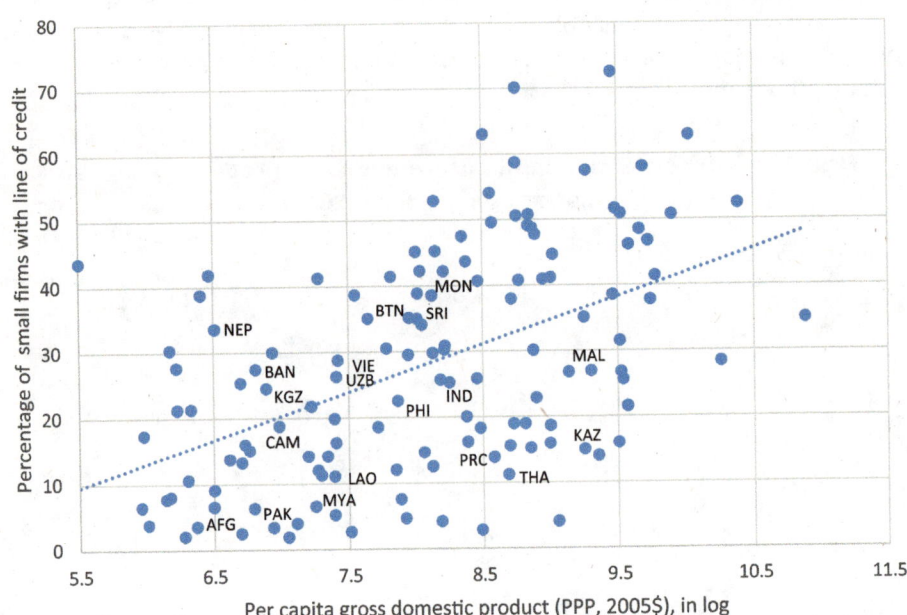

Source: World Bank Global Findex Survey, www.worldbank.org/en/programs/globalfindex.

Note: Data range from 2010 to 2017, depending on the country.

Abbreviations: AFG, Afghanistan; BAN, Bangladesh; BTN, Bhutan; CAM, Cambodia; IND, India; KAZ, Kazakhstan; KGZ, Kyrgyzstan; LAO, Lao People's Democratic Republic; MAL, Malaysia; MON, Mongolia; MYA, Myanmar; NEP, Nepal; PHI, Philippines; PPP, purchasing power parity; PRC, China; SRI, Sri Lanka; THA, Thailand; UZB, Uzbekistan; VIE, Viet Nam.

V. BARRIERS TO FINANCIAL INCLUSION

Barriers to financial inclusion can be classified as either supply side or demand side. Supply-side barriers reflect limitations on the capacity or will of the financial sector to extend financial services to poorer households or MSMEs. These can be further subdivided into three categories: market-driven factors; regulatory factors; and infrastructure limitations.

Market-driven factors include aspects, such as relatively high maintenance costs associated with small-size deposits or loans, high costs associated with providing financial services in small towns in rural areas, lack of credit data or usable collateral and lack of convenient access points. Provision of financial services in rural areas can pose particular problems in archipelagic countries such as Indonesia or the Philippines. Lack of credit data and reliable financial records worsens the problem of information asymmetry that discourages banks from lending to poorer households and MSMEs.

Regulatory factors include capital adequacy and supervisory rules that may limit the attractiveness of small-size deposits, loans or other financial products to financial institutions. Strict requirements regarding opening of branches or installing automated teller machines may also restrict the attractiveness of doing so in remote areas. Identification and other documentation requirements are important both with respect to know-your-client (KYC) requirements and monitoring for anti-money laundering/ combating the financing of terrorism (AML/CFT), but these can pose problems for poor households in countries which do not have universal individual identification systems. Regulatory requirements can also restrict the entry of microfinance institutions, such as restrictions on foreign ownership and inspection requirements.

Infrastructure-related barriers include lack of access to secure and reliable payments and settlement systems, the lack of availability of either fixed or mobile telephone communications, the lack of access to the Internet, and the lack of availability of convenient transport to bank branches or automated teller machines. Again, these can pose particular problems in archipelagic countries. Numerous studies have identified the lack of convenient transport as an important barrier to financial access (Tambunlertchai, 2017).

Demand-side factors include a lack of funds, lack of knowledge of financial products (i.e. financial literacy) and lack of trust. Lack of trust can be a significant problem when countries do not have well-functioning supervision and regulation of financial institutions or programmes of consumer protection that require, among others, adequate disclosure, regulation of collection procedures and systems of dispute resolution.

VI. APPROACHES TO PROMOTE FINANCIAL INCLUSION

Strategies for promoting financial inclusion can be implemented at the national level, as well as by central banks, financial regulatory agencies, private institutions and non-governmental organizations. Among countries in Asia, Indonesia, the Philippines and Thailand are relatively advanced, having developed broad national strategies for financial inclusion. Efforts to promote MSMEs in Thailand are well advanced and are organized through the SME Master Plan. The third master plan came into effect in 2012 and covered a five-year period ending in 2016. In South Asia, India stands out for its successful "JAM" strategy for financial inclusion with three key elements: the Pradhan Mantri Jan Dhan Yojana (PMJDY) scheme for increasing bank deposits; the Aadhaar biometric identity scheme; and the widespread use of mobile phones.

Strategies for promoting financial inclusion encompass five broad areas: (a) inclusion-oriented financial institutions; (b), subsidized funding; (c) development of innovative products and services; (d) development of innovative delivery technologies; and (e) development of innovative systems to enhance access to credit. These elements are shown in table 1 for the countries included in the present study.

Table 1. Elements of financial inclusion strategies

Country	Inclusive financial institutions	Subsidized funding	Innovative financial products and services	Innovative delivery technologies	Innovative systems to enhance credit access
Bangladesh	Cooperative societies, postal savings bank, Grameen Bank, licensed NGO-MFIs	Palli Karma Sahayak Foundation for MFIs; refinancing of bank loans to SMEs	Microdeposits, microloans, Taka Ten bank accounts for farmers, school banking program	Mobile phone banking	
India	Regional rural banks, united community banks, Local Area Banks, NBFC-MFIs	Micro Units Development and Refinance Agency Bank	No-frills bank accounts (with additional services to be added), business correspondents	Telephone bill-paying	Stock exchange platforms for SMEs, credit bureaus
Indonesia	Bank Perkreditan Rakyat, Bank Pembangunan Daerah, Bank Rakyat Indonesia		Grameen Bank-style microcredit products, Islamic microfinance products	Telephone banking, e-money	Loan guarantee programs

Table 1. *(continued)*

Country	Inclusive financial institutions	Subsidized funding	Innovative financial products and services	Innovative delivery technologies	Innovative systems to enhance credit access
Philippines	Rural banks, cooperatives, credit cooperatives, credit NGOs		Microdeposits, microloans, and microinsurance products; agents for insurance, e-money, and payments	Telephone banking, e-money	
Sri Lanka	Cooperatives, NGO-MFIs, community-based organizations, Samurdhi, rotating savings and credit associations			Telephone banking via point of sale terminal, e-remittance services	
Thailand	State financial institutions, cooperatives and occupational groups, savings groups for production, village funds			Telephone banking, e-money	Loan guarantee program, credit database (in development)

Sources: ADBI (2014); BUCFLP (2014); Barua, Kathuria and Malik (2017); Kelegama and Tilakaratna (2017); Khalily (2017); Llanto (2017); Tambunan (2017); and Tambunlertchai (2017).

Abbreviations: MFI, microfinance institution; NBFC, non-banking financial company; NGO, non-governmental organization; SMEs, small and medium-sized enterprises.

Inclusion-oriented financial institutions

Inclusion-oriented financial institutions include microfinance institutions (MFIs), state-owned banks, post offices offering financial services, credit cooperatives and community organizations. In India there are state-owned agricultural banks and local banks, such as Regional Rural Banks, United Community Banks and Local Area Banks (Barua, Kathuria and Malik, 2017). Institutions were established in Indonesia, including Bank Perkreditan Rakyat, Bank Pembangunan Daerah and Bank Rakyat Indonesia (Tambunan, 2017). In Thailand, specialized financial institutions operate as banks and cater to lower income households and smaller firms, including the Small and Medium Enterprise Development Bank of Thailand, the Bank for Agriculture and Agricultural Cooperatives and the Government Savings Bank.

Subsidized funding

Subsidizing the costs of loans is one way to make them more accessible to the unbanked. Examples include the Palli Karma Sahayak Foundation for MFIs and refinancing of bank loans to SMEs in Bangladesh and the Micro Units Development and Refinance Agency Bank in India. However, the performance of state-owned banks and government finance programmes has been mixed, and these experiences have shifted the emphasis away from specialized state-owned lenders to more market-based solutions.

Innovative products and services

Innovative products and services include various products such as no-frills bank accounts, microcredits and microinsurance, the development of agent banking and the establishment of micro branches of banks. In India there were an impressive 411.3 million new bank accounts as of 21 October 2020 (PMJDY, 2020). However, the World Bank Global Findex Survey of 2017 (Demirgüç-Kunt and others, 2018) estimated that 48 per cent of Indian bank accounts were inactive (i.e. they saw no activity during the year). This implies a far lower degree of effective financial inclusion. Unfortunately, more recent data are unavailable, although the use of bank accounts most likely increased during the COVID-19 pandemic due to government transfer programmes. The Government of Indonesia has introduced Grameen Bank-style credit products, and it offers three types of Islamic microfinance products, including a profit and loss sharing approach for credit and savings, Grameen-model Islamic microfinance and Islamic style microinsurance (Tambunan, 2017). In the Philippines, regular insurance companies and mutual benefit associations have begun to provide microinsurance and similar products to help low-income sectors to deal with vulnerability risks and catastrophic events (Llanto, 2017).

Use of agents or correspondents can help to overcome problems of distance and shortages of bank branches. For example, in India business correspondents can provide connectivity to financial services in remote and underbanked locations. However, business correspondents largely facilitate payments and have a limited role in opening deposit accounts or lending.

Innovative delivery technologies

Innovative delivery technologies, such as mobile phones, electronic money (e-money) and Internet banking, can also help to bridge distances and save time. Telephone banking has great potential as a result of the rapid diffusion of mobile phone ownership in many emerging economies. Telephone banking has enjoyed substantial success in the Philippines (ESCAP, 2014). However, use of mobile phones to pay bills in India is still quite limited at only about 2 per cent of the population, and the rate is much lower for the rural poor (Barua, Kathuria and Malik, 2017).

The development of e-money can make a substantial contribution to reducing the cost and inconvenience of making payments. Llanto (2017) notes that e-money accounts and e-money transactions have grown significantly in the past few years in the Philippines. For example, from 2010 to 2013, registered e-money accounts increased by 34 per cent to 26.7 million. Also, there are 10,620 active e-money agents performing cash-in/cash-out transactions. However, there are issues with regard to the identification and monitoring of money laundering and possible terrorism-related transactions. The developments of fintech represent the latest wave of such innovations and are described in greater detail in section 10 of the present study.

Innovative systems to enhance credit access

Informational asymmetries, such as the lack of credit data, bankable collateral and basic accounting information, discourage financial institutions from lending to MSMEs. Innovations to provide more information, such as credit databases, credit guarantee systems and rules to expand the kinds of eligible collateral, could substantially ease these asymmetries and increase the willingness of financial institutions to lend. Financial education for MSMEs could also encourage them to keep more complete and better records. Finally, the development of new investment vehicles, such as venture capital, specialized stock exchanges for MSMEs and new firms, and hometown investment trusts could expand the financing options of MSMEs.

Some Asian economies have been active in expanding and consolidating credit databases on households and MSMEs, but such efforts in most cases are still at an early stage, while such efforts have not yet started in other Asian economies. In Thailand, Tambunlertchai (2017) notes that the existing credit database of the Thai National Credit Bureau provide little credit information on low-income individuals and microenterprises. The issue of establishing a credit database for MSMEs in Thailand was raised in the SME Master Plan (2012–2016), and there have been talks, training sessions and workshops in preparation for the establishment of a credit risk database for MSMEs for the implementing agencies, such as the Thai Credit Guarantee Corporation, the Bank of Thailand and the Office of Small and Medium Enterprises Promotion.

Credit guarantees can also ease access to finance for MSMEs, although they confront a number of problems, in particular issues of moral hazard and high costs due to non-performing loans. In Thailand, the Thai Credit Guarantee Corporation offers credit guarantee products that assist MSMEs in obtaining commercial bank loans (Tambunlertchai, 2017). In Indonesia, loans to MSMEs under the programme for people/community business credit are guaranteed (70 per cent) by two insurance companies, Asuransi Kredit Indonesia and Perusahaan Umum Jaminan Kredit Indonesia, and by other companies which have voluntary joined the programme (Tambunan, 2017).

It may be difficult for some MSMEs to access equity-related financing, but some Governments have introduced measures in this area. In India both the National and Bombay Stock Exchanges set up dedicated platforms for MSMEs, and Thailand has similar programmes. One alternative is to develop hometown investment trust funds to finance local projects. Hometown investment trust funds are described in Yoshino and Kaji (2013).

VII. STRATEGIES FOR FINANCIAL INCLUSION

The previous section has shown that countries approach the issue of financial inclusion from many angles. However, strategies are needed to set priorities and coordinate overall approaches of relevant organizations. Table 2 contains a summary of the major strategies of the countries in the present study. National-level strategies are most desirable, followed by strategies of the central bank and major ministries and/or financial regulatory bodies. In Asia, Indonesia, the Philippines and Thailand have the most well-articulated financial inclusion strategies, which are incorporated in their national economic planning strategies. Bangladesh, India and Sri Lanka have long-standing policies to promote financial inclusion through devices such as loan quotas for priority sectors, but they have not articulated a national strategy. At the regulatory level, the SME Master Plan of Thailand stands out, along with the Credit Policy Improvement Project of the Philippines.

Table 2. Strategies for financial inclusion

Country	National	Central bank	Ministries/ regulators	Private sector
Bangladesh	No national strategy; legal basis for Grameen Bank; establishment of Microcredit Regulatory Authority	Taka Ten Account for farmers; expansion of rural bank branches, refinancing, mobile banking, SME financing, and school banking		
India	Priority sector lending targets; Prime Minister's People Money Scheme bank account strategy; biometric identification program	Rural branch opening rules; establishment of innovative bank types; promotion of no-frills bank accounts; business correspondents; financial education		
Indonesia	Subsidized credit and bank lending targets for micro, small, and medium-sized enterprises and farmers; establishment of Grameen-type banks and other microfinance institutions	National Strategy for Financial Inclusion (with Ministry of Finance), payment system infrastructure; financial education; credit-related information; supporting regulation; campaigns; consumer protection	Ministry of Finance (see central bank)	
Philippines	Included in Philippine Development Plan 2011–2016 to increase confidence in financial system; expand offerings of financial products; financial education	Lead government institution to formulate specific financial inclusion strategies, numerous circulars	Department of Finance-National Credit Council: Credit Policy Improvement Project	

Table 2. *(continued)*

Country	National	Central bank	Ministries/ regulators	Private sector
Sri Lanka	10% bank loan target for agriculture; creation of Samurdhi banking societies	Branch opening regulations		Commercial bank campaigns to attract savings; services for overseas workers
Thailand	Aspects included in 11th National Economic and Social Development Plan: focus on SME finance, financial education		Ministry of Finance: National Strategy for Financial Inclusion; Office of Small and Medium Enterprises Promotion: Master Plan of SME Promotion	

Sources: ADBI (2014); BUCFLP (2014); Barua, Kathuria and Malik (2017); Kelegama and Tilakaratna (2017); Khalily (2017); Llanto (2017); Tambunan (2017); and Tambunlertchai (2017).

Abbreviations: MFI, microfinance institution; NBFC, non-banking financial company; NGO, non-governmental organization; SMEs, small and medium-sized enterprises.

Financial inclusion strategies need to balance the "three legs of the stool" – adequate regulation and supervision of microfinance institutions; consumer protection; and financial education. The first two are needed to address the issue of the lack of trust in financial institutions and inadequate information provided by them, while the last is needed so that consumers can make informed decisions about how to use the products and services available to them. These issues are described in the next two sections.

VIII. REGULATORY ISSUES FOR FINANCIAL INCLUSION

Efforts to promote financial inclusion raise many challenges for central banks and financial regulators, and creative responses to these challenges could contribute substantially to promoting financial inclusion. Traditionally, central banks and regulators have been sceptical of financial inclusion and have worried about possible negative impacts on financial stability, due to the higher credit risks and lack of documentation associated with small borrowers.

However, more recent literature highlights the potentially positive implications of financial inclusion for financial stability. Khan (2011) suggests three main ways in which greater financial inclusion can contribute positively to financial stability. First, greater diversification of bank assets as a result of increased lending to smaller firms could reduce the overall riskiness of a bank's loan portfolio. This would both reduce the relative size of any single borrower in a bank's overall portfolio and reduce its volatility. Adasme, Majnoni and Uribe (2006) found that the non-performing loans of small firms have quasi-normal loss distributions, while those of large firms have fat-tailed distributions, implying that the former have less systemic risk. Morgan and Pontines (2014) found that an increased share of lending to MSMEs tended to reduce measures of financial risk, such as bank Z-scores or non-performing loan ratios.

Second, increasing the number of small savers would increase both the size and stability of the deposit base, reducing banks' dependence on non-core financing, which tends to be more volatile during a crisis. Third, greater financial inclusion could improve the transmission of monetary policy, contributing to greater financial stability. Hannig and Jansen (2010) argue that low-income groups are relatively immune to economic cycles, so including them in the financial sector will tend to raise the stability of deposit and loan bases.

Therefore, regulators need to strike a balance between the need to promote financial inclusion while guaranteeing the stability of the financial system and protecting consumers. Table 3 contains a summary of the major features of regulations related to financial inclusion in the subject countries, including regulatory agencies (predominantly central banks), identification requirements, regulation of MFIs, regulations of lending (mainly interest rate caps) and consumer protection. Two broad conclusions have emerged from the varied country experiences seen in the present study: programmes to promote financial inclusion should be aligned with financial incentives to make their implementation more effective; and regulation of microfinance should be proportionate to the financial stability risks posed by MFIs.

Table 3. Financial inclusion regulatory measures

Country	Regulatory agencies	Identification-related measures	Regulation of MFIs	Lending regulations	Consumer protection
Bangladesh	Bank of Bangladesh, Microcredit Regulatory Authority, Insurance Development and Regulatory Authority		Licensing of MFIs over certain size can take deposits	Interest rate cap, deposit rate floor	
India	Reserve Bank of India, Micro Units Development and Refinance Agency Bank	Aadhaar biometric identification programme, linked to access to microaccounts	Licensed; can convert to small bank	Lending rate caps for banks, non-bank MFIs	Reserve Bank of India: Grievance Redressal Mechanism in banks; banking ombudsman system
Indonesia	Bank Indonesia, Financial Supervisory Agency and multiple others		Multiple regulatory entities	Interest rate caps: non-collateralized credit scheme for MSMEs (KUR) (22 per cent), 5–7 per cent for agriculture/ energy programmes	National Consumer Protection Agency, Consumer Dispute Settlement Board, Credit Information Bureau

Table 3. *(continued)*

Country	Regulatory agencies	Identification-related measures	Regulation of MFIs	Lending regulations	Consumer protection
Philippines	Bangko Sentral ng Pilipinas (BSP), Insurance Commission	Easier identification requirements in cases where documentation is lacking	BSP regulates most entities; only rural banks and credit cooperatives can accept deposits	Only disclosure rules	BSP: Consumer Affairs Group; Securities and Exchange Commission; National Credit Council and National Anti-Poverty Council Microfinance Consumer Protection Guidebook
Sri Lanka	Central Bank of Sri Lanka		NGO-MFI's can register under various acts; not licensed; only cooperative societies and Samurdhi Banking Societies can take deposits		Consumer Affairs Authority; Voluntary Financial Ombudsman system; Consumer Affairs Council; Credit Information Bureau of Sri Lanka
Thailand	Bank of Thailand, Ministry of Finance, and multiple others		Various agencies depending on type of MFI, some not regulated at all	Interest rate cap of 28 per cent for specialized financial institutions, 15 per cent for non-formal lenders	Bank of Thailand: Financial Consumer Protection Centre

Sources: ADBI (2014); BUCFLP (2014); Barua, Kathuria and Malik (2017); Kelegama and Tilakaratna (2017); Khalily (2017); Llanto (2017); Tambunan (2017); and Tambunlertchai (2017).

Abbreviations: BSP, Bangko Sentral ng Pilipinas; MFI, microfinance institution; MSMEs, micro-, small and medium-sized enterprises; NGO, non-governmental organization.

Regulatory measures to promote access

Governments have relied on a number of different measures to promote financial access, but with varying degrees of success. In India, minimum quotas were set for so-called "priority sector loans" such as agriculture and MSMEs. Also the Prime Minister's Task Force on MSMEs stipulated a target of 20 per cent year-on-year credit growth to micro- and small enterprises (Barua, Kathuria and Malik, 2017). In the Philippines, banks are required to allocate at least 8 per cent of their loan portfolio for micro- and small enterprises, and at least 2 per cent for medium-sized enterprises (Llanto, 2017). In Sri Lanka, the banking sector is required to allocate 10 per cent of credit to agriculture, and the central bank required banks to open two branches in rural areas for every branch opened in metropolitan areas (Kelegama and Tilakaratna, 2017). However, without adequate incentives, banks will not achieve the targets, they will cherry pick customers within target groups, and the poorer segments will remain unserved.

Identification requirements

Banking transactions are normally subject to strict requirements regarding identification, both in view of KYC norms and the need to monitor possible cases of money laundering or terrorist financing. However, it is often difficult for people in poorer rural areas to provide proof of identification. There are two main approaches to overcoming this obstacle: (a) relaxing identification requirements; and (b) establishing a national identification system. As shown in table 3, the Philippines has moved in the direction of relaxing identification requirements when such evidence is difficult to provide. However, in India, the ambitious programme of the biometric unique identity card or 'Aadhaar' is the sole KYC document for both account opening and access to other financial products. As of 31 October 2021, 1.317 billion Aadhaar numbers had been issued to the residents of India (Unique Identification Authority of India, 2021).

Regulation of microfinance institutions

Non-government MFIs have shown that their business models can achieve satisfactory investment results in many cases, as long as the risks and costs of servicing their customer base are adequately reflected in the rates they charge. Therefore, policies should aim to maximize the potential benefits of MFIs in terms of providing financial services at an affordable cost and in an efficient way.

The observation that loans to poorer households and MSMEs have less systemic risk than do loans to large firms provides the basis for the concept of "proportionate regulation" that calls for the regulation of financial institutions commensurate with their potential benefits and risks to the financial system. Compared to other countries in the region, the Philippines has perhaps implemented this concept most thoroughly. The General Banking Act of 2000 and the National Strategy for Microfinance provided the regulatory framework for proportionate regulation and risk-based supervision adopted by the Bangko Sentral ng Pilipinas (BSP) (Llanto, 2017).

Table 3 shows that in India, Indonesia and Sri Lanka, many MFIs are not allowed to take deposits. In the Philippines, only rural banks and credit cooperatives are allowed to accept deposits (Llanto, 2017). In Bangladesh, MFIs of a certain size may be licensed and take deposits. Khakily (2017) finds that this development has improved both the efficiency of MFIs and their attractiveness to customers. It seems that more countries should consider an explicit licensing regime for MFIs to promote efficiency in the sector.

Interest rate caps

Table 3 shows that many countries impose caps on loan interest rates. In India, the charge on all bank loans given is linked to their base rate except on farm loans (300,000 Indian rupee) which are capped at 7 per cent. However, costs of making small loans to poor households and firms are inherently high, due to lack of economies of scale and information, and costs of access in remote areas. Therefore such limits can be counterproductive if they mainly act to limit supply. In this regard, the Consultative Group to Assist the Poor (2004) found that interest rate ceilings in 30 countries impeded the penetration of microcredit. The Reserve Bank of India in April 2014 removed the rate cap of 26 per cent on loans advanced by non-bank finance company MFIs, the only lenders eligible to lend through the microfinance channel (Barua, Kathuria and Malik, 2017).

In most cases, traditional money lenders are outside the range of formal financial institutions, which includes banks and MFIs. However, they still are an important source of credit for low-income households and MSMEs, and they pose a number of regulatory questions. Should they be registered or regulated? Should their interest rates be capped? How closely should they be monitored? Other issues related to disclosure and collection practices are discussed in the next subsection on consumer protection. Currently, in the Philippines BSP does not impose any interest rate caps on money lenders, relying instead only on disclosure requirements.

Consumer protection

Consumer protection programmes are seen as a necessary support for financial inclusion efforts, together with financial education and effective regulation and supervision of financial institutions. Consumer protection can help to address the issue of trust as a demand-side barrier to financial inclusion. Consumer protection programmes in the selected countries are at various stages of development. In

Thailand, the Bank of Thailand has the power to monitor consumer protection. In 2013, the Bank of Thailand opened its Financial Consumer Protection Centre to inform consumers about their rights and responsibilities, to prevent consumers from falling prey to fraudulent practices and to facilitate informed consumer decision-making.

IX. FINANCIAL LITERACY AND EDUCATION[3]

In the aftermath of the global financial crisis of 2007–2009, financial literacy and financial education are receiving increasing attention worldwide. There were sobering lessons, for example, in how the mis-selling of financial products contributed directly to the severity of the global financial crisis, both in developed economies and in Asia, which could partly be attributed to inadequate financial knowledge on the part of individual borrowers and investors. Financial education can be viewed as a capacity-building process over an individual's lifetime, which results in improved financial literacy and well-being. Financial education is also necessary to prepare for old age. Financial education for MSMEs is also very important. However, with some exceptions, Asian economies so far have only devoted limited resources to financial education.

Current situation of financial literacy in Asia

Mapping the current status of financial literacy (or financial capability) in Asia presents challenges to researchers and policymakers alike. It is a new area with limited data. The coverage of available surveys is relatively spotty, and methodologies and results are inconsistent. Only a limited number of Asian economies and target groups within them have been surveyed so far and their results vary widely. There is some relation between financial literacy and per capita income, but rankings differ significantly across different studies. Greater coverage of target groups (such as students, seniors, MSMEs and the self-employed) is needed.

Figure 3 shows the results of standardized financial literacy surveys conducted by the Organisation for Economic Co-operation and Development (OECD) International Network for Financial Education. The financial literacy score is calculated based on the number of correct answers to 21 questions regarding financial knowledge, financial behaviour and financial attitude (OECD, 2018). The vertical axis shows the financial literacy score and the horizontal axis shows per capita GDP. The figure shows a rough correlation of financial literacy with income levels, but there is still

---

[3] This section is based on Yoshino, Morgan and Wignaraja (2015). Also, see the extensive discussion of issues related to financial education in Yoshino, Messy and Morgan (2016).

wide variation. More importantly, average financial literacy levels are relatively low even in high-income countries.

Figure 3. Financial literacy score and per capita gross domestic product

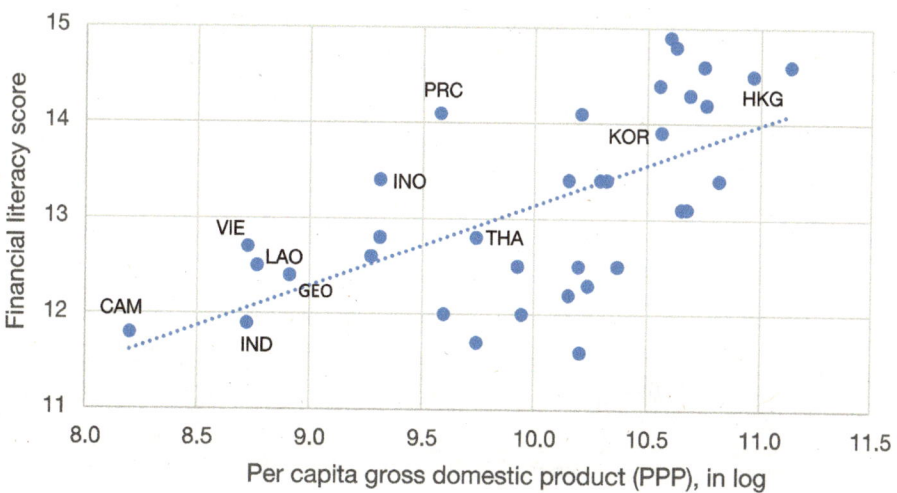

Sources: OECD (2016) and authors' estimates.

Abbreviations: CAM, Cambodia; GEO, Georgia; HKG, Hong Kong, China; IND, India; INO, Indonesia; KOR, Republic of Korea; LAO, Lao People's Democratic Republic; PPP, purchasing power parity; PRC, China; THA, Thailand; VIE, Viet Nam.

Current policies and gaps in financial education in Asia

There are still many policy gaps in Asia in the areas of financial literacy and financial education. Table 4 contains a summary of programmes, including national strategies, the roles of central banks, regulators and private programmes, and the channels and coverage of such programmes. The starting point for financial education programmes is to have a national strategy, but so far in Asia such strategies have been implemented only in India, Indonesia and Japan. Indonesia and Philippines are relatively strong compared to other countries in the area of financial education. The Philippines is in the process of finalizing its national policy. Central banks active in this area include the Reserve Bank of India, Bank Indonesia, BSP and Bank of Thailand. Financial regulators active in financial education include the Financial Services Authority of Indonesia. In Sri Lanka, however, measures to enhance financial literacy have been rather ad hoc in nature and there is no national policy on financial education.

Table 4. Policies and programmes for financial education

Country	National	Central bank	Other regulators	Private sector	Coverage	Channels
Bangladesh		Policy statement on financial literacy, but no specific strategy				
India	National Strategy on Financial Education launched by the Financial Stability and Development Council	Financial literacy project to enhance financial literacy among target groups; standardized literacy material		Bank literacy centers that work with microfinance institutions	School children, senior citizens and military personnel	Schools
Indonesia	Financial education one pillar of National Strategy for Financial Inclusion organized by Bank Indonesia and Ministry of Finance, "My Saving" programme (2010)	Financial education, "Let's go to the bank" campaign (2008)	Financial Supervisory Agency: National Financial Literacy Strategy		Students, children and youth, migrant works, fishermen, communities in remote areas, factory workers	Schools, media

Table 4. *(continued)*

Country	National	Central bank	Other regulators	Private sector	Coverage	Channels
Philippines	Included in Philippine Development Plan 2011–2016	Economic and Financial Learning Programme to promote public awareness of economic and financial issues				
Sri Lanka		Some activities	Some activities	Some activities		
Thailand		Financial education programs for individuals, SMEs	Government "Debt Doctor" programme, Office of Small and Medium Enterprise Promotion	Civil society groups, commercial banks, Bank of Agriculture and Agricultural Cooperatives, independent organizations, non-profit organizations	Generally small-scale programmes, except "Debt Doctor"	Media

Sources: ADBI (2014); BUCFLP (2014); Barua, Kathuria and Malik (2017); Kelegama and Tilakaratna (2017); Khalily (2017); Llanto (2017); Tambunan (2017); and Tambunlertchai (2017).

Abbreviations: SMEs, small and medium-sized enterprises.

The financial education programme in Indonesia is particularly well developed, as it includes cooperative efforts by the Ministry of Finance, Bank Indonesia and Financial Services Authority of Indonesia. They have developed a variety of programmes at both the national level and targeted at specific groups, including students and youth, migrant workers, fishermen, communities in remote areas and factory workers. One notable development was the TabunganKu ("My Saving") joint programme by the Ministry of Finance and Bank Indonesia that helped promote savings in bank accounts. In this programme, the Government of Indonesia established a no-frills savings account with no monthly administration frees and a low initial deposit of 20,000 rupiah for commercial banks and 10,000 rupiah for rural banks.

In India, the Financial Stability and Development Council launched the National Strategy for Financial Education in 2012. The financial literacy programme of the Reserve Bank of India has teaching materials for a variety of target groups, including students, women, rural and urban poor, and older people, and these programmes are promoted through schools. Private banks have also developed literacy centres to work with MFIs (Myrold, 2014).

In the Philippines, BSP has been active in developing strategies for financial education, and it has issued a number of circulars in this regard. The Economic and Financial Learning Programme promotes awareness of economic financial issues. The programme targets specific audiences like schoolchildren, secondary and tertiary students, overseas Filipino workers, microfinance clients and others. The Credit Surety Programme is a trust fund financed by contributions of a provincial government and a cooperative in the same province to encourage financial institutions to lend to MSMEs in the province using the surety cover as a collateral substitute. The Consumer Affairs Group of BSP has been in charge of programmes for consumer protection, and the Monetary Board approved adoption of the Financial Consumer Protection Framework to institutionalize consumer protection as an integral component of banking supervision in the country (Tetangco, 2014). In addition, The National Credit Council and the Insurance Commission oversee financial education covering microinsurance in collaboration with the National Anti-Poverty Commission (Llanto, 2017).

X. FINTECH AND FINANCIAL INCLUSION

Fintech, which is the use of software, applications and digital platforms to deliver financial services to consumers and businesses through digital devices such as smartphones, is perceived to have great potential to promote financial inclusion, reflecting its ability to deliver innovative services online cheaply and efficiently. Fintech represents the latest wave of digital finance innovation and is connected with a wide range of new technologies and digital components including big data, machine learning and artificial intelligence, online platforms, distributed ledger technology and blockchain, and the Internet of things. In 2010, G20 members endorsed the Financial Inclusion Action Plan and established the Global Partnership for Financial Inclusion to coordinate and implement it. The Financial Inclusion Action Plan was updated at the 2014 G20 Leaders Summit in Brisbane. Acknowledging the importance of fintech, the Financial Inclusion Action Plan includes a commitment to implement the G20

Principles for Innovative Financial Inclusion under a shared vision of universal access (Bank for International Settlements and World Bank Group, 2016). The COVID-19 pandemic has increased the demand for fintech services, due to factors such as lockdowns, travel restrictions and the desire to minimize person-to-person contacts.

Major categories of financial services offered by fintech firms include:

- Payments and transfers; (e-commerce payments; mobile banking, mobile wallets; peer-to-peer payments and transfers; digital currency; cross-border transactions, including remittances and business-to-business payments)

- Personal finance (robo-advisors; mobile trading and personal financial management)

- Alternative financing (crowdfunding, peer-to-peer lending, and invoice and supply-chain finance)

- Other (insurance, etc.)

Payments and transfers and alternative financing have the most obvious potential to contribute to financial inclusion. Recognizing this potential, central banks and other financial regulators have adopted a number of approaches to encourage innovation in the sector while balancing risks to financial stability, including the use of regulatory sandboxes to assess risks and benefits of new services and special licensing regimes for fintech companies.

However, fintech introduces new risks and unexpected side effects as well, especially for less educated financial consumers. Fintech users face a multitude of potential risks, including the following:

- Phishing: When a hacker impersonates an institution to convince a user to divulge personal data, such as usernames or passwords, via email or social networks;

- Pharming: When a computer virus redirects a user to a fraudulent page to divulge personal information;

- Spyware: Malicious software on the personal computer or mobile phone of a user that transmits personal data of the user;

- SIM card swap: When someone poses as the user and obtains the user's SIM card and private data stored on it.

The digital footprint of fintech users, including information they provide to digital financial service providers, may also be a source of risk, even if it does not result directly in a loss, including:

- Profiling: Users may be excluded from access to certain services based on their online data and activities;

- Hacking: Thieves may steal personal data from social networks or other online platforms.

Due to easy access to credit enabled by fintech, consumers could also face potential problems of overborrowing or excessively high interest rates. Such risks can trigger unexpected and large losses when fintech providers are not regulated or regulation is weak. Overborrowing may also harm their credit rating (Morgan, Huang and Trinh, 2019).

Central banks and other financial regulators need to take a three-pronged approach to controlling these risks, including appropriate regulation of fintech companies, regimes for consumer protection and promotion of financial literacy, including digital financial literacy (Morgan, Huang and Trinh, 2019). Without such measures, consumers may lack trust in fintech products and services, and therefore be less willing to use them.

Table 5 contains a summary of recent regulatory measures affecting the fintech sector, including measures related to identification, e-payments, alternative finance and consumer protection. Central banks are the main regulators in most cases.

Table 5. Fintech regulatory measures

Country	Regulatory agencies	Identification-related measures	Payments	Alternative finance	Consumer protection
Brunei Darussalam	Autoriti Monetari Brunei Darussalam	e-Darussalam Account is a nationwide digital authentication key that provides access to online government services	No legal requirement to register corporate mobile payment services, but generally done in practice	No P2P lending firms yet. Equity crowdfunding platform operators must apply for a Capital Market Services License.	

Table 5. *(continued)*

Country	Regulatory agencies	Identification-related measures	Payments	Alternative finance	Consumer protection
Cambodia	National Bank of Cambodia (NBC)	Piloting digitized identification system	No regulations yet for cashless payments or e-commerce	P2P lending governed by the Law on Banking and Financial Institutions, primarily under the NBC. Law on the Issuance and Trading of Non-Government Securities is the primary legislation for equity crowdfunding, including both the issuing entity and platform.	
India	Reserve Bank of India (RBI), Securities and Exchange Board of India	Aadhaar biometric identification programme, linked to access to microaccounts	Must be regulated as payment bank, or put transactions through a regulated bank	Lending platforms treated as non-bank financial companies, must obtain a 'Certificate of Registration' from RBI. Equity-based crowdfunding remains a grey area.	RBI: Grievance Redressal Mechanism in banks; banking ombudsman system

Table 5. *(continued)*

Country	Regulatory agencies	Identification-related measures	Payments	Alternative finance	Consumer protection
Indonesia	Bank Indonesia, Financial Supervisory Agency (OJK)	Electronic identity card known as e-KTP	Five Bank Indonesia Initiatives for the Payment System under Decree No.18/73/ DKom: national payment gateway; national standard for Indonesian Chip Card Specification; payment transaction processing; financial technology; and government to person social assistance	OJK regulations govern organization of technology-based P2P lending services and equity crowdfunding	National Consumer Protection Agency, Consumer Dispute Settlement Board, Credit Information Bureau
Lao People's Democratic Republic	Bank of Lao PDR	Piloting digitized identification system	Payment system operator and provider apply for business operation license		
Malaysia	Bank Negara Malaysia (BNM), Securities Commission Malaysia (SCM)	'MyKad' card incorporates both photo identification and fingerprint biometric data, but not verifiable	Digital payments governed as a payment instrument. Issuers are required to obtain prior approval from BNM	SC has appointed six operators to run P2P platforms. Equity crowdfunding firms regulated by SCM	

Table 5. *(continued)*

Country	Regulatory agencies	Identification-related measures	Payments	Alternative finance	Consumer protection
Myanmar	Central Bank of Myanmar	Digital identification regarded as national priority	Regulated either as (a) mobile banking as a traditional bank or by a Fintech company in conjunction with a traditional bank; or (b) mobile financial service, which is operator-led	P2P lending and equity crowdfunding currently not regulated	
Philippines	Bangko Sentral ng Pilipinas (BSP), Securities and Exchange Commission (SEC)	Phil-ID will collect information and biometric data including iris scans, fingerprint and facial images	BSP Circular No. 649, Series of 2009 provides guidelines for issuers as a retail payment medium. Issuers may be banks or non-banking financial institutions registered as a money transfer agent.	No specific regulations governing online P2P lending. Lending companies are under SEC. Rules covering the operation and use of equity and lending-based crowdfunding only apply to registered persons.	BSP: Consumer Affairs Group; SEC; National Credit Council and National Anti-Poverty Council Microfinance Consumer Protection Guidebook
Singapore	Monetary Authority of Singapore	Digital identification serves as an official identification document, security measures are in place to protect user identity	New Payment Services Bill aims to streamline existing regulations of payment services	Platforms which allow P2P-lending to non-accredited natural persons require a license under the Moneylenders Act. Equity crowdfunding platforms must hold a Capital Market Services license.	

Table 5. *(continued)*

Country	Regulatory agencies	Identification-related measures	Payments	Alternative finance	Consumer protection
Thailand	Bank of Thailand (BOT), SEC	Digital identification system allows institutions to electronically identify and authenticate end users, but not mandatory	Licensing of payment systems and other services such as systems for fund transfer handling, clearing or settlement for retail fund transfers, electronic cards services, e-money service and bill payment service	BOT regulates P2P lending platforms. SEC oversees the operation of crowdfunding platforms.	BOT: Financial Consumer Protection Centre
Viet Nam	State Bank of Vietnam, State Securities Commission (SSC)	Piloting digitized identification system	Third-party payment service providers (non-banks) licensed	No official legal framework for P2P lending. Equity crowdfunding platforms must obtain a license from SSC.	

Sources: CCAF, ADBI and FinTechSpace (2019).

Abbreviations: BNM, Bank Negara Malaysia; BOT, Bank of Thailand; OJK, Financial Supervisory Agency; NBC, National Bank of Cambodia; RBI, Reserve Bank of India; SCM, Securities Commission Malaysia; SEC, Securities and Exchange Commission; P2P, person to person; SSC, State Securities Commission.

XI. REGULATOR INNOVATIONS IN RESPONSE TO COVID-19 TO SUPPORT FINANCIAL INCLUSION

The COVID-19 pandemic has underlined the benefits of using fintech services. It became more difficult to travel to banks or other physical outlets to do financial transactions because of travel restrictions, lockdowns and concerns about possible infection. Governments also greatly expanded the use of online transfers to deliver financial aid more efficiently and cheaply to households and firms. In light of this, central banks and other financial regulators took numerous steps to support the use of fintech services.

One step was to ease requirements for KYC procedures. This included facilitating or permitting electronic KYC processes where they had not been permitted previously, or simplifying KYC processes and practices. Examples of measures included digital on-boarding (e.g. facilitating or permitting the use of digital identities); permission for the use of digital/electronic signatures; simplified and/or digitalized customer due diligence checks; and use of digital documents (World Bank and CCAF 2020).

Central banks provided emergency liquidity facilities to financial institutions, including fintech firms. They also provided concessional funding for commercial banks and credit institutions for lending to firms, including to MSMEs and start-ups (World Bank and CCAF 2020).

Business continuity planning measures have been a key area of focus for central banks and financial regulators in response to COVID-19. Central banks have been more focused on business continuity planning for banks than the fintech sector, while other financial regulators may be more concerned about the threats to the continued operation of fintech companies during the pandemic.

Fintech firms perceived increases in cybersecurity risks during the COVID-19 pandemic period associated with increased use of fintech. Indeed, during the fintech firms reported that they have on average experienced a 15 per cent increase in cybersecurity breaches during the pandemic (CCAF, World Bank and World Economic Forum, 2020). In light of these risks, central banks also enhanced requirements or controls, strengthened cybersecurity oversight and supervision, and made recommendations for cybersecurity protocols (World Bank and CCAF, 2020). Some regulators have gone further to draft cybersecurity guidelines while others are developing comprehensive regulatory frameworks.

Central banks and regulators have also adopted a more 'digital' approach to regulation. This includes shifting from physical processes, to using a "digital first approach" to activities such as licensing, correspondence, meetings, inspections, virtual annual general meetings and electronic submission of regulatory forms (World Bank and CCAF, 2020).

Finally, central banks and regulators have encouraged the use of fintech services by lowering the costs of payment services to consumers, especially in countries where use of mobile money is widespread. This included waiving or reducing transaction fees and increasing transaction limits or thresholds. Examples include increases in daily maximum account balance and wallet limits, and increases in contactless payment and mobile money limits. Of course, fee reductions hurt the profitability of banks and fintech firms, so are generally temporary. In the area of digital lending, providers were authorized to issue credit cards and fund operations with resources from relevant development banks to target the underserved (World Bank and CCAF, 2020).

XII. CONCLUSIONS AND WAY FORWARD

Central banks have already been active in promoting financial inclusion, often nested within national financial inclusion strategies. This reflects a number of motivations, including the desire to promote economic and financial development, but also to reduce cash transactions in order to increase transparency and reduce channels for money laundering and terrorism finance. At the same time, they have to balance encouragement of financial innovation to promote financial inclusion with the need to maintain financial stability, especially in the banking sector, adhere to AML/CFT requirements, and protect consumers. These considerations are also reflected in their approach to promoting and regulating fintech firms.

Such activities have included innovations regarding identification, KYC and AML/CFT; innovations regarding products and access; differentiated regulatory approaches for innovative financial institutions aimed at financial inclusion; and differentiated regulatory approaches for fintech firms. Central banks have developed regulatory sandboxes to test innovative products and services, and have developed tailored licensing regimes for financial inclusion firms and fintech firms.

Financial innovation requires greater knowledge and experience on the part of consumers in order to make effective use of financial products and avoid losses and other risks. Therefore, central banks have supported financial education programmes to promote financial literacy. The increasing importance of fintech points to the need for programmes to promote digital financial literacy as well. However, this area is still in its infancy and requires further policy support (Morgan, Huang and Trinh, 2019).

The COVID-19 pandemic has underlined the benefits of using fintech services. In response, central banks and other financial regulators need to take further steps to support the use of fintech services, including the following: promoting digitalization and simplification of KYC, identification and related requirements; strengthening cybersecurity measures and other consumer protection measures; and supporting innovation in digital lending while maintaining financial stability.

NOTE ON CONTRIBUTORS

Peter J. Morgan is Senior Consulting Economist and Vice Chair of Research at the Asian Development Bank Institute. Previously, he had 23 years of experience in the financial sector in Asia. His research interests are macroeconomic policy, financial sector regulation, reform, financial development, financial inclusion, fintech, financial literacy and financial education.

REFERENCES

Adasme, Osvaldo, Giovanni Majnoni and Myriam Uribe (2006). Access and Risk: Friends or Foes? Lessons from Chile. Policy Research Working Paper, No. 4003. Washington, D.C.: World Bank.

Alliance for Financial Inclusion (AFI) (2010). Financial inclusion measurement for regulators: Survey design and implementation. Bangkok.

Asian Development Bank Institute (ADBI). 2014. *Financial Inclusion in Asia: Country Surveys.* Tokyo.

Atkinson, Adele, and Flore-Anne Messy (2013). Promoting Financial Inclusion through Financial Education: OECD/INFE Evidence, Policies and Practice. OECD Working Papers on Finance, Insurance and Private Pensions, No. 34. OECD Publishing.

Bank for International Settlements and World Bank Group (2016). *Payment aspects of financial inclusion.*

Barua, Abheek, Rajat Kathuria and Neha Malik (2017). India. In *Financial Inclusion, Regulation, and Education: Asian Perspectives.* Naoyuki Yoshino and Peter Morgan, eds. Tokyo: ADBI Press.

Beck, Thorsten, Asli Demirgüç-Kunt and Ross Levine (2007). Finance, Inequality, and Poverty: Cross-Country Evidence. *Journal of Economic Growth,* vol. 12, No. 1, pp. 27–49.

Boston University Center for Finance, Law and Policy (BUCFLP) (2015). Financial Inclusion Guide.

Cambridge Centre for Alternative Finance (CCAF), Asian Development Bank institute (ADBI) and FinTechSpace (2019). *ASEAN FinTech Ecosystem Benchmarking Study.* Cambridge, United Kingdom: Cambridge Centre for Alternative Finance.

Cambridge Centre for Alternative Finance (CCAF), World Bank and World Economic Forum (2020). The Global Covid-19 FinTech Market Rapid Assessment Report. University of Cambridge, World Bank Group and the World Economic Forum.

Consultative Group to Assist the Poor (CGAP) (2004). Interest Rate Ceilings and Microfinance, The Story So Far. Occasional Paper, No. 9. Washington, D.C.

Demirgüç-Kunt, Asli and Leora Klapper (2013). Measuring Financial Inclusion: Explaining Variation Across and Within Countries. *Brookings Papers on Economic Activity,* Spring. pp. 279–321.

Demirgüç-Kunt, Asli, Leora Klapper, Dorothe Singer, Saniya Ansar and Jake Hess (2018). *Global Findex Database 2017: Measuring Financial Inclusion and the Fintech Revolution.* Washington, D.C.: World Bank. Available at https://openknowledge.worldbank.org/handle/10986/29510 License: CC BY 3.0 IGO.

Hannig, Alfred, and Stefan Jansen (2010). Financial Inclusion and Financial Stability: Current Policy Issues. ADBI Working Paper, No. 259. Tokyo: Asian Development Bank Institute.

Kelegama, Saman, and Ganga Tilakaratna (2017). Sri Lanka. In *Financial Inclusion, Regulation, and Education: Asian Perspectives.* Naoyuki Yoshino and Peter J. Morgan, eds. Tokyo: ADBI Press.

Khalily, M.A. Baqui (2017). Bangladesh. In *Financial Inclusion, Regulation, and Education: Asian Perspectives.* Naoyuki Yoshino and Peter J. Morgan, eds. Tokyo: ADBI Press.

Khan, H.R. (2011). "Financial Inclusion and Financial Stability: Are They Two Sides of the Same Coin?" Address at BANCON 2011, organized by the Indian Bankers Association and Indian Overseas Bank, Chennai, India, 4 November.

Llanto, Gilberto (2017). Philippines. In *Financial Inclusion, Regulation, and Education: Asian Perspectives*. Naoyuki Yoshino and Peter J. Morgan, eds. Tokyo: ADBI Press.

Morgan, Peter J., Bihong Huang and Long Q. Trinh (2019). The Need to Promote Digital Financial Literacy for the Digital Age. Policy Brief, T20 Japan Task Force 7: the Future of Work and Education for the Digital Age.

Morgan, Peter J., and Victor Pontines (2014). Financial Stability and Financial Inclusion. ADBI Working Paper, No. 488. Tokyo: Asian Development Bank Institute.

Myrold, Alan (2014). Innovations in India: From Agent Banking to Universal Identification. In *Financial Inclusion in Asia: Country Surveys*. Tokyo: Asian Development Bank Institute.

Organisation for Economic Cooperation and Development (OECD) (2018). "OECD/INFE Toolkit for Measuring Financial Literacy and Financial Inclusion". Paris.

Pradhan Mantri Jan Dhan Yojana (PMJDY) (2020). Progress Report. New Delhi, India: Mission-FI, Department of Financial Services, Government of India. Available at https://pmjdy.gov. in/account.

Tambunan, Tulus (2017). Indonesia. In *Financial Inclusion, Regulation, and Education: Asian Perspectives*. Naoyuki Yoshino and Peter J. Morgan, eds. Tokyo: ADBI Press.

Tambunlertchai, Kanittha (2017). Thailand. In *Financial Inclusion, Regulation, and Education: Asian Perspectives*. Naoyuki Yoshino and Peter J. Morgan, eds. Tokyo: ADBI Press.

Tetangco, Amando (2014). "Improving Financial Literacy and Increasing Financial Inclusion to Sustain Economic Growth". Speech given at the 7th General Membership Meeting of the Shareholders Association of the Philippines. Manila, 5 November. Available at www. bis.org/review/r141111f.pdf.

Unique Identification Authority of India (2021) "About UIDAI". New Delhi. Available at https://uidai. gov.in/about-uidai-unique-identification-authority-of-india.html.

United Nations, Economic and Social Commission for Asia and the Pacific (ESCAP) (2014). *Sustainable development financing: perspectives from Asia and the Pacific*. Background paper. Asia-Pacific Outreach Meeting on Sustainable Development Financing Jakarta, 10 and 11 June.

World Bank (2014). *Global Financial Development Report: Financial Inclusion*. Washington, D.C.: World Bank.

World Bank and Cambridge Centre for Alternative Finance (CCAF) (2020) *The Global COVID-19 FinTech Regulatory Rapid Assessment Report*. World Bank Group and the University of Cambridge.

Yoshino, Naoyuki, and Sahoko Kaji, eds. (2013). *Hometown Investment Trust Funds: A Stable Way to Supply Risk Capital*. Tokyo: Springer.

Yoshino, Naoyuki, Flore-Anne Messy and Peter J. Morgan, eds. (2016). *Promoting Better Lifetime Planning through Financial Education*. World Scientific books.

Yoshino, Naoyuki, Peter J. Morgan, and Ganeshan Wignaraja (2015). Financial education in Asia: Assessment and Recommendations. ADBI Working Paper, No. 534. Tokyo: Asian Development Bank Institute.

Special theme: Macroeconomic policies for inclusive sustainable development

LEARNING BY DOING: CENTRAL BANK DIGITAL CURRENCY IN THAILAND

Thammarak Moenjak

Chief Representative, Bank of Thailand London Representative Office
Email: thammarm@bot.or.th

Central bank digital currency (CBDC) has gained much attention among central banks, as it could potentially improve efficiency, inclusion and innovation in the financial system. The present paper contains a review of the CBDC journey of the Bank of Thailand (BOT), from the guiding principles, to test results of the CBDC prototypes and challenges going forward. It provides insights with regard to the introduction of CBDC into the economy, as well as how a public institution such as a central bank can go about exploring cutting-edge technologies for use in public policy.

Keywords: central bank digital currency (CBDC), digital financial infrastructures, payments systems, innovations, financial inclusion, financial stability

JEL classification: G21, G28, H31, H41, H53, O31, O36, O38

I. INTRODUCTION

In recent years, with advancements in technology and digitalization of the economy, a growing number of central banks have embarked on a journey towards introducing a central bank digital currency (CBDC). Compared to cash and traditional payment systems, CBDCs have the potential to help improve efficiency, encourage innovations and raise financial inclusion. The introduction of CBDCs to the economy, however, requires careful planning and design as CBDCs have vast potential implications on financial stability, monetary policy and the roles of financial institutions and the central bank.

The Bank of Thailand (BOT) is among the first emerging market central banks to explore the potential benefits and challenges in introducing CBDC to the economy (PwC, 2021). By 2021, BOT had conducted a total of five proofs of concept for wholesale and retail CBDC, and it is planning to introduce a live retail CBDC pilot in 2022. The present paper provides a review of the CBDC journey of BOT, from its initial goals and guiding principles, to the findings and lessons learned from proofs of concept and the plan to introduce a retail CBDC live pilot in 2022. It aims to provide insights into a variety of policy issues with regard to CBDC, and how an emerging market central bank can prepare itself and its stakeholders in CBDC development, which has the potential to improve the financial system and transform the economy.

II. BACKGROUND

The CBDC journey of BOT began in 2017, with the planning of Project Inthanon. The overarching motivation at the time was to understand how technology, particularly blockchain or distributed ledger technology (DLT), can address long-standing pain points in the financial system by improving efficiency, access and inclusion. Along the way, BOT and stakeholders gained more understanding of the technology and policy implications, as well as potential benefits and challenges. It is expected that the accumulated body of knowledge and experience has prepared BOT and stakeholders to roll out CBDC that will help address pain points in the financial system without bringing undue risks to the economy.

Guiding principles

Throughout the journey, BOT adhered to three guiding principles: learning by doing, involving a dedicated team of staff from different parts of the central bank in the various aspects of building and testing of CBDC prototypes, from information technology development, business process design and stakeholder engagement; ecosystem building, engaging relevant stakeholders, including banks, non-banks, technology providers, government agencies, foreign central banks, corporations and, ultimately, retail users in multi-faceted collaborations; and taking an iterative approach, where lessons learned from one prototype helped to build the next prototype, and designs could be drawn and redrawn based on lessons learned.

III. THE JOURNEY SO FAR

By early 2022, BOT had built and tested three categories of CBDCs, namely domestic and cross-border wholesale CBDC and retail CBDC, as shown in figure 1. Starting off with domestic wholesale CBDC, the journey branched off into cross-border wholesale CBDC, including multi-currency CBDC, followed by a series of retail CBDC projects.

Figure 1. Journey of the Bank of Thailand towards a central bank digital currency

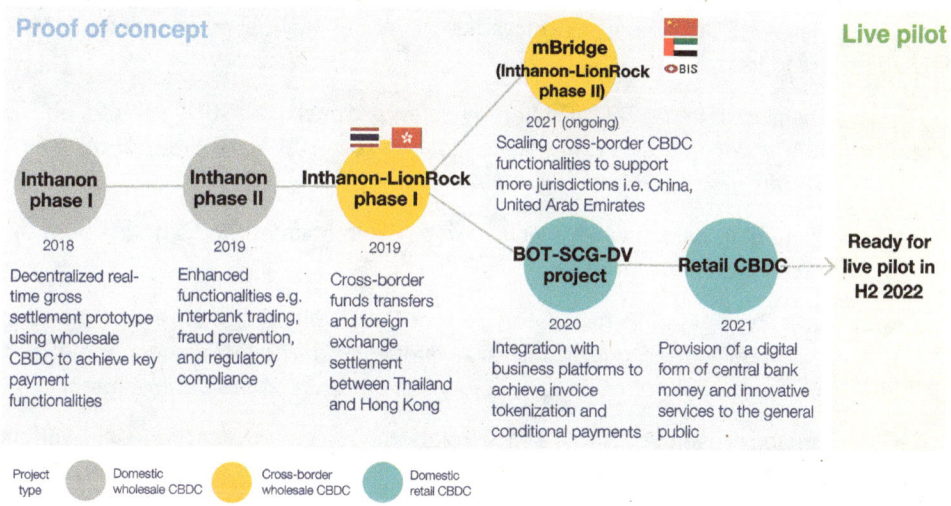

Source: BOT.

Abbreviations: BIS, Bank for International Settlements; BOT, Bank of Thailand; CBDC, central bank digital currency; DV, Digital Ventures; SCG, Siam Cement Group.

3.1 Wholesale CBDC

Wholesale CBDC refers to CBDC that is used for payments and settlement at the financial institution level (i.e. interbank payments). In Project Inthanon phase I and II, BOT tested domestic wholesale CBDC prototypes with eight domestic commercial banks. Then in collaboration with Hong Kong Monetary Authority (HKMA), BOT tested cross-border wholesale CBDC based on DLT along with a set of commercial banks in the two jurisdictions. The collaboration with HKMA has since expanded to include People's Bank of China (PBC), Central Bank of United Arab Emirates (CBUAE), and the Bank for International Settlements (BIS) in a multi-currency CBDC project for cross-border payments.

Domestic wholesale CBDC: Project Inthanon phase I

Project Inthanon phase I began in 2018 and involved BOT issuing and distributing wholesale CBDC to eight participating commercial banks (Bank of Thailand, 2019). Tests were made to see if the participants could make and settle payments among themselves and with BOT in a peer-to-peer (decentralized) manner. This contrasted with the existing real-time gross settlement system that relied on a central counterparty such as the central bank to settle the payments for the parties involved.

Technically, a prototype of a decentralized real-time gross settlement system using wholesale CBDC was created to achieve various key payment functionalities, including the following:

- Cash/bond tokenization, whereby tokenized cash (i.e. CBDC) and tokenized bonds (for use to exchange for tokenized cash) were created on a DLT platform;

- Bilateral transfers, whereby two parties could transfer CBDC/bonds between them on a DLT platform;

- Queuing mechanisms, to ensure that CBDC payments on a DLT platform could be settled according to a queue, in a decentralized manner (i.e. payments did not need to queue up at centrally at the central bank);

- Gridlock resolution, where a DLT platform could help automatically, without direct intervention from the central bank, resolve a payment gridlock;[1]

- Automated liquidity provision, whereby a bank could access liquidity from the central bank in an automated manner, by selling the bond to the central bank, whenever the bank had a cash shortage.

Results from Project Inthanon phase I showed that wholesale CBDC could be issued on a DLT platform, which potentially allowed for 24/7 wholesale payment

---

[1] A payment gridlock can occur when a payment could not be settled because the payer needed cash from another party, who directly or indirectly, needed that particular payment to be settled first, in a cyclic manner.

and settlement among the banks. Unlike the existing system, the prototype showed the potential that participating banks could settle funds among themselves without waiting for the central bank operating hours, thus improving efficiency.

Domestic wholesale CBDC: Project Inthanon phase II

Project Inthanon phase II began in 2019, and enhanced functionalities were implemented using smart contracts on a DLT platform (Bank of Thailand, 2020). Specifically, smart contracts were used to do the following:

- Automate fraud prevention for third party CBDC funds transfer on a DLT platform, ensuring that that CBDC would only automatically go to the intended third party, which would alleviate the pain point where the existing real-time gross settlement system was vulnerable to fraud, given the costly and error-prone manual inputting and verification processes involved at the customer touch points;

- Automate compliance for non-resident regulation, i.e. the amount of Thai baht to be held by each non-resident could be automatically checked and kept within regulatory limits on a DLT platform, which could also reduce costly and error-prone manual imputing and verification processes;

- Allow for interbank bond trading and repurchase agreements (repos) using CBDC on a DLT platform.

Results of Project Inthanon phase II showed vast potential of smart contracts, and enhanced functionalities such as automated fraud prevention, automated regulatory compliance, as well as atomic delivery-versus-payment in bond trading and repos could be implemented.[2] This could reduce risks related to wholesale payments, resulting in lower costs and improved efficiency.

Cross-border wholesale CBDC: Project Inthanon-LionRock phase I

The goal of Project Inthanon-LionRock was to test DLT for more streamlined cross-border funds transfers and foreign exchange settlement between Thailand and Hong Kong, China. The existing correspondent banking model often resulted in a long wait (multiple days), high costs and low transparency in cross-border payments, as cross-border funds had to pass through many steps and the steps were difficult to

---

[2] A delivery-versus-payment transaction means that the delivery of an asset would be made only if the payment for that asset is also made at the same time or prior. Borrowing a computer science term, atomic delivery-versus-payment means that the transaction is settled only if both the delivery of asset and the payment between the two parties are successful, otherwise the transaction does not take place. Conditions could be written on a smart contract to ensure that if the conditions on either the asset or the payment side are not fully satisfied, the transaction will not take place.

track. With the peer-to-peer nature of DLT, cross-border payments could potentially be made in seconds, with fewer intermediaries, more transparency and lower costs.

Project Inthanon-LionRock established a Thai baht – Hong Kong dollar corridor prototype that bridged the wholesale domestic CBDC networks of the two currencies and jurisdictions. All participating banks have their own presence and could make peer-to-peer payments via CBDC to each other. Among other things, tests were done on the following:

- Cross-border funds transfer, where peer-to-peer funds transfer could be made in an instantaneous manner;

- Atomic payment-versus-payment settlement, whereby a payment made in one currency and the receipt of another currency would need to occur together, otherwise none would occur (i.e. atomic);

- Liquidity management, whereby a queuing mechanism was used for the participating banks to set their priorities and manage their outgoing queues, and a multi-currency gridlock resolution mechanism was employed;

- Regulatory compliance, where both Thai baht and Hong Kong dollar wallets were monitored on a real-time basis, and regulations on non-residents in certain areas must be complied.

Although the test on the functionalities was successful, Project Inthanon-LionRock provided many important lessons learned. First, the 24/7 nature of the corridor network affected existing operations, since legacy systems did not run 24/7 and CBDC must be reserved for off-hour transactions. Second, the elimination of correspondent banks in cross-border transactions caused foreign exchange liquidity shortage such that the help of a liquidity provider or liquidity saving mechanism would be needed in this supposedly peer-to-peer environment. Third, the atomic nature of corridor network made it difficult to comply with jurisdiction-specific foreign exchange regulations, since regulations could be vastly different across borders. Fourth, DLT had scalability and performance limitations, as the CBDC networks still could not handle a large number of transactions per second.

Cross-border wholesale CBDC: Project Inthanon-LionRock phase II and Project mBridge

Project Inthanon-LionRock phase I showed the possibility of bilateral cross-border payment based on wholesale CBDC and revealed challenges ahead. In addition, it was also only natural to ask if wholesale CBDC could be used for cross-border payments in a multilateral manner.

In 2021, BOT, HKMA, PBC, CBUAE and BIS Innovation Hub Centre in Hong Kong, China embarked on Project Inthanon-LionRock phase II, which was renamed Project mBridge, to indicate a multi-currency CBDC bridge (BIS Innovation Hub and others, 2021). As of 2022, Project mBridge is still ongoing, with further experimentation with design choices and technology trade-offs. The goal is also to define a future road map from prototype to an open-source, production-ready system.

3.2 Retail CBDC

Retail CBDC is not used for interbank payments, but rather for payments among corporations, firms and individuals, although financial institutions might be distributors of retail CBDC. Since 2020, BOT has embarked on two proofs of concept for retail CBDC. In addition, a live pilot for retail CBDC will take place in the latter half of 2022.

Retail CBDC: CBDC for business payments

In 2020, BOT tested CBDC for corporate use with Siam Cement Group (SCG), one of the largest Thai conglomerates, and Digital Ventures, a fintech firm affiliated with Siam Commercial Bank (Bank of Thailand, SCG and Digital Ventures, 2021). A prototype was developed to test how smart contracts attached to CBDC could be used to improve supply chain financing, a prevalent business use case. Specifically, a prototype was developed where the central bank issued retail digital currency and distributed it to corporations and small and medium-sized enterprises (SMEs) via banks or payment service providers. By integrating the retail CBDC network with a business procurement platform, smart contracts could be employed with retail CBDC on the network, to create "programmable money", which could lead to greater market efficiency and more competitive funding costs for SMEs that are supplier firms to corporate buyers.

In supply chain financing, SMEs often have to wait 90–180 days for payments after delivering their products and issuing invoices to corporate buyers. While waiting for payments to arrive, SMEs may need to raise additional funds to pay for the inputs needed to continue to produce their products and fulfil additional product orders. Smaller enterprises may have limited ability to raise funds in the formal credit market, even though the corporate buyers that owe them money (as specified in the invoices) may have a very good credit rating. The inability of SMEs to raise funds based on invoices is partly because lenders may doubt invoice authenticity, or they may worry that SMEs have already used the invoice to raise funds from other lenders (i.e. double financing), which could jeopardize a lender's legal claims.

Tests were done to see if the invoices issued by SMEs could be validated and tokenized on the business procurement platform, and used as securities to raise funds from lenders in the integrated CBDC network. The fact that tokenized invoices were validated on the business procurement platform minimized the risks of fake invoices. The tokenized invoices were also used to raise funds on a DLT-based CBDC network where transactions were recorded on a blockchain; thus minimizing the risk of double financing. Furthermore, smart contracts could be written to minimize payment risk. Smart contracts could be written on the tokenized invoices such that CBDC would move from the lenders who bought the tokenized invoices to the SMEs, and once the corporate buyers made CBDC payments on the invoices, the CBDC would move directly to the lenders according to the terms set out in smart contracts.

By lowering risks associated with supply chain financing, the proof of concept demonstrated that CBDC together with smart contracts have the potential to help improve efficiency in the funding market for SMEs, allowing for greater financial inclusion. It demonstrated the vast potential of CBDC as "programmable money", whereby business logic could be embedded into complex transactions for which CBDC underlies conditional transfer of value among relevant parties.

Retail CBDC: Retail CBDC as digital banknotes

In the previous proofs of concept, whether domestic wholesale CBDC, cross-border wholesale CBDC or domestic retail CBDC for business payments, CBDC was issued, distributed and used on DLT. Although the number of stakeholders participating in the CBDC network in each test was very limited, DLT platforms showed signs of strains in terms of scalability, i.e. the ability to process a large number of transactions per second. Although DLT itself is evolving so fast that scalability may not be an issue in the future, in 2021 BOT tested a new, non-DLT approach to CBDC, i.e. the issuance of CBDC as digital banknotes.

Conceptually, digital banknotes could be perceived as digital tokens representing money issued by the central bank, and digital banknotes could be distributed by banks or payment services providers to CBDC wallets of merchants or individuals. To ensure that a retail CBDC payment is valid and that there is no double spending of the same token, public key cryptography could be used. Unlike CBDC on DLT, there is no common ledger distributed to the participants to record digital banknote transactions. Similar to CBDC on DLT, and similar to physical banknotes, however, transactions using digital banknotes could be settled peer-to-peer among the participants without the need of a central counterparty.

Unlike physical banknotes, CBDC digital banknotes could be used like debit cards or e-money to make payments through electronic interfaces such as point-of-sale machines or through online channels. Unlike debit cards or e-money that have claims on the private sector (banks and e-money providers, respectively), holders of CBDC digital banknotes would have a direct claim on the central bank, similar to holders of physical banknotes.

In this proof of concept, BOT tested prototype CBDC digital banknotes to see if they could be issued, destroyed, redeemed and used for transactions securely. The prototype was also tested to see if it could handle transaction throughputs at a scale that reflected real-life usage. The success of this proof of concept in 2021 has enabled BOT to go forward with a retail CBDC pilot in 2022, with a sizeable number of stakeholders using and processing CBDC for everyday transactions.

IV. RETAIL CBDC PILOT

The aim of the retail CBDC pilot forecasted for the latter half of 2022 is to investigate how retail CBDC might be a complementary infrastructure that helps to future-proof the Thai financial system. At a strategic level, the pilot would allow BOT to investigate how, compared to existing retail payments systems, retail CBDC would raise efficiency, innovation and financial inclusion. At a more technical level, the pilot will allow BOT to investigate if retail CBDC digital banknotes could be issued, distributed and used safely for retail transactions. Innovations to solve existing pain points will also be tested. Key issues such as cybersecurity, data privacy and transaction scalability will also be investigated.

4.1 Design characteristics

Based on a survey taken among stakeholders and BOT research (Bank of Thailand, 2021a and 2021b), BOT selected the following design characteristics for the retail CBDC pilot prototype: (a) the system will have two tiers, whereby the CBDC is issued to payment services providers (banks and non-banks) that distribute CBDC to the general public; (b) the system will be non-interest bearing; (c) there will be limits on the amount of CBDC that can be held in different types of wallets; (d) the system will be open to innovations, whereby banks and non-banks can develop applications for the CBDC infrastructure; and (e) the system will ensure appropriate levels of data privacy.

The decision to design a two-tier system was based on the desire to ensure that CBDC would not unduly disrupt the underlying financial system. Intermediaries such as banks provide valuable services to the economy (i.e. efficient allocation of funds into productive use). As such BOT deemed it inappropriate to bypass the intermediaries and issue digital banknotes directly to individuals and firms. By not directly interacting with the general public, this would also help to lessen heavy operational burdens on the central bank, as otherwise it would also need to do know-your-client (KYC) operations on a large number of users and manage a large number of CBDC wallets.

The decision to design a non-interest-bearing system for retail CBDC was based on financial stability concerns. Interest payments on CBDC would make it a direct competitor to bank accounts, disrupting the ability of the intermediaries to raise and allocate funds in the economy. Although interest payments on retail CBDC could hypothetically make monetary policy transmission much faster, since individual holders of CBDC could be directly and instantly affected by changes in interest rates paid on CBDC, this would amount to the central bank's direct intervention into the balance sheets of households and firms.

Limitations on the amount that may be held in different types of CBDC wallets reduces the possibility of bank runs. If there were no limits on the amount of CBDC to be held in the CBDC wallets, unfounded rumors could easily cause bank runs, as people could use their mobile phones any time to transfer large balances out of their bank accounts and into risk-free CBDC wallets. To allow for reasonable use of CBDC wallets, the limits could depend on the types of holders of CBDC wallets (e.g. individuals versus merchants), or different KYC levels on the wallets.

The emphasis of the pilot on openness to innovation is reflected in the architecture of the CBDC network. In contrast to wholesale CBDC that can be accessed only by banks, participating banks and non-banks would distribute digital banknotes to the general public and act as custodians of CBDC wallets. Banks and non-banks can thus develop applications for CBDC wallets customized to particular use cases. Smart contracts could be built for CBDC wallets to allow for complex, conditional payments.

On data privacy issues, BOT differentiates between identifiable personal data and transactions data. As banks and non-banks deal with KYC, BOT will not have direct access to identifiable personal data. This is similar to the existing systems in the banking industry, where BOT does not have a direct access to identifiable personal data on the bank accounts of individuals. Banks, including BOT and non-banks acting as payment service providers all need to comply with regulations on data privacy.

Another aim of the pilot is to test the security and reliability of the system, thus a limited number of users (merchants and individuals) and payment services providers (banks and non-banks) would be invited at the start. Once the results of the pilot have met pre-defined criteria, there may be an extension in terms of participants, scope and timing.

4.2 Differences between retail CBDC and existing e-payment systems

A question that often arises when discussing retail CBDC is how it would be different from the existing payment systems, including PromptPay, the existing faster payment system. PromptPay is already very popular in Thailand, as it allows a user to make payment from a mobile banking application to a bank account that is linked with the recipients' mobile phone number or linked with a QR code, free of charge.

By the end of 2021, there were more than 66.9 million registered PromptPay bank accounts (Thairath Online, 2021). Furthermore, in April 2021 BOT and the Monetary Authority of Singapore launched the world's first linkage of real-time payment systems, PromptPay-PayNow, enabling the transfer of funds between the two countries using only a mobile phone number (Bank of Thailand and Monetary Authority of Singapore, 2021).

At first glance, there may seem to be few differences between making payments using retail CBDC or PromptPay, as both use a mobile phone application. The key differences, however, are the underlying payment and settlement system architecture and how the transactions are processed. Such differences could have vast implications on innovations that build on the payment infrastructure.

The existing faster payment systems, including PromptPay, are centralized, and payments between banks are settled at a central switch. These payments require interactions with the core information technology infrastructure of the payer and payee banks. Typically, a fund would be debited from the payer's account at one bank and credited into the payee's account at another bank. As a bank's core information technology infrastructure typically houses millions of accounts, it cannot be readily modified to accommodate customized debiting or crediting for individual accounts. Specifically, it would not be easy, or even possible, to write smart contracts on legacy bank accounts to allow for complex, customized and automated payments among them.

In contrast, payments using retail CBDC would be settled on a peer-to-peer basis. The transfer of value between two CBDC wallets would occur as soon as the payer instructs her CBDC wallet to make a transfer to the payee's wallet. There would be no need for a centralized switch, nor for integration with the core information technology infrastructure for banking (except where an individual wants to move funds between her retail CBDC wallet and her own bank account). As such, smart contracts could be written to allow for complex, customized and automated payments among the retail CBDC wallets. The decentralized nature of retail CBDC allows for the possibility of programmable money to be ready for implementation. As retail CBDC payment and settlement occur on a peer-to-peer basis, new financial services providers have the potential to propose innovative payment solutions through smart contracts written on retail CBDC wallets, uninhibited by legacy information technology systems or barriers-to-entry that might be imposed upon by the company that owns a centralized payment switch.

4.3 Possible pilot use cases

To encourage innovation, BOT invited private sector participants to propose use cases. Participating banks and non-banks may identify pain points of their customers, whether individuals or merchants, and provide solutions using retail CBDC. As of early 2022 there has yet to be a decision on the retail CBDC pilot use case, but an oft-cited possibility is the targeted government welfare payment, as it could explore actual use of smart contracts.

In Thailand, during the COVID-19 pandemic, the Government implemented several COVID-19 relief schemes for citizens and merchants using "Pao Tang", a smartphone application. For example, the Government introduced a scheme in 2020, whereby Pao Tang users could deposit funds and use the application to pay for goods and services from registered merchants, including street vendors, at half price. The Government paid the other half to the merchants (Bangprapa and Theparat, 2022). In a scheme to stimulate domestic tourism, the Government introduced "Thai-Teaw-Thai" to subsize bookings at registered hotels and hostels for Pao Tang users (Worrachaddejchai, 2021). The schemes were very popular, and by the end of 2020, there were approximately 40 million accounts on Pao Tang (Banchongduang, 2020).

The success of Pao Tang suggested that citizens may be willing to embrace digital welfare payment schemes. The pilot use case for retail CBDC could be the implementation of more refined, complex government welfare schemes based on smart contracts. Smart contracts could be written on CBDC wallets to implement more granular welfare schemes with eligibility criteria for participants, goods and services, and timing.

V. CONCLUSION: LESSONS AND CHALLENGES AHEAD

Central banks around the world are exploring CBDC, whether domestic wholesale, cross-border wholesale, or retail CBDC. The experience of BOT can offer important lessons for other central banks in the Asia-Pacific region, especially in emerging markets.

The journey of BOT so far has shown that CBDC has the potential to raise efficiency, inclusion and innovation for the financial system. Given that CBDC could also deeply affect financial stability, monetary policy and the roles of financial institutions and central banks, BOT is proceeding in a measured and gradual manner. Through learning-by-doing, ecosystem building and an iterative approach, BOT has built its capability along with the capacity of stakeholders to reap the benefits of CBDC while mitigating risks that might arise. The retail CBDC pilot in 2022 is expected to add to the body of knowledge and experience and help to build a road map for a possible future CBDC roll-out.

A key challenge after the retail CBDC pilot in 2022 will be to integrate all the knowledge and experience gained from each proof of concept and the pilot, to make an informed decision whereby domestic wholesale CBDC, cross-border CBDC and retail CBDC could be integrated, and complement and coexist with existing payment systems. This will be an ongoing journey, as technology and the financial landscape continue to evolve.

Going forward, for actual deployment in the economy, wholesale and retail CBDC might not need to be introduced together in one-go. However, a well thought-out sequential introduction might be warranted. Again, the three guiding principles, i.e. learning by doing, ecosystem building and an iterative approach, should help BOT to introduce CBDC in an orderly and secure manner without jeopardizing the financial sector stability.

Lessons learned from the CBDC journey can also be applied to other public institutions in their efforts to introduce digital technologies. Moreover, CBDC could be seen as digital infrastructure that can help improve efficiency, inclusion and innovation of the financial sector. Similar to physical infrastructure, digital infrastructure is a public good that often requires public sector initiative.

Unlike physical infrastructures such as bridges, tollways or airports that can be built and run by a particular entity (public, private or public-private), digital infrastructure, including CBDC, often require a network of participants to build and run their own parts of the infrastructure based on common standards and protocols. For example, to make an automated peer-to-peer transaction on a CBDC network, participating banks will need the ability to develop and run CBDC wallets and write smart contracts that share common standard and protocols. Furthermore, as digital infrastructure can evolve much faster than physical infrastructure, all the relevant stakeholders will need to regularly come together in order to make timely infrastructure adjustments. The CBDC journey of BOT has reflected the importance of learning by doing, ecosystem building and taking an iterative approach for public institutions in the development of digital infrastructure.

ACKNOWLEDGEMENTS

The author would like to thank those involved in the CBDC journey of BOT. Such a journey has so far involved not only the BOT team, but also the participating commercial banks, information technology vendors, Thai public agencies, foreign central banks, as well as non-banks and the public, who responded to BOT surveys and public consultations. In particular, the author wishes to thank Veerathai Santiprabhob, Sethaput Suthiwartnarueput, Mathee Supapongse, Vachira Arromdee, Chantavarn Sucharitakul, Amporn Sangmanee, Titanun Mallikamas and Chayawadee Chai-anant, for their guidance from the beginning of the BOT's CBDC journey, and the rest of

BOT Digital Currency Team for their tireless effort to introduce CBDC to improve efficiency, inclusion and innovation in the Thai financial sector. Any errors found in this paper are the author's alone.

NOTE ON CONTRIBUTORS

Thammarak Moenjak is Chief Representative, Bank of Thailand (BOT) London Representative Office, and Senior Advisor to the BOT central bank digital currency team. Thammarak is the author of *Central Banking: Theory and Practice in Sustaining Monetary and Financial Stability,* John Wiley and Sons, 2014, which has been translated into Mandarin.

REFERENCES

Banchongduang, S. (2020). KTB eyes 40m users under government projects. *Bangkok Post,* 6 November.

Bangprapa, M., and C. Theparat (2022). Relief schemes set to kick off earlier. *Bangkok Post,* 25 January.

Bank of Thailand (2019). "Inthanon Phase I: An application of Distributed Ledger Technology for a Decentralised Real Time Gross Settlement system using Wholesale Central Bank Digital Currency". Available at www.bot.or.th/Thai/PaymentSystems/Documents/Inthanon_Phase1_Report.pdf.

_____ (2020). *Inthanon Phase II: Enhancing Bond Lifecycle Functionalities and Programmable Compliance Using Distributed Ledger Technology.* Bank of Thailand. Available at www.bot.or.th/English/FinancialMarkets/ProjectInthanon/Documents/Inthanon_Phase2_Report.pdf.

_____ (2021a). *Retail Central Bank Digital Currency: Implications on Monetary Policy and Financial Stability.* Available at www.bot.or.th/Thai/PressandSpeeches/Press/News2564/n6064t_annex.pdf.

_____ (2021b). *The Way Forward for Retail Central Bank Digital Currency in Thailand.* Available at www.bot.or.th/Thai/digitalcurrency/documents/bot_retailcbdcpaper.pdf.

Bank of Thailand and Monetary Authority of Singapore (2021). "Thailand and Singapore Launch World's First Linkage of Real-time Payment Systems". Joint press release. Available at www.bot.or.th/Thai/AboutBOT/Activities/Documents/290464_JointPress/JointPress29042021_EN.pdf.

Bank of Thailand, SCG and Digital Ventures (2021). "Central Bank Digital Currency: The Future of Payments for Corporates". Available at www.bot.or.th/English/FinancialMarkets/ProjectInthanon/Documents/20210308_CBDC.pdf.

BIS Innovation Hub Hong Kong Centre, Hong Kong Monetary Authority, Bank of Thailand, People's Bank of China, Central Bank of the United Arab Emirates (2021). *Inthanon-LionRock to mBridge: Building a multi CBDC platform for international payments.* Available at www.bis.org/publ/othp40.pdf.

PwC (2021). "PwC Global CBDC Index". First edition. Available at www.pwc.com/gx/en/industries/financial-services/assets/pwc-cbdc-global-index-1st-edition-april-2021.pdf

Thairath Online (2021). PromptPay daily transaction reached 94 billion baht, with 66.9 million users (in Thai language). Available at www.thairath.co.th/business/finance/2261591.

Worrachaddejchai, D. (2021). Bargains galore at Thai Teaw Thai fair. *Bangkok Post,* 4 March.

INVITED PAPER

Invited paper

IMPACT OF CLIMATE CHANGE AND VARIABILITY ON FOOD SECURITY IN THE ASIA-PACIFIC REGION

A. Mukherjee, S. Saha, S. C. Lellyett and A.K.S. Huda
Corresponding author: A.K.S. Huda

Email: s.huda@westernsydney.edu.au

The Asia-Pacific region is highly disaster prone and susceptible to climate variability and extremes due to widely varying geography from coastal territories to mountainous areas, and tropical to polar climates. Long-term food security in this region necessitates estimation of future food production, including the assessment and adoption of adaptation/mitigation strategies. The present paper serves to highlight climate variability of the recent past and for future projected scenarios, and its impact on food production. It serves to recommend adaptive climate-smart agricultural measures, from local practices to policy level initiatives to help address 2030 Agenda for Sustainable Development and future food security of the Asia-Pacific region.

Keywords: food security, climate change, climate variability, Asia-Pacific, climate-smart agriculture

JEL classification: Q01

I. INTRODUCTION

The Asia-Pacific region is highly susceptible to changes in climate variability, with extensive coastlines, many small island countries, and a widely varying geography from low-lying coastal territories to elevated mountainous areas, and tropical to polar climates. According to the sixth assessment report of the Intergovernmental Panel on Climate Change (IPCC) intensifying greenhouse gas (GHG) emissions have affected all continents and most oceans, with many natural systems disrupted by climate change, particularly increases in temperature. Evidence is seen in rising carbon dioxide concentrations, global mean temperatures and sea levels, and changing precipitation patterns. Relative to 1850–1900, global mean surface temperature by 2100 is likely to increase by 1.4°C to 4.4°C under five different GHG emissions scenarios (Shared Socioeconomic Pathways (SSP), SSP1-1.9 to SSP5-8.5). The frequency and intensity of heavy precipitation events have increased since the 1950s. The average annual global land precipitation is projected to increase by 0–13 per cent under emissions scenarios (SSP1-1.9 to SSP5-8.5) by 2081–2100, relative to 1995–2014. Intensity and frequency of hot extremes including heatwaves, plus agricultural and ecological droughts, are likely to increase in some regions in the future (IPCC, 2021). Sea levels rose by 0.20 m between 1901 and 2018. Given Asia-Pacific topography, this poses an existential threat to many countries in the region.

There is growing consensus that under future climate change scenarios and in the absence of adaptive measures severe impacts on crop production can be expected. Negative impacts for coastal regions are expected to be exacerbated, with overall losses of production and increased food security risks. Causes include the additive effects of erosion, increased contamination of groundwater and estuaries by saltwater incursion, tropical cyclones and storm surges, heat stress and drought. For crops where the Asia-Pacific region accounts for a significant proportion of world production, the impacts will not only be local, but also global. Similar impacts are possible for livestock production. Pacific Island Countries and other nations dependent upon fisheries face potential yield and species loss due to climate change induced alteration of turbidity, salinity and temperature (Barnett, 2020).

The present paper provides a consolidated view detailing important climate change impacts and how they can affect food security. Food security has four main dimensions: physical availability; economic and physical access to food; food utilization; and stability of the other three dimensions over time (FAO, 2015). The focus of the present paper is on the first dimension, physical availability, which largely depends on production. It provides an outline of how mitigation and adaptation measures are inextricably linked to the achievement of the Sustainable Development Goals (SDGs) embodied in the 2030 Agenda for Sustainable Development. Acknowledging the importance of this and other top-down policy frameworks for action, the present paper serves to propose that complementary local and broad scale implementation of climate-smart agricultural practices throughout the Asia-Pacific region are essential for achieving and ensuring sustainable agriculture and food security.

Section II covers past changes and trends of climate; section III examines future climate projections; section IV documents likely impacts of climate change on food security; section V covers agriculture and sustainable development policy in the Asia-Pacific region; and section VI provides conclusions and makes recommendations.

II. CLIMATE: PAST CHANGES AND TRENDS

Global surface temperature has increased faster since 1970 than in any other 50-year period over at least the past 2,000 years. Hot extremes (including heatwaves) have become more frequent and more intense across most land regions since the 1950s, while cold extremes (including cold waves) have become less frequent and less severe (IPCC, 2021). The frequency and intensity of heavy precipitation events have increased since the 1950s over most land areas for which observational data are sufficient for trend analysis, and human-induced climate change is likely the main driver.

2.1 Temperature

Relative to 1850–1900, the rise in global average surface temperature accelerated from +0.89°C for 2001–2010, to +1.09°C for 2011–2020. Larger increases were seen over land than sea, for instance, +1.59°C versus +0.88°C during 2011–2020. As reported by IPCC (2012), since 1950, cold days and nights in the Asia-Pacific region have decreased in number, warm days and nights have increased in number, and heat wave frequency has increased.

2.2 Precipitation

The frequency of occurrence of more intense rainfall in many parts of Asia has increased while the number of rainy days and total annual amount of precipitation has declined. Precipitation trends, including extremes, are characterized by strong variability, with both increasing and decreasing trends observed in different parts of the Asia-Pacific region and in different seasons (Hijioka and others, 2014). In northern Asia, observations indicate some increasing trends of heavy precipitation events, but in Central Asia, no coherent trends were found. In West Asia, a weak but non-significant downward trend in mean precipitation was observed in recent decades, and an increase in intense weather events. In South Asia, seasonal rainfall shows a declining trend in inter-decadal variability, with more frequent relative rainfall deficits in monsoons. The frequency of heavy precipitation is increasing, while light rain events are decreasing. In South-East Asia, annual total wet-day rainfall along with extreme rainfall has increased. In Peninsular Malaysia during the southwest monsoon season, total rainfall and the frequency of wet days decreased, but rainfall intensity increased over much of the region. During the northeast monsoon total rainfall and the frequency of extreme rainfall intensity increased over the peninsula.

During 1961–2000, locations to the northeast of the South Pacific Convergence Zone became wetter, while locations to the southwest became drier.

III. CLIMATE: FUTURE PROJECTIONS

3.1 Temperature

Under the Representative Concentration Pathway (RCP) scenarios for GHG emissions through the year 2100, changes in projected mean annual temperature exceed 2°C above the 1961–1990 baseline over most land areas by 2050 under the high-emissions scenario, RCP8.5, and range from greater than 3°C in South and South-East Asia, to greater than 6°C in high latitudes by 2100. Projected changes are less than 2°C above the same baseline by both 2050 and 2100 under the lower emissions scenario, RCP2.6, with the exception of 2°C to 3°C rises in the highest latitudes (Hijioka and others, 2014). The projections show not only rising average temperatures, but also rising numbers of hot days.

According to the IPCC Sixth Assessment Report Summary for Policymakers, (IPCC, 2021) global surface temperature will continue to increase until at least mid-century under all emissions scenarios considered. Projections show that every additional 0.5°C of global warming will cause increases in the intensity and frequency of extremes, including heatwaves (very likely), heavy precipitation (high confidence) and drought intensity and frequency in some regions (medium confidence).

It is widely accepted now that many changes in the climate system correspond to increasing global surface temperature.

3.2 Precipitation

A 7 per cent global increase in extreme daily precipitation events is projected for each 1°C of warming (high confidence). The proportion of intense tropical cyclones (category 4–5) is projected to increase globally (IPCC, 2021). Average annual global land precipitation is projected to increase by 0–5 per cent under SSP1-1.9, and by

1–13 per cent under SSP5-8.5 by 2081–2100 relative to 1995–2014. Increases are projected in high latitudes, the equatorial Pacific and parts of the monsoon regions, but decreases are projected in parts of the subtropics and tropics for SSP2-4.5, SSP3-7.0 and SSP5-8.5 (very likely). Monsoon precipitation is projected to increase globally in the medium to long term, particularly in South Asia, South-East Asia and East Asia (high confidence).

3.3 Sea level rise

Global mean sea level rise of 0.20 m during 1901–2018 has occurred due to ice loss on land and thermal expansion caused by ocean warming. Thermal expansion accounted for 50 per cent of sea level rise during 1971–2018 while accelerating losses from glaciers contributed 22 per cent, ice sheets 20 per cent and changes in land-water storage 8 per cent (IPCC, 2021). The average rate of rise was 1.3 mm yr–1 during 1901–1971, increasing to 1.9 mm yr–1 during 1971–2006, and further increasing to 3.7 mm yr–1 during 2006–2018 (high confidence). Approximately two thirds of global coastline have a projected relative rise within ±20 per cent of the global mean increase. The Asia-Pacific region is highly vulnerable to rising sea levels, which increase the risk of floods. Some Pacific Island Countries have experienced a rate of sea level rise that is four times the global average (Nurse and others, 2014).

In the Asia-Pacific region, sea level is expected to rise 3–16 cm by 2030 and 7–50 cm by 2070 (Preston and others, 2006). With a sea level rise of 40 cm by 2100, the population facing floods in coastal areas will increase from 13 million to 94 million, with 60 per cent of that population found in South Asia (Bangladesh, India, Pakistan, Myanmar and Sri Lanka) and 20 per cent found in South-East Asia (Indonesia, the Philippines, Thailand and Viet Nam).

IV. CLIMATE IMPACTS ON FOOD SECURITY

Climate change will affect all four dimensions of food security: availability; accessibility; utilization; and stability (figure 1). An IPCC Special Report found that climate-related risks to food security are projected to increase with global warming of 1.5°C and increase further with global warming of 2°C (IPCC, 2018). Shifts in land suitability will likely lead to an increase in suitable cropland at higher latitudes and a decline of cropland at lower latitudes. Fluctuating crop yields and local food supply will make achieving food security more difficult. Semi-arid and subhumid regions will be affected most, reducing yields of crops, livestock and productivity. Potential price increases and negative income effects associated with climate change also have implications for food accessibility (ADB, 2013).

Figure 1. Diagram of climate change influence on food security

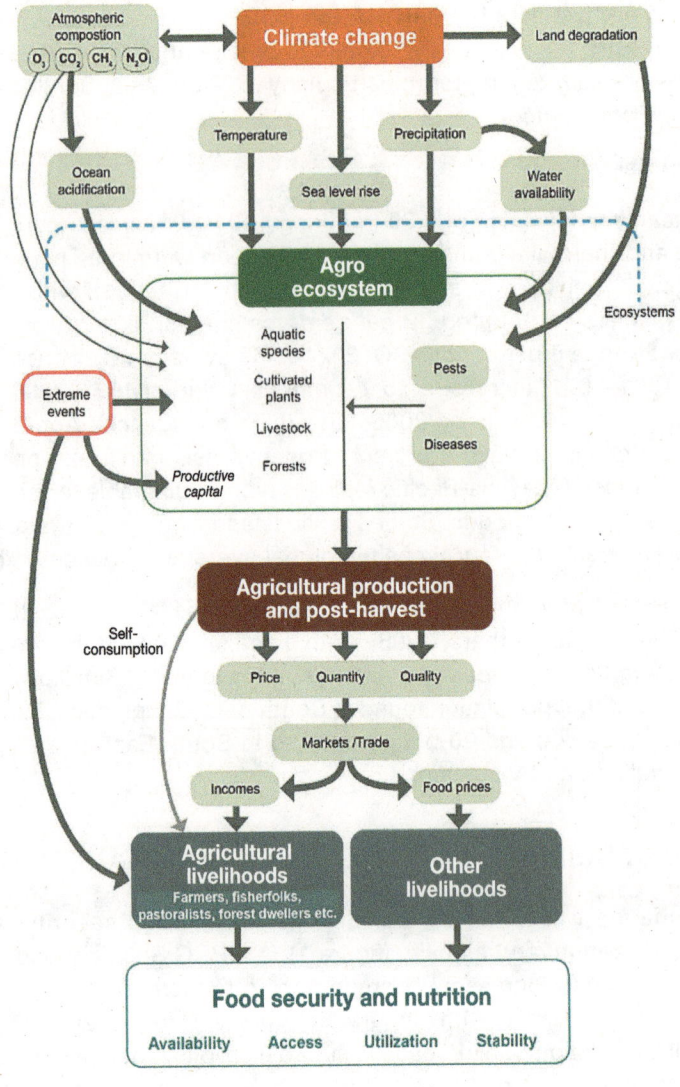

Source: FAO (2015).

4.1 Crop production

Since the IPCC Fifth Assessment Report, studies have demonstrated strong relationships between observed climate variables and crop yields that indicate expected future warming will have severe impacts on crop production (Mavromatis, 2015). Climate and crop simulations indicate that climate changes during 1981-2010 have decreased global mean yields of maize, wheat, and soybeans by 4.1, 1.8 and 4.5 per cent, respectively, relative to preindustrial climate, even when carbon dioxide fertilization and agronomic adjustments are considered (Iizumi and others, 2018). Dryland settlements are vulnerable to climate change driven food security risks, with drylands constituting over 40 per cent of the earth's land area, and home to 2.5 billion people. Agricultural production in the Pacific Island Countries is likely to be adversely affected by climate change in a number of ways. The effects of climate change are highly heterogeneous with some regions gaining, nevertheless the overall effect is negative.

Cereals in South Asia. In South Asia, for example, climate change will likely bring a substantial reduction in aggregate crop production. Cereal's production could be decreased up to approximately 31, 24, 25 and 6 per cent (figure 2) by 2050 as compared to 2011, in Bangladesh, Pakistan, Sri Lanka and India respectively (Alvi and others, 2021).

Figure 2. Change in cereal production by 2050 compared to 2011 under climate change scenario

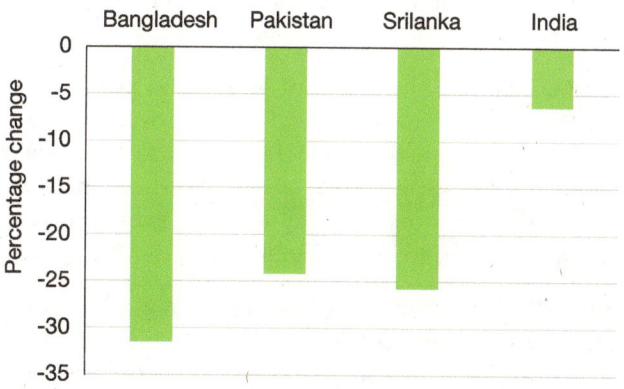

Source: Alvi and others (2021).

Rice. On average, rice yields are projected to decline. By 2050 in South Asia climate change could reduce irrigated crop yields of rice (14–20 per cent), wheat (32–44 per cent); maize (2–4 per cent) and soybeans (9–18 per cent) relative to 2010 (Rosegrant, Tokgoz and Bhandary, 2013). Yoon and Choi (2020) reported that irrigation requirements for rice in the Republic of Korea under RCP4.5 would decrease by 2100 because of an increase in projected rainfall, but under RCP8.5 rainfall decreases therefore increasing the need for irrigation. Rice yields in the Republic of Korea were projected to decrease monotonically from the 2020s to the 2040s due to the increase in days that could cause high temperature damage (Kim and others, 2021). Warming and increasing extreme climate events are expected to reduce crop yields, including rice production in China, threatening food security. Chinese rice growth duration is anticipated to decease by >30 days by the end of the twenty-first century, and average rice yield will decline approximately 5, 7 and 15 per cent respectively in the periods 2011–2040, 2041–2070 and 2071–2100 (Ding and others, 2020).

Wheat in Australia. Variations in average growing season temperature of ±2°C in wheat growing regions of Australia could reduce production by 50 per cent (Asseng and others, 2015). Zheng and others (2012) showed Australian wheat life cycles could be shortened by up to 42 days by 2050. Simulations by Hochman, Gobbett and Horan (2017) for 50 sites showed that, other factors held constant, declines in rainfall and rising maximum temperatures account for a potential water-limited yield decline of 27 per cent during 1990–2015, with elevated carbon dioxide concentrations avoiding a further 4 per cent loss. Actual yields however experienced a modest growth over the period, mainly due to an unprecedented rate of technological gains – underlining the value of investing in technological adaptation and mitigation strategies.

Maize. Negative impacts on maize yields are projected (-4 to -14 per cent) compared to 1981–2010 in China (Xiao and others, 2020) and (-11 to -27 per cent) compared to 1982–2012 for West Bengal, India (Shrivastava, Panda and Chakraborty, 2021).

Groundnut and soybean (rainy season) and wheat and chickpea (post-rainy season) in India. Results from an Asia-Pacific Network project in India (Huda and others, 2012) showed that increasing temperature trends are likely to reduce rainy-season crop yields by approximately 10–15 per cent and post-rainy season crop yields by approximately 20–25 per cent. As a result, breeding heat tolerant wheat and chickpea varieties needed to be strengthened.

Wheat-maize in China. Increasing temperatures in China have favoured wheat-maize systems in the north, while rice-based systems in the south are disadvantaged. Maize varieties with a longer growing season for northern China are less frost tolerant and breeding is required to overcome this deficiency. The Government of China established a disaster fund to deal with extreme weather events as part of an adaptation strategy. Research should concentrate on practices to reduce GHG emissions and water use by rice and to ensure biological nitrogen fixation (Huda and others, 2012).

Generally, across maize, sunflowers, wheat and rice, most projected climate change related yield losses around the world could be explained by a shortened growth duration.

For coastal communities, severe droughts, intense floods, saltwater incursion of ground water and estuaries, plus tropical cyclones and associated storm surges reduce both crop yields and total production, increasing the risk to food security. Tropical cyclones are a significant cause of lost agricultural production (Barnett, 2020). As agriculture is the main source of food, livelihood and income for many Pacific island communities, extreme weather events can have a highly critical impact.

In a sea level rise scenario of 1 m, up to 7.7 million ha of croplands would be submerged, while in a 3 m scenario, up to 16.1 million ha would be lost. Rice is expected to be the most affected, losing 4.9 million ha under the 1 m scenario and 10.5 million ha under the 3 m scenario, followed by wheat (0.6 million ha and 1.2 million ha) and maize (0.5 million ha and 0.9 million ha). Given the cultivation of 150 million ha of rice, the forecasted losses would significantly affect global rice production and, hence, prices (ADB, 2013).

South Asia, East Asia and the Pacific are consistently found to suffer in terms of reduced crop yields by 2080 under RCP8.5. Impacts may be more severe for South Asia than for East Asia and the Pacific.

4.2 Fruits and vegetables

The effect of climate change on vegetable crops was estimated to be similar to the effect on grain crops. The initial effect of increased carbon dioxide on vegetables is mostly beneficial for production, but it may alter quality parameters. Heat stress due to higher temperatures reduces fruit numbers produced by fruiting vegetables, and it speeds up the development of annual vegetables, thereby shortening their time for photo assimilation. Luck and others (2012) reported that relative to 1972–2010, by 2050 the productivity of potato crops in India may be reduced by 23–30 per cent (Nadia district) and 28–32 per cent (Hooghly district) and in Bangladesh by 7–26 per cent (Bogra district) and 18–31 per cent (Munshiganj district). In Australia, relative to the same period, there is a chance of small yield reductions (3 per cent) in tropical Queensland, and <1 per cent in temperate Victoria. Potato production will likely become more reliable over southern Australia. Tuber formation in sweet potato is significantly reduced at temperatures above 34°C. Projected temperature increases of 2.0°C–4.5°C by 2100 could significantly reduce sweet potato production in lowland areas of Papua New Guinea but may increase cacao production in Vanuatu and Fiji while increased flooding may affect sugar cane production in Papua New Guinea and Solomon Islands (Bell and others, 2016).

4.3 Crop protection

Direct impacts of climate change on pests include alteration of reproduction, development, survival and dispersal, whereas indirect impacts include the relationships between pests, their environment and other insect species such as natural enemies, competitors, vectors and mutualists (Prakash and others, 2014). Warren and others (2018) estimated that about 49 per cent of insects, some of which are considered agricultural pests or disease vectors while others are considered mutualists, will change the spatial ranges within which they thrive by about 50 per cent by 2100 given a 3.2°C increase in the global average temperature. If warming can be limited to 2°C the estimate of affected insect species reduces to 18 per cent.

According to Deutsch and others (2018), warming will accelerate the growth of wheat-pest populations in temperate climates. For rice grown in tropical zones a decrease in the growth of rice-pest populations is predicted, while for maize grown in both temperate and tropical regions mixed responses in pest population growth could be expected. Overall, the estimated likely net effect is for crop yield reductions. By 2100 under 2°C of global warming, the pest-related global yield losses from wheat, rice and maize are likely to increase by 46 per cent, 19 per cent and 31 per cent, respectively, when compared to current levels of loss. Furthermore, each additional degree of temperature rise could cause global yield losses to increase by a further 10–25 per cent, due to insect pests (Dunne, 2018).

Hence adaptation and mitigation strategies are crucial. Huda and others (2007) noted that integrated pest management approaches should be complemented with pest epidemiology and consideration of local socioeconomic capacity. They caution that responses such as the use of herbicides, pesticides or other biological approaches need careful optimization to minimize negative externalities such as pollutant damage or unintended ecological damage.

Integrated pest management related research in the Asia-Pacific region undertaken by Huda and others (2009) demonstrated the feasibility of identifying specific quantitative pest/disease-climate relations for location-specific selected pests and diseases. Relationships displaying high correlations between climate and incidence of disease were developed for late leaf spot in peanuts for India and Cambodia; alternaria blight in mustard for India and Bangladesh; and sclerotinia in canola for Australia and India. These relationships enabled identification of critical climate-related decision thresholds to inform adaptation or mitigation strategies.

Earlier onset of potato late blight is likely in future decades in India, Bangladesh and Australia. Disease severity is likely to reduce by 5–7 per cent in 2031–2040 compared to 1981–2010 in West Bengal, India. However, in growing areas of Bangladesh, disease severity could shift in either direction. Increases of up to 12 per cent are expected in northern Bangladesh and reductions of around 7 per cent in central Bangladesh. Potato late blight is expected to be less problematic in the tropical north than elsewhere in Australia (Luck and others, 2012).

4.4 Overall impacts on food security

The physical availability dimension of food security depends on domestic production and imports. Declining per capita food production is a function of several factors: population growth; private and public investment in agriculture; availability of labour, water and land; input costs; and disasters.

Across Pacific Island Countries, in the decade up to 2006 per capita food production declined and dependence on imported foods increased, including cereals which are virtually all imported. Indeed, this has affected trade deficits, and total food availability in the Pacific islands is increasingly becoming a function of the ability to pay for food imports (Barnett, 2020). The Hindu-Kush Himalayan region is experiencing an increase in extremes, with farmers facing more frequent floods and prolonged droughts that have decreased yields and increased food insecurity (Hussain and others, 2016).

A summary of the impacts of climate change on yield of major food sources in selected Asia-Pacific countries is provided in table 1.

Table 1. Impact of climate change

(a) On change in crop yield by mid to late twenty-first century

Crop	Region/Country	Change in yield (percentage)	Base year	Reference
Rice	South Asia	-14% to -20%	2010	Rosegrant, Tokgoz and Bhandary (2013)
	China	-5% to -15%	2002–2012	Ding and others (2020)
	India	-2 to -15%	2005	Teng, Caballero-Anthony and Lassa (2016)
	Pakistan	-7 to -18%	1960–2004	Iqbal and others (2009)
	Viet Nam	-6 to -24%	2013	Teng, Caballero-Anthony and Lassa (2016)
	Indonesia	Wetland rice: -3 to -6% Dry land rice: -2 to -4%	1976–2011	Khairulbahri (2021)
	Global average impact	-10 to -25% per +1°C temp	2003-2008	ADB (2021)

Table 1. *(continued)*

Crop	Region/Country	Change in yield (percentage)	Base year	Reference
Wheat	South Asia	-32% to -44%	2010	Rosegrant, Tokgoz and Bhandary (2013)
	China	-36 to -41%.	2006–2012	Wang and others (2021)
	India	Irrigated: -1 to -8% Limited irrigation: -4 to -36%	1986–2005	Daloz and others (2021)
	Bangladesh	-7 to -35%	2000–2019	Islam and others (2022)
	Pakistan	+18 to +48%	2006–2015	Alvar Beltran (2021)
	South West Australia	-26% to -49%	1980–2010	Taylor and others (2018)
Maize	South Asia	-2% to -4%	2010	Rosegrant, Tokgoz and Bhandary (2013)
	China	-4 to -14%	2001–2009	Xiao and others (2020)
	India (West Bengal)	-11 to -27%	1982–2012	Shrivastava, Panda and Chakraborty (2021)
Soyabean	South Asia	-9% to +18%	2010	Rosegrant, Tokgoz and Bhandary (2013)

(b) On global sea level rise and crop area loss (million ha)

Sea level rise	Rice	Wheat	Maize	Reference
+1 metre	4.9	0.6	0.5	ADB (2013)
+3 metre	10.9	1.2	0.9	ADB (2013)

Analysis of yield projection estimates against the most recently available statistical data (2019) of the Food and Agriculture Organization of the United Nations (FAO) (FAOSTAT, 2022) can provide an indication of the relative effort and investment that might be considered in addressing findings such as those in table 1.

Rice. China, India and Viet Nam represent 28, 24 and 6 per cent, respectively, of global rice production (FAOSTAT, 2022). Projected losses of 10, 9 and 15 per cent, respectively (figure 3) may lead to 3, 2 and 1 per cent reductions in global rice production, warranting the development of policies and plans to address the situation. As rice is a staple food, reduced production would increase the hunger index.

Figure 3. Expected change of overall rice yield under future climate scenario by 2100

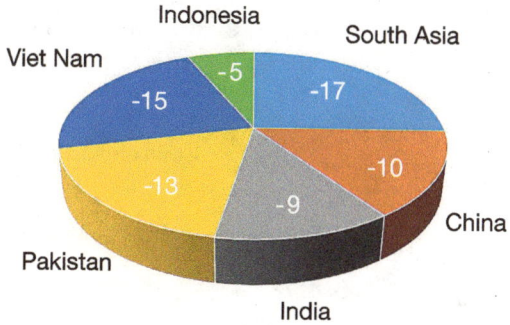

Source: See references in table 1.

Wheat. Asia contributes around 44 per cent of global wheat production, of which China (17.5 per cent) and India (13.5 per cent) occupy the major share. A projected reduction in wheat yield for China of 39 per cent will be a great threat to global food supply (figure 4). In India non-irrigated wheat will suffer a reduction in productivity of approximately 20 per cent, which could be minimized with judicious irrigation management.

Figure 4. Expected change of overall wheat yield under future climate scenario by 2100

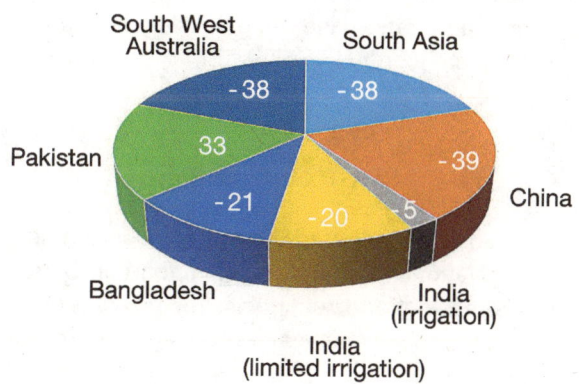

Source: See references in table 1.

Maize. As China contributes 23 per cent of global maize production, a 9 per cent decline in its productivity (figure 5) corresponds to a 2 per cent reduction in global production, which will be a concern for food security. Similarly, the contribution of India to global production may be reduced to 1.9 per cent from 2.4 per cent (FAOSTAT, 2022).

Figure 5. Expected change of overall maize yield under future climate scenario by 2100

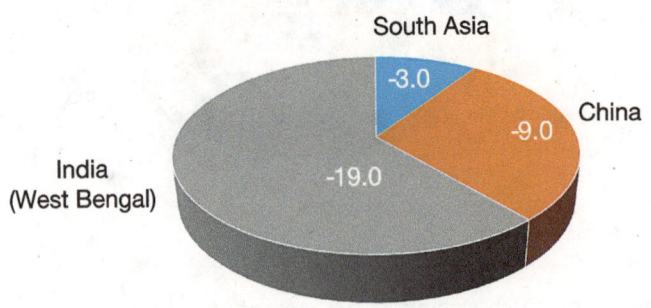

Source: See references in table 1.

In summary, comparing the limited data available in figures 3, 4 and 5 to FAO statistical data provides a basis for identifying where targeted investments could be beneficial. For example, in India to offset climate related wheat losses an effective strategy could centre on investments in irrigation and crop water use efficiency.

Comprehensive coverage of the entire Asia-Pacific region and the discernment of the relative merits of investment across the full spectrum of geographies, agricultural production and potential adaptation and mitigation strategies is beyond the scope of the present paper and is a worthy topic for further investigation.

V. AGRICULTURE AND SUSTAINABLE DEVELOPMENT POLICY IN THE ASIA-PACIFIC REGION

The present section highlights selected Sustainable Development Goals and policy measures of the United Nations Framework Convention on Climate Change for the agriculture sector in addressing food security issues relevant to climate change and endorses the bottom-up approach of climate-smart agriculture as a practical means toward implementation.

Agriculture features prominently in the 2030 Agenda. It is relevant to each of the 17 Sustainable Development Goals. Rapidly rising population rates, limited arable land and diminishing natural resources across the Asia-Pacific region will impose significant economic reliance on the agriculture sector for long-term sustainability.

Sustainable Development Goal 2 considers the adequacy of food production. Agricultural productivity has risen in many Asian countries, but opportunity remains to lift productivity further. However, there is also a dominance of small-holder farmers in the agriculture sector of many countries within the Asia-Pacific region, who are often unable to afford the costs, lack adequate access to capital, have varying levels of education and access to the support of national extension services, research and development infrastructure to engender and sustain the adoption of better technological farming systems. This is a major risk to the achievement of Goal 2, which includes ending hunger and ensuring access by all people to safe, nutritious and sufficient food all year round by 2030.

According to FAO (2021), hunger as measured by the prevalence of undernourishment globally increased from 630 million to 690 million between 2014 and 2019. By extrapolation, this trend could reach more than 840 million people by 2030, including 330 million people in Asia.

Agriculture still accounts for a significant proportion of gross domestic product (GDP) in many countries across the Asia-Pacific region, especially those recognized as developing countries. For those countries, structural transformation is central to achieving overall sustainable national economic growth and full productive employment for all, which are aims of Sustainable Development Goal 8. Truelove and others (forthcoming) cite value chain analysis and modelling as providing a sound basis upon which to develop and enact plans for guiding structural adjustments.

Responsible climate action will provide substantial opportunities for modernizing infrastructure, creating new jobs, and promoting greater prosperity. Coordinated efforts will be required to achieve the targets enumerated under the 17 Sustainable Development Goals. The aim of the 26th session of the Conference of the Parties to the United Nations Framework Convention on Climate Change (UNFCCC) in 2021 was to accelerate action toward meeting the goals of the Paris Agreement. Doing so would assist in addressing Goal 13 regarding urgent action to combat climate change and its impacts. The Conference of the Parties emphasized the need for more lending to help poor countries shift out of fossil fuel based energy generation (aligning with Goal 7), to build societies better adapted to the impacts of climate change and to recover from damage caused by extreme weather events. Notably, besides biomass and bioenergy, other forms of renewable energy substitution for fossil fuels (e.g. wind, solar, geothermal, hydroelectric) are increasingly being adopted by producers and applied to practices such as conservation tillage and precision farming (e.g. fertilizer and chemical application and precision irrigation) to further reduce GHG emissions (Ahmed and others, 2017).

Climate-smart agriculture provides a set of practical responses that can scale from locally based actions through to broad-scale policy application, contributing towards and complimenting high level actions such as the Sustainable Development Goals and initiatives of UNFCCC. The Koronivia Joint Working Group for Agriculture at the Conference of the Parties highlighted that actions should be inclusive of strategies and modalities to scale up implementation of best practices, innovations and technologies to increase resilience and sustainable production in agricultural systems (UNFCCC, 2021).

Climate-smart agriculture is defined as an integrated approach to managing cropland, livestock, forests and fisheries that aims to support food security under projected climate change through sustainable and equitable transitions of agricultural systems and livelihoods (Aggarwal and others, 2018). It is designed to increase productivity and income through enhancing the ability of communities to adapt to climate change and weather extremes, and decreasing GHG emissions (Steenwerth and others, 2014).

Huda and others (2012) highlighted how an understanding of the impact of climate change on key crops could enable Asia-Pacific farmers (in India, China and Australia), community workers and policy agencies to work together in better preparing for and adapting to climate change, through changes to existing policies and practices. It was identified that adaptation measures such as supplementary irrigation, breeding new heat- and drought-tolerant seed varieties and concentrating agriculture in geographically suited locations would be effective. Sustainable adaptation strategies explored for paddy ecosystems included relocation of croplands, shifting planting dates and developing new varieties, along with smart management of water and fertilizer (Ding and others, 2020; Yoon and Choi, 2020).

Transplantation date shifts and raising drainage outlets were evaluated as pragmatic and robust strategies to mitigate climate change impacts on paddy rice cultivation (Kim and others, 2021). Heat tolerant varieties were identified as a preferred adaptation strategy for subtropical regions. Recently, sweet potato has been cultivated as part of food security and climate change adaptation projects in Pacific communities due to its climatic and ecological resilience (McGregor and others, 2016).

While greater fertilizer use may help maintain or increase food production, it may also result in greater overall GHG emissions, not to mention increases in pollutants or potential soil degradation effects. Nevertheless, increased nutrient use efficiency through adoption of better management practices can assist in maintaining and increasing yield, contributing to both food security and climate change mitigation (Sapkota and others, 2017). Mixed farming systems integrating crops, livestock, fisheries and agroforestry could also help maintain crop yields in the face of climate change, assisting in the adaptation to changes in climate variability and minimizing GHG emissions by improving the nutrient flows (Newaj, Chaturvedi and Handa, 2016).

Options to increase resilience to climate risks include livelihood diversification within and across fisheries, aquaculture and agriculture. In Bangladesh, fishing pressure on post-larval prawns has increased as displaced farmers have shifted to fishing following saltwater intrusions of agricultural land (Ahmed Occhipinti-Ambrogi and Muir, 2013). Adaptation strategies proposed by FAO (2014) include the introduction of fishponds in areas susceptible to flood and drought; cage fish aquaculture in human-made reservoirs; transition to different species, polyculture and integrated systems for diversification and resilience systems; combined rice-fish farming; and transitions to alternative livelihoods. In terms of mitigation, Ahmed and others (2017) found that conversion of 25 per cent of total aquaculture area to integrated aquaculture-agriculture ponds has the potential to sequester 95.4 million tonnes of carbon per year.

Soil carbon sequestration together with biological nitrogen fixation has been shown to improve land health and underlying ecosystem services. Further enhancement is possible through improved agricultural land management practices such as incorporation of trees (agroforestry, fruit crops, etc.) within farms or in hedges (manure addition, green manures, cover crops, etc.). This promotes greater soil organic matter and nutrient content (and thus soil organic carbon) and improves soil structure. Such measures have the potential to reduce GHG emissions from the agroforestry sector by up to 0.1–5.7 gigatons per year (Griscom and others, 2017).

All of the above results are within the remit of climate-smart agriculture and are of great importance not only for food security, but also for the sustainable use of water resources (Ding and others, 2020). Changes in temperature and precipitation, and increased evapotranspiration may require significant increases in irrigation for many countries and regions. However, having sufficient water resources is a prerequisite, with water itself a central management issue for climate change. Increasing or adjusting irrigation requirements is another potentially effective adaptation measure.

Huda and others (2019) conducted a multi-faceted climate-smart livelihood improvement programme at two small-holder agriculture-based villages in West Bengal, India, to implement many of the above-mentioned strategies. Dependence on seasonal monsoon rainfall was removed through enhancement of local water resources, enabling diversification of crops from wet season rice only to a variety of year-round crops. Mushroom and worm cultivation were introduced, along with fish farming, planting of fruit trees on water resource bunds and a range of new soil nutrient management practices. Built upon a base of sustainable practices adopted by the villagers, the result was a movement from largely subsistence farming to fledgling small commercial enterprises attracting diversified year-round income, improved diets for villagers and the active participation of women in the workforce.

Rosegrant, Tokgoz and Bhandary (2013) posit that the entire climate change-related increase in childhood malnutrition in Pacific Island Countries could be eliminated through a policy package, including: (a) an increase in research and extension spending (up to 2 per cent of agricultural GDP); (b) optimization of crop varieties to climate change; (c) increasing the use of nitrogenous fertilizers from 30 to 50 kg/ha; and (d) applying public incentives to increase fish and livestock production.

Since so many people in the Asia-Pacific region are not receiving adequate nutrition through their diets, regional production, availability and affordability of nutritious foods will almost certainly need to increase to eradicate malnutrition in line with Goal 2.

VI. CONCLUSIONS AND RECOMMENDATIONS

Widespread recent research for selected major crops across the Asia-Pacific region strongly supports a growing consensus around forecasts of an overall decline in yields by the mid to late twenty-first century unless extensive adaptive and mitigative actions are taken and sustained. Given that the region accounts for a substantial portion of global production, forecasted declines constitute a threat to global food security. Further assessment of yield expectations for all agricultural outputs across the region is required to discern the relative merits of investments.

The forecasted impacts on agriculture are set against a backdrop of rapidly increasing populations and recently observed increases in poverty. For many countries and communities across the region, these factors coincide with a high economic and livelihood dependence on the agriculture sector. Moreover, many of the economies in question are still developing with agriculture sectors characterized by a high proportion of small-holders that are currently ill-placed to compete sustainably beyond their local communities. Thus, in many cases across the region, it will be central to reform and restructure agriculture and the infrastructure and relationships upon which agriculture depends, to address the climate change and sustainable development challenges which are inextricably linked.

Top-down approaches embodied within the IPCC process and 2030 Agenda are essential to meeting these challenges, yet they are insufficient alone. In terms of adaptive measures to boost agricultural productivity and livelihoods, the following suite of climate-smart agricultural measures and strategies can be enacted either bottom up or at scale:

- Suitable crop(s) selection under changing climate variability, based upon local climate, geography and available/planned infrastructure;

- Livelihood diversification within and across fisheries, aquaculture and agriculture;

- Adaptation of crops to environmental stresses, including cropping systems and varieties designed to match water availability with crop water requirements and avoid exposure to extreme temperature and limited water supply conditions during critical crop development phases;

- Breeding or genetic engineering of new varieties with better adapted phenology, such as heat and salt tolerance, shorter maturity duration and pest-disease resistance;

- More efficient and sustainable water and nutrient management practices, noting that integrated watershed management will play a major role in sustaining productivity;

- Quantification of specific pest-disease-climate-location relationships, and use of identified critical climate-decision thresholds against climate projection data to inform adaptation and mitigation strategies;

- Projected changes in yield across countries/regions and all major crops should be used along with historic FAO statistical data to inform the relative investment and effort in adaptation and mitigation strategies that should be made, spatially and by crop across the Asia-Pacific region;

- Enhancement of renewable energy substitution for fossil fuels (e.g. wind, solar, geothermal, and hydropower) in agricultural production systems;

- Increased integration of agroforestry (fruits crop) in agriculture production systems.

In practice the scoping, design and implementation of such measures necessitate collaboration between multidisciplinary experts, governments and producers. It may also call for international collaboration, as best practices in several areas may have been developed and implemented outside the Asia-Pacific region. In any case the food-security risks highlighted in the present paper for the Asia-Pacific region are not unique. For example, Kray and others (2022) showed that global warming of 3°C on average by 2050 could cause up to 30 per cent of maize growing areas in Africa to be lost due to climate change.

The opportunistic uptake of suggested measures in a bottom-up fashion by individual producers and their local communities will have a cumulative positive effect and change the livelihoods of those directly involved. However, optimizing the benefits on a broader scale across the Asia-Pacific region (with consequential global positive externalities) will require coordinated planning, implementation and investments from States, nations, and regional areas, each customized to suit their particular circumstances. Where they are involved, special attention should be given to enabling small-holder farming communities with infrastructure, capacity-building and financial means to sustainably adopt new practices, and this should include assistance in opening and servicing new markets.

NOTE ON CONTRIBUTORS

Asis Mukherjee, Assistant Professor, Bidhan Chandra Krishi Viswavidyalaya, India, has 15 years teaching, research and extension experience. His research interests cover crop-water productivity, climate change, crop modelling and yield forecasting. He has 74 publications and was awarded with an Endeavour Fellowship, 2016 for Post-Doctoral research at Western Sydney University, Australia.

Salil Saha, Agrometeorologist, India Meteorology Department sponsored Agrometeorology Field Unit, Uttar Banga Krishi Viswavidyalaya, India. He is responsible for preparing weather forecast based Agro-Advisory bulletins and dissemination to block level farming communities. His research interests span microclimate, crop weather modelling and agricultural water management.

Stephen C. Lellyett is an expert in application of climate information to industry and societal problems; spent 30 years with the Australian Bureau of Meteorology including as NSW State Director, and lead for major clients and projects. For over a decade he participated in Expert Teams of the United Nations World Meteorological Organization's Commission for Agrometeorology.

Abul Kalam Samsul Huda, Adjunct Associate Professor, Western Sydney University, Australia, has 40 years teaching, research and outreach experience. He focuses on climate-smart agriculture research for livelihood improvement. He has 294 publications and led/initiated 24 major externally funded projects. He is a Fellow of the American Society of Agronomy.

REFERENCES

Aggarwal, P.K., and others (2018). The climate-smart village approach: framework of an integrative strategy for scaling up adaptation options in agriculture.

Ahmed, N., and others (2017). Can greening of aquaculture sequester blue carbon? *Ambio,* vol. 46, No. 4, pp. 468–477.

Ahmed, N., A. Occhipinti-Ambrogi, and J.F. Muir (2013). The impact of climate change on prawn postlarvae fishing in coastal Bangladesh: socioeconomic and ecological perspectives. *Marine Policy,* vol. 39, pp. 224–233.

Alvi, S., and others (2021). An integrated assessment model for food security under climate change for South Asia. *Heliyon,* vol. 7, No. 4.

Asian Development Bank (ADB) (2013). *Food Security in Asia and the Pacific.* Manila.

Asseng, S., and others (2015). Rising temperatures reduce global wheat production. *Nature Climate Change,* vol. 5, No. 2, pp. 143-147.

Barnett, J. (2020). Climate change and food security in the Pacific Islands. In *Food Security in Small Island States,* J. Connell and K. Lowitt, eds. Singapore: Springer (pp. 25–38).

Bell, J.D., and others (2016). Climate change and Pacific Island food systems: the future of food, farming and fishing in the Pacific Islands under a changing climate.

Daloz, A.S., and others (2021). Direct and indirect impacts of climate change on wheat yield in the Indo-Gangetic plain in India. *Journal of Agriculture and Food Research,* vol. 4.

Deutsch, C.A., and others (2018). Increase in crop losses to insect pests in a warming climate. *Science,* vol. 361, No. 6405, pp. 916–919.

Ding, Y., and others (2020). Adaptation of paddy rice in China to climate change: The effects of shifting sowing date on yield and irrigation water requirement. *Agricultural Water Management,* vol. 228.

Dunne, Daisy (2018). Rise in insect pests under climate change to hit crop yields, study says. *Carbon Brief,* 30 August. Available at www.carbonbrief.org/rise-in-insect-pests-under-climate-change-to-hit-crop-yields-study-says.

Food and Agriculture Organization of the United Nations (FAO). (2014). *The State of Food Insecurity in the World 2014.* Rome.

_____ (2015). *Climate Change and Food Security: Risk and Responses.* Rome.

_____ (2021). *The State of Food Security and Nutrition in the World 2021.* Available at www.fao.org/3/cb4474en/online/cb4474en.html.

FAOSTAT (2022). Food and Agriculture data. Available at www.fao.org/faostat/en/#home.

Griscom, B.W., and others (2017). Natural climate solutions. *Proceedings of the National Academy of Sciences,* vol. 114, No. 44, pp. 11645–11650.

Hijioka, Y., and others (2014). Asia. In *Climate Change 2014: Impacts, Adaptation, and Vulnerability. Part B: Regional Aspects. Contribution of Working Group II to the Fifth Assessment Report of the Intergovernmental Panel on Climate Change.* Cambridge University Press.

Hochman, Z., D.L. Gobbett, and H. Horan (2017). Climate trends account for stalled wheat yields in Australia since 1990. *Global Change Biology,* vol. 23, No. 5, pp. 2071–2081.

Huda, A.K.S. (ed.) (2009). Climate and Crop Disease Risk Management: An international Initiative in the Asia-Pacific Region (Project ARCP2007-06CMY-Huda). Asia-Pacific Network for Global Change Research.

Huda, A.K.S., and others (2007). Examples of coping strategies with agrometeorological risks and uncertainties for Integrated Pest Management. In *Managing Weather and Climate Risks in Agriculture*, Mannava V. K. Sivakumar and Raymond P. Motha, eds. Berlin: Springer.

____ (2012). Food security and climate change in the Asia-Pacific Region: evaluating mismatch between crop development and water availability. *APN Science Bulletin*, vol. 2, pp. 42–48.

____ (2019). Australia-India Collaboration for Improving Farmers' Livelihood through Climate-Smart Agriculture. Proceedings of the National Seminar on "Sustainable Resource Management for Enhancing Farm Income, Nutritional Security and Livelihood Improvement". Visva-Bharati University, Sriniketan, West Bengal, India, 1–3 February.

Hussain, A., and others (2016). Household food security in the face of climate change in the Hindu-Kush Himalayan region. *Food Security*, vol. 8, pp. 921–937.

Iizumi, T., and others (2018). Crop production losses associated with anthropogenic climate change for 1981–2010 compared with preindustrial levels. *International Journal of Climatology*, vol. 38, Issue 14, pp. 5405–5417.

IPCC (2012). Managing the Risks of Extreme Events and Disasters to Advance Climate Change Adaptation. A Special Report of Working Groups I and II of the Intergovernmental Panel on Climate Change. C.B. Field, and others, eds. Cambridge University Press.

____ (2018). Summary for Policymakers. In *Global Warming of 1.5°C. An IPCC Special Report on the Impacts of Global Warming of 1.5°C Above Pre-Industrial Levels and Related Global Greenhouse Gas Emission Pathways, in the Context of Strengthening the Global Response to the Threat of Climate Change*. V. Masson-Delmotte, and others, eds.

____ (2021). Summary for policymakers. In *Climate Change 2021: The Physical Science Basis. Contribution of Working Group I to the Sixth Assessment Report of the Intergovernmental Panel on Climate Change*. V. Masson-Delmotte, and others, eds.

Iqbal, M.M., and others (2009). *Climate Change and Rice Production in Pakistan: Calibration, Validation and Application of CERES-Rice Model*. Islamabad: Global Change Impact Studies Centre.

Islam, A.F.M. Tariqul, and others (2022). Adaptation strategies to increase water productivity of wheat under changing climate. *Agricultural Water Management*, vol. 264.

Khairulbahri, M. (2021). Analyzing the impacts of climate change on rice supply in West Nusa Tenggara, Indonesia. *Heliyon*, vol. 7, No. 12.

Kim, Dong-Hyeon, and others (2021). Paddy rice adaptation strategies to climate change: Transplanting date shift and BMP applications. *Agricultural Water Management*, vol. 252.

Kray H.A., and others (2022). "The urgency and benefits of climate adaptation for Africa's agriculture and food security". Brookings, 24 March.

Luck, J., and others (2012). The effects of climate change on pests and diseases of major food crops in the Asia Pacific region. Asia-Pacific Network for Global Change Research.

Mavromatis, T. (2015). Crop–climate relationships of cereals in Greece and the impacts of recent climate trends. *Theoretical and Applied Climatology*, vol. 120, No. 3–4, pp. 417–432

McGregor, A., and others (2016). Vulnerability of staple food crops to climate change. In *Vulnerability of Pacific Agriculture and Forestry to Climate Change*. Queensland: University of the Sunshine Coast.

Newaj, R., O.P. Chaturvedi, and A.K. Handa (2016). Recent development in agroforestry research and its role in climate change adaptation and mitigation. *Indian Journal of Agroforestry*, vol. 18, No. 1, pp. 1-9.

Nurse, L.A., and others (2014). Small islands. In *Climate Change 2014: Impacts, Adaptation, and Vulnerability. Part B: Regional Aspects. Working group II Contribution to the Fifth assessment Report of the Intergovernmental Panel on Climate Change,* V.R. Barros, and others, eds. Cambridge University Press.

Prakash, A., and others (2014). *Climate Change: Impact on Crop Pests.* Odisha, India: Applied Zoologists Research Association (AZRA), Central Rice Research Institute.

Preston, B.L., and others (2006). Climate change in the Asia/Pacific region: a consultancy report prepared for the climate change and development roundtable. Commonwealth Scientific and Industrial Research Organisation.

Rosegrant, M.W., S. Tokgoz, and P. Bhandary (2013). The new normal? A tighter global agricultural supply and demand relation and its implications for food security. *American Journal of Agricultural Economics,* vol. 95, Issue 2, pp. 303–309.

Sapkota, T.B., and others (2017). Soil organic carbon changes after seven years of conservation agriculture based rice-wheat cropping system in the eastern Indo-Gangetic Plain of India. *Soil Use and Management,* vol. 33, Issue 1, pp. 81–89.

Shrivastava, R.K., R.K. Panda, and A. Chakraborty (2021). Assessment of climate change impact on maize yield and yield attributes under different climate change scenarios in eastern India. *Ecological Indicators,* vol. 120.

Steenwerth, Kerri L., and others (2014). Climate-smart agriculture global research agenda: scientific basis for action. *Agriculture and Food Security,* vol. 3.

Taylor, C., and others (2018). Trends in wheat yields under representative climate futures: Implications for climate adaptation. *Agricultural Systems,* vol. 164, pp. 1-10.

Teng, P.P., M. Caballero-Anthony, and J.A. Lassa (2016). The future of rice security under climate change.

Truelove, R.N., and others (forthcoming). Agricultural value-chains in developing economies: a theoretical framework. In *Sustainable Food Value Chain Development in Context of SDGs: Perspectives from Developing and Emerging Economies,* S.A. Narula and S.P. Raj, eds. Springer Nature.

United Nations Framework Convention on Climate Change (UNFCCC) (2021). Sustainable land and water management, including integrated watershed management strategies, to ensure food security. FCC/SB/2021/3. Agenda Item 8 – Koronivia Joint Work on Agriculture.

Wang, X., and others (2021). Adaptation of winter wheat varieties and irrigation patterns under future climate change conditions in Northern China. *Agricultural Water Management,* vol. 243.

Warren, R., and others (2018). The projected effect on insects, vertebrates, and plants of limiting global warming to 1.5°C rather than 2°C. *Science,* vol. 360, No. 6390, pp. 791–795.

Xiao, D., and others (2020). Climate change impact on yields and water use of wheat and maize in the North China Plain under future climate change scenarios. *Agricultural Water Management,* vol. 238.

Yoon, P.R., and J.Y. Choi (2020). Effects of shift in growing season due to climate change on rice yield and crop water requirements. *Paddy and Water Environment,* vol. 18, No. 2, pp. 291–307.

Zheng, B., and others (2012). Breeding for the future: what are the potential impacts of future frost and heat events on sowing and flowering time requirements for Australian bread wheat (Triticum aestivium) varieties. *Global Change Biology,* vol. 18, No. 9, pp. 2899–2914.

EARLY CAREER RESEARCHERS

Early career researchers

FACTORS AFFECTING CONSUMER BEHAVIOUR IN MOBILE FINANCIAL SERVICES IN BANGLADESH

Afnaan Ahmed, S.M. Raihan Uddin and S.M. Rifat Hassan

Corresponding author: Afnaan Ahmed
Email: afnaan.ahmed@northsouth.edu; afnaanahmed@gmail.com.

The aim of the present paper is to identify the determinants of consumer behaviour of mobile financial services (MFS) in Bangladesh. Data used in the study were collected through an online survey. A total of 1,460 users of MFS in Bangladesh participated in the survey during 2021. The findings of the study show that perceived usefulness has the strongest impact on customer satisfaction, followed by perceived safety and perceived ease of use. Customer satisfaction, however, has the strongest impact on both continuance intention and recommendation intention, followed by perceived usefulness and personal innovativeness. The findings have important policy implications for financial inclusion.

Keywords: mobile financial services, customer satisfaction, fintech, entrepreneurial firm, consumer behaviour

JEL classification: D91, G21, O16

I. INTRODUCTION

Global advancement in telecommunication technology has transformed the lifestyle of people and the way businesses are conducted. E-business, e-commerce and m-business (mobile business) have grown rapidly in recent years. The popularity and demand for mobile businesses are increasing rapidly due to the lasting development and cost reduction of mobile and Internet technologies all over the world (Lee and others, 2012).

The digital economy provides several advantages for small and medium-sized enterprises to develop. These prospects extend to the financial industry, as fintech firms continue to enter the market with new, innovative and more user-friendly financial services or products than incumbents (Gazel and Schwienbacher, 2020). The growing fintech industry has substantial impacts on the financial sector; particularly in payment systems, wealth management, crowdfunding, lending, capital markets and insurance. The advent of new products, channels, business models as well as innovative ways to service delivery has changed the financial services industry. Increased client awareness and expectations, digitalization, favourable regulation and cost-cutting demands have amplified the impact of fintech disruptions (Zarrouk, El Ghak and Bakhouche, 2021).

Mobile financial services (MFS) in Bangladesh have been growing in the past decade (Parvez, Islam and Woodard, 2015). During the ongoing COVID-19 pandemic, a steady influx of new MFS users have increased the number of transactions and amount of fund transfers (Bangladesh Bank, 2021). Rocket, the mobile financial service by Dutch-Bangla Bank Limited, started on 31 March 2011.The mobile financial services application, bKash, by BRAC Bank Limited, started on 21 July 2011. Nagad, the digital financial service, was launched by the Bangladesh Post Office on 11 November 2018, and it started operations on 26 March 2019.

As of April 2021, there were 15 banks offering MFS in Bangladesh, with more than 1 million agents, more than 96 million registered clients and more than 36 million active accounts. The average number of daily transactions is above 10 million, and more than 21 billionBangladesh taka (BDT) is transacted daily. In 11 months from March 2020 to January 2021, the number of MFS users increased by 18 million (Bangladesh Bank, 2021). In terms of average amount of daily transactions, the mobile financial industry experienced a compound annual growth of approximately 20 per cent within a span of five years (from December 2015 to December 2020). During the COVID-19 pandemic, due to health concerns of the physical handling of banknotes, many people started using MFS to minimize health risks (Tasreen, 2021).

In light of the above, the aim of the present paper is to identify the determinants of consumer behaviour of MFS in Bangladesh. That is, it serves to explain customer satisfaction, continuance intention and recommendation intention of MFS applications. Section II provides a brief overview of MFS in Bangladesh and the impact of the COVID-19 pandemic on its expansion. The rest of the present paper is organized as follows: section III provides a literature review; section IV explains research design and methodology; section V presents findings; and section VI concludes with policy implications and limitations of the study.

II. MOBILE FINANCIAL SERVICES INDUSTRY IN BANGLADESH

Starting its journey in March 2011, the provision of financial services through mobile phones has expanded rapidly in Bangladesh. The mobile banking business has become quite popular in the past decade. It is now widely used in throughout the country. The private sector Dutch-Bangla Bank was the first to launch this service (Rocket). Later, bKash was launched as a subsidiary of BRAC Bank offering MFS. Over the following years, more banks launched separate financial services projects on mobile phones. By the end of 2021, 15 banks were providing MFS in Bangladesh.

Thus, MFS have experienced a sustained growth in Bangladesh. The industry has become a top solution for all kinds of financial transactions, from sending and receiving money to paying for services like electricity, water, gas, telephone, retail purchases, transportation, education and medical bills. People of all economic classes have gained access to MFS, thus accelerating financial inclusion in Bangladesh (Khalid, Ichihashi and Gani, 2020; Bangladesh Bank, 2021).

There are now more than 100 million mobile banking customers across the country. As reported by Bangladesh Bank, they transacted more than BDT 712 billion as of May 2021. The average value of transactions daily stands at more than BDT 22 billion. Never before had so many transactions taken place in a single month through MFS (Bangladesh Bank, 2021).

The number of bKash subscribers is more than 50 million. bKash claimed that the average value of daily transactions through bKash was more than BDT20 billion during the month of May 2021. The daily average transactions through Rocket are approximately BDT5 billion. Rocket now has more than 24 million subscribers. SureCash service by Rupali Bank has more than 20 million subscribers. In April 2021, Nagad crossed the mark of 40 million subscribers and daily average transactions through Nagad went past the mark of BDT4 billion. The general public is opting for MFS for small financial transactions during the COVID-19 pandemic (*Dhaka Tribune*, 2021).

As of January 2021, the total number of subscribers to MFS in the country was approximately 140 million. However, the number of active users is close to only 50 million. Nonetheless, in a country of 120 million adult citizens, this number is significant.

Instead of going to the bank, people are now resorting to mobile banking for various daily needs. Mobile banking is being used for small transactions, especially for paying various service bills (electricity, water, gas and telephone), fees for educational institutions, online shopping, government allowance, pension, bus-train-plane ticket purchases, insurance premium, mobile recharge and various grants. Almost all banks provide MFS and facilitate deposits into mobile banking accounts.

Credit card or bank loan instalments are also being deposited through MFS or mobile phones. Thus, everywhere in the country – from the capital city to remote villages – mobile phones in the hands of people of all walks of life provide access to bank services. The time and labour required in the past to receive services at bank branches have been significantly reduced due to the rapid development and expansion of MFS (Uddin, 2021).

According to the e-Commerce Association of Bangladesh, there are 100 e-commerce entrepreneurs and 8,000 businesses operating through Facebook. As a result, Facebook has influenced the majority of the e-commerce market size, and MFS have become a fantastic tool of transactions for these online firms, particularly those that run their enterprises through Facebook pages (Chowdhury and others, 2019).

Comparison among the service providers

Another challenge of digital financial services is the pricing of the services. For cash out through agents, most service providers charge a tariff of 1.85–2 per cent of transaction amounts, excluding Nagad, which reduced its cash out from agent tariff to 1.149 per cent of the transaction amounts in October 2020, causing a massive influx of new subscribers. A tariff of 1.85–2 per cent is not inexpensive enough for many lower income and marginal people. Consumer groups and industry experts have urged Bangladesh Bank to implement ceilings for MFS tariffs (New Age, 2020; Haroon, 2021; The Daily Star, 2020a).

Table 1. Mean values of selected variables by different service providers

Variables	Mean values		
	bKash	Nagad	Rocket
Perceived usefulness	7.646	7.584	7.460
Perceived ease of use	7.495	7.724	7.521
Perceived safety	7.625	7.641	7.507
Monetary value	7.550	7.699	7.607
Connectivity	7.600	7.768	7.469

Table 1. *(continued)*

Variables	Mean values		
	bKash	**Nagad**	**Rocket**
Customer satisfaction	7.588	7.668	7.498
Continuance intention	7.612	7.646	7.493
Recommendation intention	7.619	7.648	7.488

Table 1 serves to illustrate that there are no significant differences among the providers in the mean values of the variables.

Impacts of COVID-19 on digital payments

The onset of the COVID-19 pandemic in March 2020 led to massive lockdowns across the country, with more and more people using MFS to purchase essential goods and services. Thus, the pandemic pushed the digital payment ecosystem of Bangladesh to new heights.

Following the outbreak of the pandemic, public panic and business shutdowns led to a dip in economic activities, but soon transactions increased steadily. The increase in MFS payments was most noticeable, as access to MFS has become easier over time.

Although the epidemic reduced business across the country, the rise in digital payments indicates that more and more people are moving to digital payment services for their business and daily transactions. The transition to digital payment services both encouraged financial inclusion and helped to enhance COVID-19 hygiene practices through contactless payments. In addition, essential services such as grocery delivery and online shopping have benefited greatly from the convenience, ease and growth of digital payment services.

In addition to money transactions, the number of accounts for all services also increased. There was a huge increase in customers of both MFS and Internet banking (*The Daily Star,* 2020b).

According to a study on customer perceptions of MFS, lower physical access and cost barriers allow a considerably larger proportion of the public to use basic formal sector deposit and payment services and assist many small company owners to receive payments and grow their businesses (Chowdhury and others, 2019). The same study observed a trend among entrepreneurs to launch their businesses using a variety of websites in recent years. Facebook and e-commerce pages encourage payments via mobile banking services. Therefore, MFS providers are trying to make their services more user-friendly.

Future of digital finance in Bangladesh

Though the MFS industry is a rapidly growing sector in Bangladesh, further progress is impeded by several issues, and the lack of interoperability among the different service providers is one of the most important barriers. Bangladesh Bank was scheduled to implement interoperability among MFS providers in October 2020, but the process was postponed due to technical issues. Interoperability should include MFS systems and encompass commercial banks and card terminals (ATMs).

Mobile subscribers in Bangladesh number more than 150 million. However, 15 per cent of the total population of the country has not yet received traditional banking services. More than 50 per cent of the economy is informal. As these barriers are removed, people will be more motivated to enter the formal economy, thus facilitating financial inclusion.

The use of digital financial services has increased since the COVID-19 pandemic began. The usage rate of digital financial services will increase far more when proper interoperability is implemented (Mujeri and Azam, 2018; Murtuza, 2021).

Table 2 contains a summary of MFS services in Bangladesh. However, statistics from Bangladesh Bank do not incorporate the data of Nagad. Nagad operates under the authority of the Bangladesh Post Office. As of 29 June 2021, Nagad has operated under an interim license from Bangladesh Bank, and this is why the financial statements of Nagad are not incorporated in official MFS statistics of Bangladesh Bank (Alo, 2021).

Table 2. A snapshot of MFS in Bangladesh as of April 2021

Description	Number, April 2021
Banks currently providing services	15
Agents (millions)	1.062
Registered clients (millions)	96.476
Active accounts (millions)	36.749
Total transactions (millions)	304.979
Daily average transactions (millions)	10.166
Information by service type	**Amount, April 2021** *(billion Bangladesh taka)*
Total transactions	634.789
Daily average transactions	21.160
Inward remittance	2.120

Table 2. *(continued)*

Information by service type	Amount, April 2021 *(billion Bangladesh taka)*
Cash in transaction	190.234
Cash out transaction	164.212
P2P transaction	190.342
Salary disbursement (business to people)	24.046
Utility bill payment (people to business)	9.624
Merchant payment	27.586
Government payment	7.338
Others	19.286

Source: Bangladesh Bank (2021).

Over the past few years in Bangladesh, rapid growth in technological advances, including Internet usage rates, has opened up a wide range of opportunities for businesses and services to prosper. One of the notable trends in Bangladesh is the increase in digital payments. These changes have subsequently encouraged a digital ecosystem and added value to the overall economy.

The COVID-19 pandemic was a game changer in the national digital payment ecosystem due to the need for contactless payments. In addition to facilitating trade, the government also helped distribute digital payments to needy people during the COVID-19 pandemic.

III. CONCEPTUAL ISSUES AND VARIABLE SECTIONS

According to the CFA Institute, fintech or financial technology, refers to technological advances in the design and delivery of financial services and products. One example of how technology in finance is advancing is the use of big data, artificial intelligence (AI), and machine learning to evaluate investment opportunities, optimize portfolios and manage risks. Therefore, by focusing on the requirements of the customers, the desired outcome of fintech can be attained. Moreover, the fintech can provide tailored and actionable advice to investors with greater ease of access and at a lower cost (CFA Institute, 2022).

Moreover, fintech accompanies a new pattern in which information technology drives financial industry innovation. Fintech is regarded as a game-changing invention that has the potential to upend established financial markets. By integrating finance and technical innovations, MFS contributes to a new aspect of fintech entrepreneurship (Lee and Shin, 2018).

Moreover, adequate access to information in particular on various areas of finance, including the business climate and the company strategy, plays a significant role in the success of fintech (Zarrouk, El Ghak and Bakhouche, 2021).

Because digitalization affects not only the type of entrepreneurial opportunities created but also how these opportunities are best pursued by entrepreneurs, including more collaborative forms of activity development, start-ups in heavily impacted sectors are said to operate under different organizational and network structures than traditional firms. This impact is likely to spread to the banking business, where innovative financial technologies have emerged (Gazel and Schwienbacher, 2020).

Several studies have been conducted to investigate the user perceptions and influencing factors of usage intention towards MFS in different countries across the globe. Customer satisfaction is influenced by multiple factors, such as perceived usefulness, perceived ease of use, monetary value, safety, task fit, connectivity, personal innovativeness and absorptive capacity (Omigie and others, 2020; Khan, Mahmud and Lima, 2020). Customer satisfaction has a positive impact on the continuance intention (Omigie and others, 2020).

Perceived ease of use

Perceived ease of use is defined as the degree to which a user believes that using a system would be effortless for them. Several studies have shown that perceived ease of use positively impacts customer satisfaction (Simiyu and Kohsuwan, 2019; Le and others, 2020; Bakri, 2020).

Perceived safety

Perceived safety is defined as the user's level of comfort and perceptions of risk, without thinking about standards or safety history. Several studies have indicated that perceived safety positively impacts customer satisfaction (Zhao and Bacao, 2021; Alkhaldi, 2019; Aye and Soe, 2020; Daragmeh, Sági and Zéman, 2021).

Monetary value

Monetary value is defined as how much a service is reasonable in regard to cost of using that. Several studies have found that monetary value positively impacts customer satisfaction (Baabdullah and others, 2019; Sankaran and Chakraborty, 2021; Zhang and others, 2019).

Task fit

Task fit is defined as the interdependence among users, systems and activities carried out by users to produce the required output. Several studies have revealed that task fit positively impacts customer satisfaction (Baabdullah and others, 2019; Zhao and Bacao, 2021; Xiong and others, 2020).

Connectivity

Connectivity is defined as the extent to which users believe that they can access and use the service anytime and anywhere. Several studies have indicated that connectivity positively impacts customer satisfaction (Chang and others, 2020; Abadi, Saeednia and Khorshidi, 2021; Banker and Parmar, 2020).

Personal innovativeness

Personal innovativeness is defined as the user's inclination to try out new technology. Several studies have found that personal innovativeness positively impacts customer satisfaction, intention to repurchase or continue usage and intention to recommend the service to others (Avornyo and others, 2019; Reiting and others, 2020; Geebren and Jabbar, 2021).

Absorptive capacity

Absorptive capacity is defined as the ability to obtain, absorb and integrate knowledge, so it can be utilized. Several studies have found that absorptive capacity positively impacts customer satisfaction and intention to repurchase or continue usage (Lee and others, 2012; Shin and Lee, 2021; Kalinic and others, 2019; Routray and others, 2019).

Customer satisfaction

Customer satisfaction is described as an overall evaluation based on the complete purchase and consuming experience, with an emphasis on perceived product or service performance relative to pre-purchase expectations over time (Kaur and Kiran, 2014). Previous studies have indicated that customer satisfaction positively impacts intention to repurchase or continue usage and intention to recommend the service to others (Poromatikul and others, 2019; Le and others, 2020; Omigie and others, 2020).

Continuance intention

Continuance intention is defined as the user's intention to continue using the service (Luqman, Razak and Ismail, 2014). Previous studies have indicated that continuance intention is positively affected by perceived usefulness (Jumaan, Hashim and Al-Ghazali, 2020; Puriwat and Tripopsakul, 2021; Rabaa'i and AlMaati, 2021), personal innovativeness (Avornyo and others, 2019; Liébana-Cabanillas and others, 2021), absorptive capacity (Routray and others, 2019; Alhassan and others, 2020) and customer satisfaction (Alzahrani, Beloff and White, 2021; Chang and others, 2020).

Recommendation intention

Intention to recommend is defined as the likelihood that the users would recommend and say positive things about the service to others (Leppäniemi, Karjaluoto and Saarijärvi, 2017). Previous studies have found that intention to recommend is positively affected by perceived usefulness (Chaouali and others, 2019; Akinwale and Kyari, 2020), personal innovativeness (Liébana-Cabanillas, Molinillo and Japutra, 2021; Kaur and others, 2020) and customer satisfaction (Sankaran and Chakraborty, 2021; Barbosa and others, 2021).

IV. RESEARCH DESIGN AND RESEARCH METHODOLOGY

The extant literature suggests how the variables are related. Having reviewed the literature, the following models for explaining customer satisfaction, continuance intention and recommendation intention of MFS application are proposed focusing on 11 variables.

Customer satisfaction: dependent on perceived usefulness, perceived ease of use, perceived safety, monetary value, task fit, connectivity, personal innovativeness and absorptive capacity variables. Their hypothesized relations are shown in figure 1.

Figure 1. Proposed model for explaining customer satisfaction

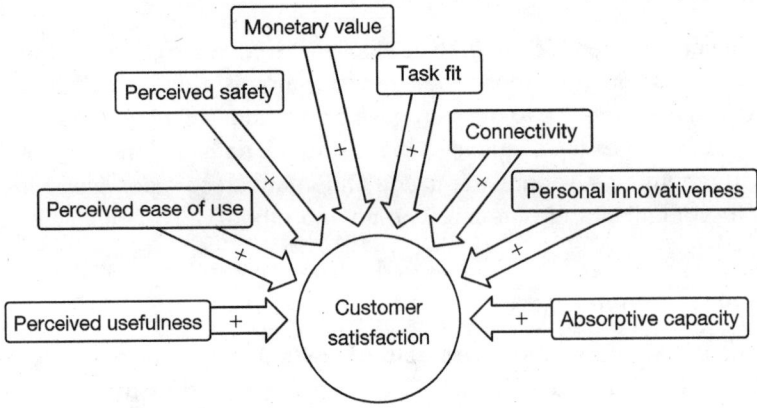

H1: Perceived usefulness, perceived ease of use, perceived safety, monetary value, task fit, connectivity, personal innovativeness and absorptive capacity have positive impacts on customer satisfaction of MFS application.

Continuance intention: influenced by perceived usefulness, personal innovativeness, absorptive capacity and customer satisfaction. Their hypothesized relations are shown in figure 2.

Figure 2. Proposed model for explaining continuance intention

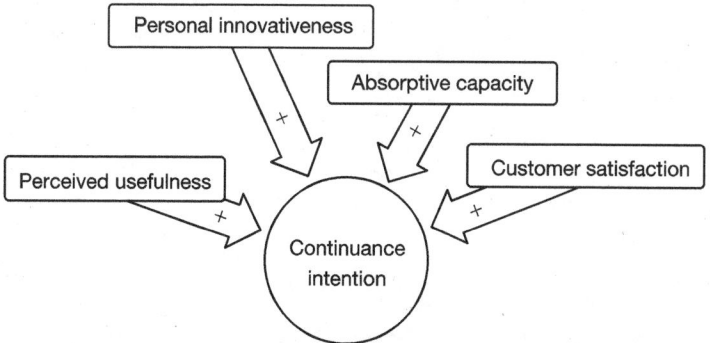

H2: Perceived usefulness, personal innovativeness, absorptive capacity and customer satisfaction have positive impacts on continuance intention of MFS application.

Recommendation intention: depends on perceived usefulness, personal innovativeness and customer satisfaction. Their hypothesized relations are shown in figure 3.

Figure 3. Proposed model for explaining recommendation intention

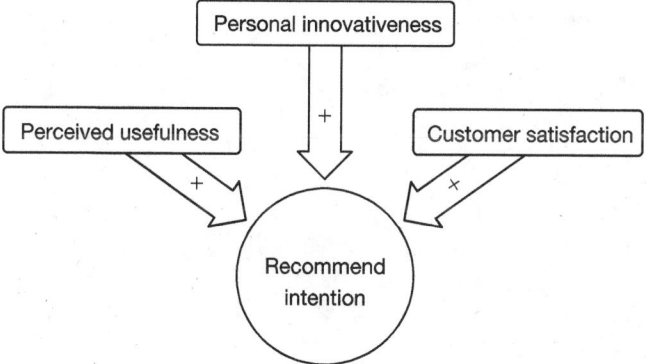

H3: Perceived usefulness, personal innovativeness and customer satisfaction have positive impacts on recommend intention of MFS application.

Instrument development

The study adapted tools from earlier studies to match the context of mobile banking in Bangladesh. The scale items are scored on an 11-point Likert scale, with 0 indicating strongly disagree and 10 indicating strongly agree. Instruments from the study by Lee and others (2012) are used to measure perceived usefulness, perceived ease of use, monetary value, task fit, connectedness, personal innovativeness and absorptive capacity factors. The study by Omigie and others (2020) was used to develop the variables of perceived safety, customer satisfaction, continuance intention, and recommend intention. IBM SPSS version 27 was used to analyse the data.

Data collection

Data used in the present study were collected through an online survey. The population is the users of MFS in Bangladesh. A total of 1,460 respondents participated between 1 April 2021 and 24 June 2021. The respondents of the study are subscribers of the three leading MFS providers in Bangladesh – bKash, Nagad and Rocket.

Table 3 contains the descriptive statistics of the demographic characteristics of respondents. The sample consists of 60.48 per cent male and 39.52 per cent female; 51.30 per cent of the sample are below the age of 30 and the majority have a university or higher level of education (67.88 per cent).

The highest frequency of use of MFS is once or twice per week (32.81 per cent), followed by 3 to 4 times per week (28.97 per cent). The most frequently used service is sending and receiving money (47.53 per cent), followed by paying bills and making other payments (23.42 per cent). The most often used mobile network operator is Grameenphone (46.03 per cent), followed by Robi (29.38 per cent). The most preferred mobile financial service is bKash (45.07 per cent), followed by Nagad (40.48 per cent) and Rocket (14.45 per cent).

Table 3. Descriptive statistics of demographic characteristics

Demographics		n = 1 460	Percentage
Gender	Male	883	60.48
	Female	377	39.52
Age	Below 30	749	51.30
	30 to 40	426	29.18
	40 to 50	207	14.18
	Above 50	78	5.34
Education: level completed	Secondary school	78	5.34
	Higher secondary school	391	26.78
	Bachelor's degree	697	47.74
	Master's degree	294	20.14
Monthly income (Bangladesh taka)	Less than 10,000	469	32.12
	10,000 to 25,000	658	45.07
	25,000 to 50,000	325	22.26
	Above 50,000	8	0.55
Mobile financial service usage frequency	Every day	101	6.92
	3 to 4 times a week	423	28.97
	1 to 2 times a week	479	32.81
	1 to 2 times a month	362	24.79
	Less than 1 time a month	95	6.51
Most frequent used mobile financial service	Send and receive money	694	47.53
	Mobile recharge (top up)	165	11.30
	Cash in and cash out	259	17.74
	Bills and other payments	342	23.42
Most frequent mobile financial service usage place	Home	297	20.34
	Office	230	15.75
	School	158	10.82
	Vehicle	86	5.89
	Anytime, anywhere	689	47.19
Telecommunication company	Grameenphone	672	46.03
	Robi	429	29.38
	Banglalink	328	22.47
	Teletalk	31	2.12
Mobile financial service	bKash	658	45.07
	Nagad	591	40.48
	Rocket	211	14.45

Table 4. Tariff of leading MFS providers (Bangladesh taka)

Service	bKash	Nagad	Rocket	SureCash
Cash out from agent (per 1 000)	18.50	11.49	18.00	18.00
Cash in	Free	Free	Free	Free
Send money	Free	Free	Free	4.00

Source: Official websites of bKash, Nagad, Rocket and SureCash.

Table 4 shows that Nagad has the lowest cash out (from agent) tariff among the leading MFS providers. Nagad decreased the cash out (from agent) charge to 1.149 per cent in October 2020, resulting in large number of new subscribers in subsequent months.

V. EMPIRICAL ANALYSIS AND FINDINGS

Hypothesis testing

Table 5. Variable names and designated symbols

Variable name	Symbol
Perceived usefulness	PU
Perceived ease of use	PE
Perceived safety	PS
Monetary value	MV
Task fit	TF
Connectivity	CT
Personal innovativeness	PI
Absorptive capacity	AC
Customer satisfaction	CS
Continuance intention	CI
Recommendation intention	RI

Table 6. Reliability statistics

Cronbach's alpha	Number of items
0.857	11

Proposed model for customer satisfaction

$$CS = \beta_0 + \beta_1 * PU + \beta_2 * PE + \beta_3 * PS + \beta_4 * MV + \beta_5 * TF + \beta_6 * CT + \beta_7 * PI + \beta_8 * AC$$

$H1: \beta_i > 0, \text{ for } i = 1,2,3,4,5,6,7,8$

Table 7. Model summary

R	R squared	Adjusted R squared	Standard error of the estimate
0.990	0.980	0.980	0.158

Predictors: (Constant), AC, TF, PE, PI, MV, PU, CT, PS

Table 8. ANOVA

Model	Sum of squares	Degrees of freedom	Mean square	F statistic	Significance
Regression	1810.033	8	226.254	9097.935	0.000
Residual	36.085	1451	0.025		
Total	1846.117	1459			

Dependent variable: CS
Predictors: (Constant), AC, TF, PE, PI, MV, PU, CT, PS

Table 9. Coefficients

Model	Unstandardized coefficients		Standardized coefficients	t statistic	p>|t|
	Beta	Standard error	Beta		
(Constant)	-0.283935	0.031		-9.082	0.000
PU	0.249451	0.003	0.382	93.378	0.000
PE	0.149195	0.003	0.230	56.868	0.000
PS	0.214739	0.003	0.339	81.765	0.000
MV	0.105549	0.003	0.168	41.503	0.000
TF	0.089685	0.003	0.139	35.190	0.000
CT	0.135984	0.003	0.211	51.762	0.000
PI	0.034513	0.003	0.054	13.465	0.000
AC	0.058925	0.003	0.090	22.923	0.000

Dependent variable: CS

$$CS = -0.283935 + 0.249451 * PU + 0.149195 * PE + 0.214739 * PS + 0.105549 * MV + 0.089685 * TF + 0.135984 * CT + 0.034513 * PI + 0.058925 * AC$$

Table 9 shows that perceived usefulness, perceived ease of use, perceived safety, monetary value, task fit, connectivity, personal innovativeness and absorptive capacity have statistically highly significant positive impacts on customer satisfaction. Perceived usefulness has the strongest impact on customer satisfaction, followed by perceived safety, perceived ease of use, connectivity, monetary value, task fit, absorptive capacity and personal innovativeness. The intercept (β_0) has a value of -0.284 which is also statistically highly significant. The model has an R-squared value of 0.980 indicating that 98 per cent of the variance in customer satisfaction can be explained by the explanatory variables.

Proposed model for continuance intention

$$CI = \beta_0 + \beta_1 * PU + \beta_2 * PI + \beta_3 * AC + \beta_4 * CS$$

$H2: \beta_i > 0$, for $i = 1,2,3,4$

Table 10. Model summary

R	R squared	Adjusted R squared	Standard error of the estimate
0.983	0.967	0.966	0.217

Predictors: (Constant), CS, AC, PI, PU

Table 11. ANOVA

Model	Sum of squares	Degrees of freedom	Mean square	F statistic	Significance
Regression	1 977.281	4	494.320	10 514.669	0.000
Residual	68.403	1 455	0.047		
Total	2 045.684	1 459			

Dependent variable: CI
Predictors: (Constant), CS, AC, PI, PU

Table 12. Coefficients

Model	Unstandardized coefficients		Standardized coefficients	t statistic	$p > \lvert t \rvert$
	Beta	Standard error	Beta		
(Constant)	-0.032201	0.041		-0.791	0.429
PU	0.277506	0.005	0.404	58.963	0.000
PI	0.192991	0.004	0.289	53.542	0.000
AC	0.034415	0.004	0.050	9.392	0.000
CS	0.499553	0.008	0.475	60.488	0.000

Dependent variable: CI

$$CI = 0.277506 * PU + 0.192991 * PI + 0.034415 * AC + 0.499553 * CS$$

β_0 is omitted because it is not statistically significant.

Table 12 shows that perceived usefulness, personal innovativeness, absorptive capacity, and customer satisfaction have statistically highly significant positive impacts on continuance intention. Customer satisfaction has the strongest impact on continuance intention, followed by perceived usefulness, personal innovativeness and absorptive capacity. The intercept (β_0) has a value of -0.032201 which is not statistically significant. The model has an R-squared value of 0.983 indicating that 98.3 per cent of the variance in continuance intention can be explained by the explanatory variables.

Proposed model for recommendation intention

$$RI = \beta_0 + \beta_1 * PU + \beta_2 * PI + \beta_3 * CS$$

$$H3: \beta_i > 0, \text{ for } i = 1,2,3$$

Table 13. Model summary

R	R squared	Adjusted R squared	Standard error of the estimate
0.988	0.975	0.975	0.188

Predictors: (Constant), CS, PI, PU

Table 14. ANOVA

Model	Sum of squares	Degrees of freedom	Mean square	F statistic	Significance
Regression	2 027.504	3	675.835	19 182.321	0.000
Residual	51.298	1 456	0.035		
Total	2 078.802	1 459			

Dependent variable: RI
Predictors: (Constant), CS, PI, PU

Table 15. Coefficients

Model	Unstandardized coefficients		Standardized coefficients	t statistic	p>|t|
	Beta	Standard error	Beta		
(Constant)	0.038966	0.034		1.134	0.257
PU	0.303743	0.004	0.439	74.805	0.000
PI	0.206789	0.003	0.307	66.280	0.000
CS	0.484874	0.007	0.457	72.082	0.000

Dependent variable: RI

$RI = 0.303743 * PU + 0.206789 * PI + 0.484874 * CS$

β_0 is omitted because it is not statistically significant.

Table 15 shows that perceived usefulness, personal innovativeness and customer satisfaction have statistically highly significant positive impacts on recommendation intention. Customer satisfaction has the strongest impact on recommendation intention, followed by perceived usefulness and personal innovativeness. The intercept (β_0) has a value of -0.038966 which is not statistically significant. The model has an R-squared value of 0.975 indicating that 97.5 per cent of the variance in recommend intention can be explained by the explanatory variables.

VI. CONCLUSION: POLICY IMPLICATIONS AND LIMITATIONS

The study finds that the factors influencing continuance intention and recommendation intentions of MFS in Bangladesh include customer satisfaction, perceived usefulness and personal innovativeness. Customer satisfaction is determined by perceived usefulness, perceived ease of use, perceived safety, monetary value, task fit, connectivity, personal innovativeness and absorptive capacity. Customer satisfaction is the key factor influencing continuance intention and recommendation intention. Therefore, both regulators and service providers should endeavour to ensure a high degree of customer satisfaction. This would entail enhanced customer protection on the part of the regulators while providers offer user-friendly customer services, including expeditious resolution of customer complaints.

From the technology acceptance perspective, the study findings indicate that people are accepting and absorbing MFS technology. Although the MFS industry in Bangladesh is growing, it faces challenges regarding lack of interoperability and pricing regulations. Implementing suitable guidelines and proper monitoring and establishing interoperability among MFS providers and commercial banks are actions Bangladesh Bank must take for the MFS industry to reach its zenith in terms of financial inclusion and equitable economic development.

The study has some limitations. Firstly, the gender distribution of the study subjects is male dominated (60.48 per cent). However, as reported by Bangladesh Bank, the demographics of MFS users in Bangladesh show that the number of male subscribers is much higher than female ones. Therefore, from the gender perspective, the study subjects may or may not approximately represent the study population.

Secondly, only 5.34 per cent of the respondents have secondary school or lower level of education, 94.56 per cent of the respondents have completed higher secondary school or higher level of education. More than one third of the Bangladeshi population has secondary school or lower level of education (UNICEF, 2020). Thus, most likely, the study subjects are not a close representation of the study population, as the sample is biased towards higher secondary school or higher level of education.

Thirdly, the study did not investigate the potential effects of demographic characteristics, such as gender, age, education level completed and income of respondents. Studies show that age, gender and income can influence continuance intention and recommendation intention. Therefore, additional investigation through alternative models is needed to better explain the customer satisfaction, continuance intention and recommendation intention. Future research may incorporate the effects of demographic factors such as age, gender, education level, income level and urban/rural population to investigate and differentiate significant variances of consumer perceptions and usage behaviour among diverse user groups of MFS.

NOTE ON CONTRIBUTORS

Afnaan Ahmed is a Lecturer in the Department of Management, North South University, Bangladesh. She has an MA degree in Social Development from the University of Sussex, the United Kingdom. She worked as a research associate in BRAC Development Institute (BDI), a research division of BRAC University, and published an annual report on the BRAC Social Development Programme.

S. M. Rifat Hassan is a Lecturer in the Department of Business Administration, European University of Bangladesh, Dhaka. His research interests include but are not limited to corporate risk and profitability, capital structure, financial technology (Fintech), and fundamental and technical analysis of equities.

S. M. Raihan Uddin is a Lecturer in the Southeast Business School, Southeast University, Bangladesh. He has an MBA (HRM) degree from BRAC University, Bangladesh.

REFERENCES

Abadi, M., H. Saeednia, and A. Khorshidi (2021). Presenting a model of customer experience management in mobile banking industry for commercial banks customers in Dubai. *Journal of Optimization in Industrial Engineering,* vol. 14, No. 2, pp. 215–223.

Akinwale, Y.O., and A.K. Kyari (2020). Factors influencing attitudes and intention to adopt financial technology services among the end-users in Lagos State, Nigeria. *African Journal of Science, Technology, Innovation and Development,* pp. 1–8.

Alhassan, A., and others (2020). Consumer acceptance and continuance of mobile money. *Australasian Journal of Information Systems,* vol. 24.

Alkhaldi, A.N. (2019). A proposed model for determining the customer's use of mobile banking services in Saudi Arabia: toward the differential role of gender. *International Journal of Business and Information,* vol. 14, No. 1.

Alo, J.N. (2021). Nagad does not meet license conditions for third time. *The Business Standard,* 29 June.

Alzahrani, A., N. Beloff, and M. White (2021). IMMBA – An integrative model for mobile banking adoption: the case of Saudi Arabia. Conference paper. 3rd International Congress on Human-Computer Interaction, Optimization and Robotic Applications. 11–13 June, Turkey.

Avornyo, P., and others (2019). Factors affecting continuous usage intention of mobile banking in Tema and Kumasi. *International Journal of Business and Social Science,* vol. 10, No. 3.

Aye, A.C., and K.N.N. Soe (2020). The mediating role of perceived value on the relationship between service quality and loyalty: the private banking case in Myanmar. *TNI Journal of Business Administration and Languages,* vol. 8, No. 1, pp. 88–100.

Baabdullah, A.M., and others (2019). Consumer use of mobile banking (M-Banking) in Saudi Arabia: Towards an integrated model. *International Journal of Information Management,* vol. 44, pp. 38–52.

Bakri, M.H. (2020). Factors of acceptance of mobile banking in Malaysia. *International Journal of Human and Technology Interaction,* vol. 4, No. 2, pp. 13–22.

Bangladesh Bank (2021). Mobile Financial Services (MFS) comparative summary statement of March 2021 and April 2021. Available at www.bb.org.bd/en/index.php/financialactivity/mfsdata.

Banker, A., and H. Parmar (2020). A study on determinants for measuring the impact of service quality parameters of e-banking. *Solid State Technology,* vol. 63, No. 6, pp. 22608–22616.

Barbosa, H.F., and others (2021). The use of fitness centre apps and its relation to customer satisfaction: a UTAUT2 perspective. *International Journal of Sports Marketing and Sponsorship.*

CFA Institute (2022). "Fintech in investment management" online course.

Chang, Y.H., and others (2020). Customer satisfaction on mobile banking in Perak, Malaysia. Thesis. Universiti Tunku Abdul Rahman.

Chaouali, W., and others (2019). Reconsidering the "what is beautiful is good" effect: When and how design aesthetics affect intentions towards mobile banking applications. *International Journal of Bank Marketing.*

Chowdhury, A.Y., and others (2019). Role of mobile financial service in promoting online small business in Bangladesh. *IETI Transactions on Social Sciences and Humanities,* pp. 2–5.

Daragmeh, A., J. Sági, and Z. Zéman (2021). Continuous intention to use E-Wallet in the context of the COVID-19 pandemic: integrating the health belief model (HBM) and technology continuous theory (TCT). *Journal of Open Innovation: Technology, Market, and Complexity,* vol. 7, No. 2, p. 132.

Dhaka Tribune (2021). Nagad surpasses 40 million user landmark, 400C in daily transactions, 20 April.

Gazel, M., and A. Schwienbacher (2020). Entrepreneurial fintech clusters. *Small Business Economics,* vol. 57, No. 2, pp. 883–903.

Geebren, A., and A. Jabbar (2021). Factors that influence customer trust and satisfaction in mobile banking: a problematization approach. *International Journal of E-Business Research,* vol. 17, No. 3, pp. 66–82.

Haroon, J.U. (2021). Rationalising high MFS charges. *The Financial Express,* 2 February.

Jumaan, I.A., N.H. Hashim, and B.M. Al-Ghazali (2020). The role of cognitive absorption in predicting mobile internet users' continuance intention: an extension of the expectation-confirmation model. *Technology in Society,* vol. 63(C).

Kalinic, Z., and others (2019). A multi-analytical approach to peer-to-peer mobile payment acceptance prediction. *Journal of Retailing and Consumer Services,* vol. 49, pp. 143–153.

Kaur, N., and R. Kiran (2014). Customer satisfaction and customer loyalty in E-Banking in India: the intricacies of relationship. *Journal of Business and Management,* vol. 16, No. 9, pp. 6–13.

Kaur, P., and others (2020). Why do people use and recommend m-wallets? *Journal of Retailing and Consumer Services,* vol. 56.

Khalid, B.K.M., M. Ichihashi and M.O. Gani (2020). Consumer Adoption of Mobile Financial Services (MFS) in Bangladesh: A Randomized Conjoint Experiment. *IDEC DP2 Series,* vol. 10, No. 5, pp. 1–29.

Khan, A.G., M.S. Mahmud, and R.P. Lima (2020). Investigating the relationship between service quality and customer satisfaction of BKash in Bangladesh. *International Journal of Financial Services Management,* vol. 10, No. 1, pp. 1–17.

Le, T.T., and others (2020). Factors affecting users' continuance intention towards mobile banking In Vietnam. *American Journal of Multidisciplinary Research and Development,* vol. 2, No. 4, pp. 42–51.

Lee, I., and Y. J. Shin, (2018). Fintech: ecosystem, business models, investment decisions, and challenges. *Business Horizons,* vol. 61, No. 1, pp. 35-46.

Lee, Y.K., and others (2012). A unified perspective on the factors influencing usage intention toward mobile financial services. *Journal of Business Research,* vol. 65, No. 11, pp. 1590–1599.

Leppäniemi, M., H. Karjaluoto, and H. Saarijärvi (2017). Customer perceived value, satisfaction, and loyalty: the role of willingness to share information. *The International Review of Retail, Distribution and Consumer Research,* vol. 27, No. 2, pp. 164–188.

Liébana-Cabanillas, F., S. Molinillo, and A. Japutra (2021). Exploring the determinants of intention to use P2P mobile payment in Spain. *Information Systems Management,* vol. 38, No. 2, pp. 165–180.

Liébana-Cabanillas, F., and others (2021). Examining the determinants of continuance intention to use and the moderating effect of the gender and age of users of NFC mobile payments: a multi-analytical approach. *Information Technology and Management,* vol. 22, No. 2, pp. 133–161.

Luqman, A., R.C. Razak, and M. Ismail (2014). A review on mobile commerce continuance intention studies and its underlying model. *Journal of basic applied scientific research,* vol. 4, No. 30, pp. 1–9.

Mujeri, M.K., and S. E. Azam (2018). Interoperability of digital finance in Bangladesh: challenges and taking-off options. Roundtable Background Paper. Institute for Inclusive Finance and Development and United Nations Capital Development Fund.

Murtuza, H.M. (2021). MFS interoperability in limbo. *New Age,* 17 May.

New Age (2020). Nagad cuts cash-out charge to Tk 9.99, 2 October.

Omigie, N.O., and others (2020). Understanding the continuance of mobile financial services in Kenya: the roles of utilitarian, hedonic, and personal values. *Journal of Global Information Management,* vol. 28, No. 3, pp. 36–57.

Parvez, J., A. Islam, and J. Woodard (2015). Mobile financial services in Bangladesh: a survey of current services, regulations, and usage in select USAID projects. Dhaka, Bangladesh: USAID.

Poromatikul, C., and others (2019). Drivers of continuance intention with mobile banking apps. *International Journal of Bank Marketing.*

Puriwat, W., and S. Tripopsakul (2021). Explaining an adoption and continuance intention to use contactless payment technologies: during the COVID-19 pandemic. *Emerging Science Journal,* vol. 5, No. 1, pp. 85–95.

Rabaa'i, A. A., and S. AlMaati (2021). Exploring the determinants of users' continuance intention to use mobile banking services in Kuwait: extending the expectation-confirmation model. *Asia Pacific Journal of Information Systems,* vol. 31, No. 2, pp. 141–184.

Reiting, P., and others (2020). Drivers and influencing factors in mobile payment acceptance. Paper presented at 10th Euro-American Conference on Telematics and Information Systems, 25–27 November, Aveiro, Portugal.

Routray, S., and others (2019). A move towards cashless economy: a case of continuous usage of mobile wallets in India. *Theoretical Economics Letters,* vol. 9, pp. 1152–1166.

Sankaran, R., and S. Chakraborty (2021). Factors impacting mobile banking in India: empirical approach extending UTAUT2 with perceived value and trust. *IIM Kozhikode Society and Management Review.*

Shin, S., and W.J. Lee (2021). Factors affecting user acceptance for NFC mobile wallets in the US and Korea. *Innovation and Management Review.*

Simiyu, S.C., and P. Kohsuwan (2019). Understanding consumers' mobile banking adoption through the integrated technology readiness and acceptance model (TRAM) perspective. *Human Behavior, Development and Society,* vol. 20, No. 4, pp. 29–40.

Tasreen, Z. (2021). The MFS industry is sprightlier today than it was two years ago. And it is thanks to Nagad. *Dhaka Tribune,* 26 March.

The Daily Star (2020a). Cut cash-out charge for mobile banking, 15 November.

        (2020b). Digital Bangladesh 2021: payment systems and fintech, 26 September.

Uddin, A.K.M. Zamir (2021). MFS industry swells riding on low-income groups. *The Daily Star,* 4 May.

United Nations Children's Fund (UNICEF) (2020). Bangladesh Education Fact Sheets.

Xiong, J., and others (2020). Enhancing loyalty to mobile payment services: an empirical study. *Issues in Information Systems,* vol. 21, No. 2.

Zarrouk, H., T. El Ghak, and A. Bakhouche (2021). Exploring economic and technological determinants of FinTech start-ups' success and growth in the United Arab Emirates. *Journal of Open Innovation: Technology, Market, and Complexity,* vol. 7, No. 1, p. 50.

Zhang, K.Z., and others (2019). Spillover effects from web to mobile payment services: the role of relevant schema and schematic fit. *Internet Research,* vol. 29, No. 6, pp. 1213–1232.

Zhao, Y., and F. Bacao (2021). How does the pandemic facilitate mobile payment? An investigation on users' perspective under the COVID-19 pandemic. *International Journal of Environmental Research and Public Health,* vol. 18, No. 3.

POLICYMAKERS' CORNER

Policymakers' corner

CHALLENGES OF MONETARY POLICY IN A DEVELOPING COUNTRY

Salehuddin Ahmed

Email: asalehuddin@gmail.com

For a central bank to be successful in regulating the financial sector, it must have relevant and pragmatic policies. It should ensure that all financial institutions, including banks, comply with prudential and management norms. Both internal and external factors are making it difficult for Bangladesh Bank to monitor and regulate the financial sector, especially banks. Bangladesh Bank has to move away from its present conventional stance towards a heterogeneous, unconventional and implementable approach. It must strike a balance showing an appropriate professional stance while avoiding the negativity of politically motivated reforms in a highly technical domain.

Keywords: prudential regulation, reform, financial sector, central bank independence

JEL classification: E42, E44, E58

Introduction

Monetary policy is an important tool to help to accelerate economic development, especially in developing countries. Through monetary policy statements (MPSs), central banks set the policy dealing with monetary targets, instruments and implementation. The central bank of Bangladesh, Bangladesh Bank, is solely responsible for monetary policy functions.

Starting from January 2006, MPSs are usually given for six months: January to June and July to December. Exceptions have been made in only few cases when a one-year MPS was issued. The most recent one-year MPS was unveiled in July 2020 for the 12-month period of fiscal year 2020/21.

The tasks of Bangladesh Bank are enormous and its functions are stated in the vision and mission statements. The vision statement is as follows:

"to develop continually as a forward-looking central bank with competent and committed professionals of high ethical standards, conducting monetary management and financial sector supervision to maintain price stability and financial system robustness, supporting rapid, broad based inclusive economic growth, employment generation and poverty eradication in Bangladesh."

Bangladesh Bank is carrying out its functions as the country's central bank as per the following mission statements:

- "Formulating monetary and credit policies;

- "Managing currency issue and regulating payment system;

- "Managing foreign exchange reserves and regulating the foreign exchange market;

- "Regulating and supervising banks and financial institutions, and advising the Government on interactions and impacts of fiscal, monetary and other economic policies."

The main purposes of Bangladesh Bank are monetary policy functions, bankers' bank, the banker of the Government and regulators as well as the supervisor of commercial banks. Most central banks have dual functions like those of Bangladesh Bank. Therefore, the performance of the economy as a whole and that of the different sectors are closely linked with the performance of Bangladesh Bank.

The vision and mission of Bangladesh Bank are quite appropriate but putting them into action has faced serious challenges and limitations. In the context of Bangladesh

Bank, the debates on macroeconomic issues centred around how Bangladesh Bank can set up monetary targets without political pressure and how far monetary policy can be implemented without any political and structural limitations.

The authority of Bangladesh Bank regarding the constituent banks and financial institutions has recently shown some limitations in controlling corruption and increasing non-performing loans, lack of good governance, weak management and finally erosion of public faith on banks. It seems Bangladesh Bank, due to both internal (within the bank itself) and external (outside the purview of the bank) hurdles, is finding itself difficult to exert effective control.

The pressure groups of stakeholders, namely Bangladesh Association of Bankers-an association of bank owners and the Association of Bankers, Bangladesh-an association of chief executive officers and managing directors of banks, play vital roles in the regulatory aspects of the banking sector. Even the chamber bodies representing business enterprises, such as the Federation of Bangladesh Chambers of Commerce and Industry and the Bangladesh Garment Manufacturers and Exporters Association also work as pressure groups on policies and procedures.

In Bangladesh, there is a dual system of control of the banking sector. The state-owned commercial banks, such as Sonali, Rupali, Janata and Agrani, and specialized banks, such as Bangladesh Small Industries and Commerce (BASIC) Bank Limited, Bangladesh Krishi Bank, Bangladesh Development Bank Limited, and some statuary banks, such as Ansar VDP Unnyan Bank and Karmasangsthan Bank, are controlled by the Bank and Financial Institution Division of the Ministry of Finance.

Nevertheless, all private commercial banks, foreign banks, non-bank financial institutions are regulated by Bangladesh Bank. The dual system of control has often resulted in uncoordinated weak policy measures for banks regulated by the Government. Bangladesh Bank has serious limitations to enforce prudential and management norms in these banks, which have made the whole banking sector weak and vulnerable through the "domino effect".

The time has come to reform and revitalize the financial sector (comprising banks, financial institutions and capital market), to make the role of banks in financial intermediation more proactive to financially excluded enterprises and to introduce more innovative financial products, such as hedging, factoring and securitization. The time has also come to look into the foreign exchange management of Bangladesh.

In this policy note, I shall briefly review some key reforms in the regulatory environment and outline what further reforms are needed to make Bangladesh Bank more efficient and effective in discharging its tasks; I shall highlight some structural issues that need to be addressed. Finally, I shall reflect on the issue of central bank independence and the need for prudential regulation in the context of complex development challenges.

Regulatory reforms so far

Banks and financial institutions in Bangladesh have been working under diversified regulatory development over the past few years. These developments were a result of felt needs on the part of the regulators, mainly Bangladesh Bank, to bring about efficiency and discipline in the financial sector. The main regulatory developments are partly discussed below:

- Regarding reform of monetary policy tools, the first step was to make the monetary policy more effective and relevant to the economy. Instruments like "repo", "reverse repo", "open market operations" to auction government securities and foreign exchange management tools were built in MPS of Bangladesh Bank. The first MPS was formally announced to the public by Bangladesh Bank in January 2006. The policy statement was independently prepared by Bangladesh Bank, without any intervention of the Government. After that, an MPS was issued in January and July of every year, demonstrating the autonomy of the central bank.

- In January 2015, Basel-III was phased in and complete capital ratios were implemented from the beginning of 2019.

- Risk management guidelines on environmental and climate change, for banks, were distributed. A green banking policy was released as well.

- Stress-testing guidelines were published for banks and financial institutions to evaluate the resilience of banks and financial institutions under various negative conditions.

- Banks had to introduce a distinct risk management unit to manage risk thoroughly and intensively.

- Banks were ordered to form a distinct capital market subsidiary. They are now being carefully controlled in terms of capital market activities.

- Guidelines have been issued to increase bank involvement in corporate social responsibility.

- Guidelines for moneychangers, insurance companies and postal transfers have already been circulated to meet the international standard on anti-money-laundering and combating the financing of terrorism.

Needed reforms

Allow me to name some aspects which Bangladesh Bank should take into account for its future stance and policies for the financial sector:

- Monetary policy should be for six months, not one year, mainly because rapid changes are taking place on domestic and external fronts.

- Setting inflation as a policy target should not be overemphasized. Inflation and growth can be achieved through the coordination of monetary and fiscal policies and other sectoral policies, such as export policy, industrial policy and investment policy.

- The policy rates should be revisited and excess liquidity in the banks should be taken care of. In the absence of investment demand and lack of opportunities in expanding businesses, Bangladesh Bank should take steps in liquidity management policies of the banks.

- The rate of exchange of Bangladesh taka and the operation of foreign exchange market should be analysed and quick action to be taken by Bangladesh Bank. I am not advocating to align the nominal effective exchange rate fully with real effective exchange rate, but the relationship between the two and the fundamental factors to be taken into account to monitor movements of the nominal effective exchange rate. The global situation with the United States dollar and other hard currencies and the recent move by China to delink its currency from the dollar have created an atmosphere which Bangladesh cannot ignore.

- Finally, Bangladesh Bank should look into the impact of COVID-19 on the economy and future challenges, remove injustice and inequality created because of misplaced priorities focused on growth only, facilitate employment generation and increase access to finance by small businesses, farmers and marginal people.

Structural issues to be considered

Having said all the things above, I would like to point out some basic issues, which Bangladesh Bank must consider for formulating its policies and guidelines, including the next MPS and subsequent ones, because the following issues cannot be resolved within a short period.

The first is the transmission mechanism of monetary policy, which is the effect of macropolicy on the micro level, such as households and business enterprises. There is one middle level through which any macropolicy passes, that is the meso level, which consists of markets and institutions, such as banks, financial institutions, merchant bankers and brokers for the capital market; regulatory agencies, such as Bangladesh Bank, Bangladesh Energy Regulatory Commission and Bangladesh Securities and Exchange Commission; and promoting agencies, such as Bangladesh Investment Development Authority and Export Promotion Bureau.

Unless these institutions function effectively, no monetary or fiscal policy measures will be properly implemented for effective impact on the desired entities. Therefore, what we need are structural reforms. There are four major weaknesses in this regard. First, as pointed out above, Bangladesh has problems with institutions, however they are defined.

Second, our goods and services markets are exposed to international influences, which have become more acute due to globalization and then due to the COVID-19 pandemic. The recent crisis between the Russian Federation and Ukraine has given rise to unsettling situations both in international political and economic orders. Until now the policy stance of Bangladesh Bank has been "growth supportive needs while attaining the targeted inflation" (Bangladesh Bank, 2020).

Against this background, our monetary policy has to be formulated and implemented in earnest. Bangladesh, like many other developing countries, is faced with a fluid situation and the consequent uncertainties. Therefore, a country's monetary policy, moving away from conventional accommodating or contractionary policies towards a heterogeneous, unconventional and implementable policy should be taken.

Third, volatility has risen out of domestic macroeconomic and political imperatives, greater incidence of default risk, corruption and lack of accountability in the banks and financial institutions. Fourth, there is poor protection of small and marginal borrowers, lending and deposit operations made under administrative guidance and pressure groups working to create undue influence on the banks and even the central bank.

Central bank independence and prudential regulatory functions

Central bank autonomy is a debatable but crucial issue. However, for Bangladesh Bank to achieve its objectives, such as controlling inflation, increasing employment, ensuring economic stability and better financial management, it must be free from all external influences. Thus, Bangladesh Bank should be fully autonomous in all its functional and decisional activities.

Some attributes of interdependence are whether the central bank can refuse credit to the Government; whether it can meet its expenses without depending on the Government; whether its Governor or Board of Directors can function independently; whether its Governor is independent in following monetary policy; whether it is free to choose its monetary instruments; and finally, whether it is free to regulate the banking policy and banks.

To have an independent and effective Bangladesh Bank, three major steps are necessary: (a) a strong and independent central bank with more focus on core banking issues, (b) a well thought out set of prudential and managerial norms of the central bank that are not subject to frequent changes due to external political or administrative pressure, and (c) a system of prompt corrective actions for management of crises and legal or administrative actions against persons responsible for crises in a particular bank or the banking system as a whole.

It must be pointed out that a balance must be made between the regulation and independence of a bank. This means that banks should neither be overregulated nor should they be left alone to enjoy complete freedom, which often results in banking disasters. This point has been very aptly articulated in a book co-auhored by Jean Tirole, the Nobel Prize winner of Economics in 2014 (Dewatripont, Rochet and Tirole, 2010).

It is important to keep in mind what financial regulation is meant to achieve. The most important objective is to protect depositors, investors, the general public and the real economy (real goods and services) as a whole. The second rationale for regulation is to minimize the domino effect of the systematic risks of the financial institutions which destroys the foundation of economic activities resulting in the loss of real output, lower growth, higher unemployment and reduction of human welfare. Good governance in the banking sector is an important agenda of our country, especially in the present context of the crisis in the banking sector. Transparency and accountability have recently become an issue of greater concern in the context of the public and private responsibility of managing banks.

A perfect example of lack of both transparency and accountability are Sonali and BASIC Bank Limited scams where both borrowers and officials colluded in a non-transparent manner and siphoned off huge amounts of public money. Those responsible for such fraud have not yet been subjected to strong administrative and legal actions. In fact, they benefited from perverse incentives, and honest and dedicated people working in the same bank and elsewhere were marginalized and pushed back into oblivion.

For Bangladesh Bank to be successful in regulating the financial sector, it has to have relevant and pragmatic policies, prudential and managerial norms and ensure that these are fully followed by all banks and financial intuitions. Discretionary powers or ad hoc measures should be avoided to safeguard the independence and autonomy of Bangladesh Bank. The typical case of policy versus discretion has to be resolved with the strong stance of Bangladesh Bank where policies and rules will be supreme, and not the discretionary powers of any individual and agency. The time has come for Bangladesh Bank to strike a balance, showing an appropriate professional stance while avoiding the danger of politically motivated actions in a highly technical domain.

Concluding remarks

The policy stances towards the financial sector of Bangladesh resulted from action on two fronts. On the one hand, the stakeholders, mainly business people, clients of banks and other users (internal and external), articulated the need for and the kind of changes required in the sector. On the other hand, in response to the stakeholders' demands, the policymakers (politicians and advisors to the Government), initiated the process of reform and change on their own (Muqtada, 2018). Therefore, changes to take the country forward took place in different phases. However, the challenge of backing the tasks to be undertaken by political will remains, and the actions to be taken should be based on facts, data and knowledge of the decision maker and implementers.

The policies and activities of the financial sector directly impact productive activities, covering both income and employment, and income and asset distribution. The indirect impacts of the financial sector operate through its effects on the fiscal and monetary policy stances. In this context, the macropolicy stances and the financial sector are critical to the accelerated and sustainable development of Bangladesh.

Some features of the economy of Bangladesh also impede in deriving optimum results of monetary policy. These are related mainly to the transmission mechanism mentioned earlier. First, the rate of financial inclusion is low at approximately 55 per cent of the population compared to more than 90 per cent in developed countries. Low monetization limits the efficacy of monetary policy. Second, low market sensitivity to the rate of interest of financial institutions is a reason for the low impact of monetary policy. Third, the policy rates, such as the repo rate and reserve money ratio, are not very effective as pointed out by a recent study (ADB, 2021) because of the predominance of national savings certificates and government borrowing from the banks. Fourth, other savings and investment instruments, such as national savings certificates and credit by microfinance institutions, are not affected much by the monetary policy. Unless the amount of money and rate of interest used in such financial instruments are used in formulating monetary policy, its efficacy will remain limited.

In a real-world situation, extraordinary independence and full autonomy of the central bank may not be easily achieved. Therefore, a central bank like Bangladesh Bank can minimize political and other external pressure by constantly engaging with politicians and policymakers and gaining public support for actions which may make it autonomous and effective. Whether in good or bad times, supervisors always face pressure from lobbyists and politicians that can undermine the stability of the financial system.

NOTE ON CONTRIBUTORS

Salehuddin Ahmed (PhD, McMaster University) is a Professor at BRAC Business School, BRAC University, Dhaka and former Governor of the Bangladesh Bank (2005–2009). He has worked as a Consultant for ADB, APDC, ESCAP, FAO, ILO, UNCRD, UNDP, UNESCO and the World Bank. He is on advisory bodies of several government and non-government agencies in Bangladesh. He was a lecturer at Dhaka University before joining the Civil Service of Pakistan and served in government departments in various capacities.

REFERENCES

Asian Development Bank (ADB) (2021). Monetary policy transmission mechanism of Bangladesh, ADB South Asia Working Paper Series, No. 86. Manila.

Bangladesh Bank (2020). *Monetary Policy Review December 2020*. Dhaka.

Muqtada, M. (2018). Macroeconomic policy, price stability and inclusive growth in Bangladesh. CPD Working Paper, No. 115.

Dewatripont, M., J.C. Rochet and, J. Tirole (2010). *Balancing the Banks: Global Lessons from the Financial Crisis*. Princeton and Oxford: Princeton University Press.

Policymakers' corner

MAINSTREAMING THE SUSTAINABLE DEVELOPMENT GOALS IN INDONESIA: AN EXPERIENCE FROM THE MINISTRY OF DEVELOPMENT PLANNING 2016-2019

Bambang Brodjonegoro

Former Minister of Finance, Minister of National Development Planning, and Minister of Research and Technology, Government of Indonesia
Email: bambrodjo@gmail.com

The Sustainable Development Goals (SDGs) improved and expanded the Millennium Development Goals (MDGs). One of the lessons learned from MDGs is that the 2030 Agenda for Sustainable Development needed to be more comprehensive, far-reaching and people-centred. Therefore, the Sustainable Development Goals embrace the principles of universal, integrated and interrelated social, economic and environmental dimensions of development. Moreover, progress towards the Sustainable Development Goals should benefit all people, especially the vulnerable, and the achievement of the Goals should involve all stakeholders, and that ambition is contained in the pledge to leave no one behind.

During my time as Minister of National Development Planning (BAPPENAS), the engagement of stakeholders was crucial in mainstreaming the Sustainable Development Goals in all activities, not only in the government work plan but also in private institutions, universities and communities. In three parts, this article will explain the current condition of progress towards the Sustainable Development Goals, the experience during my time as the Minister of BAPPENAS as well as the steps BAPPENAS took to address relevant issues, which are reducing stunting and improving sanitation access.

The 17 SDGs entail a wholesome quality of life, including eradicating poverty, improving food security, ensuring a healthy life, attaining quality education, promoting gender equality, ensuring access to clean water and sanitation, making progress towards clean energy, promoting sustainable economic growth, fostering innovation in industry, reducing inequality, creating sustainable cities, ensuring sustainable consumption, tackling climate issues, conserving marine life, protecting land life and its environment, promoting inclusive organizations and strengthening the global partnership for sustainable development.

The United Nations, as a global organization, has ongoing partnerships with Governments to ensure SDG achievement in all sectors. Some key activities that have been implemented are capacity-building, knowledge sharing, data collection and analysis, direct support to the authorities in terms of policymaking and other supporting functions. The Government of Indonesia is continuously striving to fulfil the commitment to achieve the Sustainable Development Goals and implement the 2030 Agenda, consistent with the aim of becoming a high-income country. However, the achievement of SDG targets since 2020 has slowed with the impact of COVID-19, particularly in several key sectors.

According to the 2021 voluntary national review of progress towards the Sustainable Development Goals in Indonesia, the national poverty rate increased to 10.19 per cent in 2020 from 9.22 per cent in 2019 due to the pandemic, most notably affecting women, people in rural areas and older people. The child poverty rate increased from 11.76 per cent in 2019 to 12.23 per cent in 2020. From 2015 to 2019, the Gini coefficient fell from 0.402 to 0.380 but increased to 0.385 in 2020 due to the pandemic. Indonesia strengthened social spending from 12.3 per cent of the national budget in 2019 to 12.7 per cent in 2020, the highest ever recorded.

The formulation of development plans and actions in recovering from COVID-19 needs to be supported by sufficient financial capacity. In this case, countries worldwide need to encourage financing efforts to accelerate the recovery and ensure the achievement of the Sustainable Development Goals by 2030. The Government's limited fiscal capacity during the pandemic, compounded by the various expenditures needed to address the health and economic crisis in the short term, has forced the Government to reform its financing strategy to keep its long-term development plans on track.

One strategy that can be applied to encourage the completion of development financing is a blended financing scheme. This scheme aims to mobilize private capital flows to projects that contribute to sustainable development while still providing financial returns to investors. In this case, decision makers need to develop an attractive SDG financing ecosystem for private investors. Steps that can be taken to support this effort include strengthening financial institutions to support SDG financing, creating multilateral platforms and multi-stakeholder partnerships, strengthening the role of multilateral development banks in supporting SDG financing for developing countries, intensifying efforts to increase philanthropic contributions and developing SDG debt swaps and various other innovative financing instruments.

Multiple actions can be taken to close the funding gap for the Sustainable Development Goals, including increasing official development assistance and private funding, expanding blended finance and enhancing collaboration between the Group of Seven (G7) and the Group of Twenty (G20) countries. We must also consider moving beyond gross domestic product (GDP) and traditional measure of economic growth to address the problem, with a focus on inclusivity, sustainability and resiliency. Therefore, the discourse on financing and good practices that have been proven to strengthen financial institutions for financing development need to be supported.

The blended finance scheme has been used since my time at BAPPENAS. One of the examples was the development of the partnership scheme that involves business in the agriculture sector, which was called Partnership for Indonesia Sustainable Agriculture. The scheme successfully increased farmers' productivity from 12 to 71 per cent, equal to 400,000 ha of farmland, and increased the farmers' income by 15–80 per cent. Meanwhile, private companies benefited from having excellent quality products and a sustainable supply chain.

Another example of the implementation of blended finance in Indonesia was launching the Power Plant Micro Hydro in Jambi Province. The power plant provides access to electricity for four remote villages, with 803 households and 4,448 people. The Ministry of Energy and Mineral Resources, Amil Zakat National Agency, Bank of Jambi and the United Nations Development Programme collaborated on the power plant and exemplified well-organized collaboration between government, civil society organizations, private sector, philanthropy and academia. They were also involved in creating the national SDG action plan. With their involvement, the national action plan will have a framework that can be implemented across sectors, including the financing aspect and business aspect, and the drivers to achieve the indicators and goals.

Collaboration efforts in realizing the Sustainable Development Goals are also the key to eradicating stunting in Indonesia. Stunting is a cross-sectoral issue that is related to the health sector and to other sectors, such as clean water and sanitation access, social assistance and food fortification. Stunting is not just the impaired growth of children that affects the achievement of Goal 3 (Good health and well-being), as the failure to reduce stunting will also hinder our efforts to achieve several other Goals, including Goal 4 (Quality education), Goal 1 (No poverty), Goal 8 (Decent work and economic growth), and Goal 10 (Reduced inequalities).

To integrate all of the line ministries' efforts in tackling the stunting problem in Indonesia, BAPPENAS proposed a National Strategy to Accelerate Stunting Reduction 2018–2024. The stunting reduction strategy focuses on two types of interventions.

The first type is nutrition sensitive, such as providing clean water, sanitation, food access, education services and women's empowerment. The second type is nutrition-specific, including micronutrient supplementation and supplementary feeding. These two types of interventions showed promising results, considering the prevalence of children under 5 years of age affected by stunting decreased from 30.8 per cent in 2018 to 27.7 per cent in 2019. However, the collaboration of stakeholders still needs to be improved continuously to achieve the stunting target of 14 per cent that was set in the Medium-term National Development Plan (RPJMN) 2020–2024.

As mentioned above, safely managed water, sanitation, and hygiene (WASH) are recognized as an essential priority, not just to achieve SDG 6, but also to drive progress across other goals related to health, education, nutrition and economic sectors. Especially in this time when illness caused by lack of drinking water and sanitation causes more deaths than war, WASH services are essential for people. However, access to safely managed WASH has not been fully realized in many countries, including Asia-Pacific countries, as more than 300 million people are still without improved drinking water sources, and nearly 1.5 billion people still lack access to sanitation services in the Asia-Pacific region (ESCAP, 2018).

As for Indonesia, in 2020, 44 per cent of the population had access to improved drinking water sources. Approximately 55 per cent had access to improved sanitation, and approximately 17 per cent defecated in the open. Currently, access to drinking water in Indonesia has reached 72 per cent, and access to improved basic sanitation has reached 68 per cent. Despite the increase of around 2 per cent per year from 2010, at present, the figure still shows a significant challenge: approximately 69 million people do not have access to clean water, and 80 million people do not have access to sanitation, including around 27 million people still practicing open defecation.

We realize that improving our access to water and sanitation can lead us to a more significant impact. Safely managed water and sanitation are proven to decrease diarrhoea and stunting. We were shown that the proportion of households without access to improved sanitation had strong correlation to stunting prevalence. Moreover, poor water and sanitation also lead us to decrease productivity. The *Economic Impacts of Sanitation in Indonesia* (2008) estimated the overall economic costs of poor sanitation in Indonesia to be $6.3 billion per year, equivalent to 2.3 per cent of GDP.

The Government of Indonesia committed to achieving the SDG 6 targets and implemented five central policies in the RPJMN 2020–2024: (1) improving regulation, institutional capacity, and governance; (2) increasing commitment of local key decision makers; (3) developing infrastructure and services according to regional characteristics and needs; (4) strengthening partnerships and increasing alternative financial resources; and (5) promoting hygiene behaviour at the community level to achieve safe access to water and sanitation. Understanding the significant contribution of WASH to preventing virus transmission, the WASH programme is also positioned as a critical component of the COVID-19 countermeasure targeted to accelerate economic recovery and social reform.

The Government of Indonesia believes in the convergence of the efforts of different stakeholders to achieve the SDGs. Cross-sectoral and multi-stakeholder partnerships have been recognized as vital for SDGs achievement. Therefore, it is crucial to provide an enabling environment that allows cross-sectoral and multi-stakeholder partnerships to flourish. The first step towards an enabling environment is applying a multisectoral approach in development planning and budgeting that is holistic, integrative, thematic and spatial (HITS principle). This enabled the integration line ministries' programmes and activities to achieve national priorities.

The second enabler is a multi-stakeholder coordination platform, realized through establishing the National Coordination Team of SDGs consisting of all relevant stakeholders, including the Government, philanthropy and business, academia and civil society, as mandated in Presidential Decree No. 59 Year 2017. Having this multi-stakeholder representation, active involvement and engagement of all stakeholders throughout the process, from planning, implementation, and monitoring and evaluation, can be assured. The third and the last enabler as explained before is formulating multi-stakeholder action plans, such as the stunting national strategy, and innovative financing mechanisms, such as blended finance.

NOTE ON CONTRIBUTORS

Bambang Brodjonegoro was Minister of Finance (2014–2016), Minister of National Development Planning (2016–2019), and Minister of Research and Technology (2019–2021), Government of Indonesia. He has a PhD degree in Urban Planning from the University of Illinois at Urbana-Champaign. He began his career as an academic at the Faculty of Economics and Business, University of Indonesia, and was appointed Dean in 2005.

REFERENCES

United Nations, Economic and Social Commission for Asia and the Pacific (ESCAP) (2018). Inequality of opportunity in Asia and the Pacific: water and sanitation. Social Development Policy Papers, No. 2018-05. Bangkok.

BOOK REVIEW

Book review

HOW TO ACHIEVE INCLUSIVE GROWTH

Edited by Valerie Cerra, Barry Eichengreen, Asmaa El-Ganainy, and Martin Schindler, Oxford University Press, 23 March, 2022, 912 pages, ISBN: 9780192846938, Price: $145.00 (Hardcover). Also available in: Oxford Scholarship Online

Type in the words "inclusive growth" into Google and the search engine will return more than 9 million hits. Everyone seems to be in favour of it, from official sector institutions like the Organisation for Economic Co-operation and Development (OECD) to private sector firms like McKinsey. The definition of the term from OECD is succinct: "Inclusive growth is economic growth that is distributed fairly across society and creates opportunities for all." That does not seem too controversial, but it marks a departure from the standard practice in macroeconomists to focus on boosting growth rather than worrying about how it is distributed. Nobel Laureate Robert Lucas wrote that "of the tendencies that are harmful to sound economics, the most seductive, and in my opinion the most poisonous, is to focus on questions of distribution."

The view that boosting aggregate output through structural reforms was of paramount importance was shared by policymakers and international institutions, and embodied for instance in the OECD's famous *Going for Growth* reports, a series that started in 2005. By 2017, the series stressed the importance of "addressing the concerns of those bearing the costs of reforms, and ensuring that the gains are widely shared."

A similar transformation appears underway at the International Monetary Fund (IMF). The Washington Consensus that has long guided IMF policy advice to countries does not refer to distributional concerns. Now, however, IMF has issued a hefty tome – approximately 900 pages – on how countries can achieve inclusive growth. In so doing, IMF cannot be accused of joining the bandwagon; it has to some extent led the band. Building on a decade-long effort at IMF, *How to Achieve Inclusive Growth* takes major steps forward in organizing IMF views and its broad policy advice to countries.

The book's roots

In December 2010, a Tunisian fruit vendor set himself on fire, unleashing a movement for a more inclusive society that came to be known as the Arab Spring.

In September 2011, the Occupy Wall Street movement captured headlines, with its slogan "We are the 99 per cent" drawing attention to extreme inequalities of income and wealth. Rather than sticking to its knitting and ignoring these developments, IMF drew on past analytic work and argued that inequality could be inimical to sustained growth (Ostry and Berg, 2011). This was followed by work showing that many of the areas in which IMF provided policy advice were themselves the drivers of inequality. Chief among these were fiscal policy and capital account liberalization, both of which were shown to increase inequality (Ball and others, 2013; Furceri, Loungani and Ostry, 2019), thus setting up a trade-off between the goals of efficiency and equity. Revisiting its advice on labour market policies (Blanchard, Jaumotte and Loungani, 2014) IMF did extensive work on the need for financial inclusion. This body of work is summarized in Ostry, Loungani and Berg (2019).

How to Achieve Inclusive Growth goes beyond documenting the interactions of growth and inequality and the impacts of policies on inequality to providing an extensive discussion of how policies can be designed to achieve inclusive growth. One distinctive feature of the book is the extensive use of outside experts. Three IMF economists and noted academic Barry Eichengreen edited the book, and two thirds of the 22 individual chapters of the book are co-authored by eminent experts—Richard Rogerson on labour markets, Giovanni Peri on migration, Nora Lustig on public expenditure and Raquel Fernandez on gender equality, to name a few. Superstar economists like Joseph Stiglitz and Nick Stern also co-author respective chapters on the distributional aspects of technological progress and climate change (with a foreword by Jeff Sachs). This lends considerable credibility to the endeavour. Another welcome feature is the inclusion of authors from other institutions, not just the World Bank but also the International Labour Organization and the World Trade Organization.

Seeing the forest

Though inclusive growth is becoming more accepted within macroeconomics, so far there is no canonical model that defines the term and sets out the key parameters that drive it—there is no equivalent of the Solow model (or an endogenous growth model) for inclusive growth. In the absence of a model, chapter 1 makes a valiant attempt to give the book a common structure. It lays out an inclusive growth framework in the form on a flow chart

The top part of the chart illustrates the production of incomes by the private sector using inputs of labour, capital and technology. These inputs come from domestic sources as well as through global sources, that is though migration, capital flows, and trade and technology transfers across borders. Goods and services are produced and sold in markets, and inclusive growth "requires fair and competitive marketplaces". Government inputs are shown at the bottom part of the chart. The Government "contributes inputs and establishes the right conditions for growth and for inclusion", including an overall governance framework, a political system, macroeconomic stability and public services (for which it raises taxes).

Government policies and provision of public services, for instance those that increase access to health, education and finance, affect the 'pre-distribution' phase of production – labelled as 'pre-fiscal outcomes' in the middle of the chart. In the production phase, as correctly noted in the chapter, "governments shape the functioning of the market and the incentives firms and individuals face in their employment, investment and innovation decisions". After production and the distribution of market income, the government can use tax and spending instruments to redistribute income "to increase the welfare of the very poorest and reduce income disparities according to the weights that the society places on equality" – labelled as 'post-fiscal outcomes' in the chart.

Beyond aggregate measures of inequality, the sharing of economic benefits – either though pre-distribution or redistribution policies – can be analysed along other dimensions. These are shown along the right-hand side of the chart, including race and gender, region and generation (including generations yet to come). The final element of the framework is a "feedback loop" from the distribution of outcomes to future production through labour supply, savings and entrepreneurship, including through its impact on the next generation.

A look at some trees

In addition to providing an illustration of the inclusive growth framework, the chart contains a list of the book chapters. Each item in the chart is discussed in a chapter of the book (and, in a few cases, more than one chapter). Specifically, following a chapter on the interlinkages between measures of growth and measures of inclusion, chapters 3–5 are on contributions to growth and inclusion associated with each of the main factors of production, chapters 7–9 are on the integration of factor and goods markets across national boundaries, chapters 10–15 are on the role of government in fostering inclusive growth, and chapters 16–20 are on inequalities in outcomes across genders, regions and generations. Chapter 21 includes case studies of countries or regions that improved inclusive growth through a holistic set of policies. While Nordic countries epitomize some of the best practices in inclusive growth policies, some developing countries have achieved some success. The concluding chapter contains a useful recap of the book. Every chapter of the book makes for rewarding reading. Each provides a good overview of the literature and, as the title of the book promises, a comprehensive discussion of the policies needed to achieve inclusive growth.

The chapters on the design of fiscal policies, not surprisingly, are very strong as IMF is on its home turf. But they perhaps do not give sufficient voice to the criticisms of civil society on the regressive aspects of some IMF advice (e.g. advice on VAT) or that IMF corporate guidance on fiscal policies is not reflected in its country-level policy advice, particularly when countries are in IMF programmes. A review by the Independent Evaluation Office concluded that IMF needed to be more sensitive to social and distributional consequences in its policy advice to countries in IMF programmes (IEO, 2021).

Other areas show how far IMF has come in its policy stance. As noted earlier, IMF reworked its labour market advice to countries at the onset of the Great Recession to achieve a better balance between equity and efficiency (Duval and Loungani, 2021). The evolution continues in this book, in which IMF notes that for the vast majority of individuals, payment from selling their labour services in the labour market is the single most important source of income and "for this reason, the labour market has a key role to play in achieving inclusive growth." Encouragingly, the authors suggest that "there are important areas where achieving inclusivity is a win-win proposition: that is, where making labour markets more inclusive also enhances economic efficiency and growth. Discrimination is an important such area." This is consistent with the striking findings of Hsieh and others (2019), who found that the lowering of barriers to entry for women and African Americans accounted for a quarter of the growth of per capita income in the United States of America since 1960. Other policies to provide protection to workers will often face important trade-offs between equity and efficiency. For example, employment protection legislation may provide protection for currently employed workers while diminishing access for young workers entering the labour market. Likewise, collective bargaining may reduce narrow wage differentials among union members but widen disparities between unionized and non-unionized workers (Betcherman, 2012).

The chapter on the equity and efficiency effects of financial globalization is another example of how far IMF and the profession have come over the past decade. While theory "suggests that trade flows and capital flows have the same distributional effects ... this does not appear to be the case in practice". Recent studies suggest that inequality has risen with financial globalization in both advanced and developing countries. At the same time, the efficiency effects to financial globalization are not guaranteed; it promotes growth in countries only when there are strong institutions and effective policy and regulatory frameworks. The chapter concludes that financial globalization should be carefully sequenced and coupled with other social and economic policies that help to level the distributional playing field.

It seems churlish to point out that this long book could have been made longer yet by the inclusion of a chapter on monetary and macroprudential policies and inequality. Both have been shown to generate substantive distributional effects (Furceri, Loungani and Zdzienicka, 2018; Koedijk, Loungani and Monnin, 2018). The latest ESCAP report stresses that amid shrinking fiscal space, central banks may need to step up and consider "the distributional impacts of monetary policy, managing reserves with social gains in mind, and exploring central bank digital currency for financial inclusion."

Overall, this is a remarkable attempt by IMF to provide in one comprehensive book – and made available freely in electronic format – what is known about the linkages between growth and distribution, and how countries that want to go for not only growth but inclusive growth can try to achieve their goal.

NOTE ON CONTRIBUTORS

Prakash Loungani, Independent Evaluation Office, International Monetary Fund.

REFERENCES

Ball, L.M., and others (2013). *The distributional effects of fiscal consolidation.* International Monetary Fund.

Berg, Andrew G., and Jonathan D. Ostry. Inequality and unsustainable growth: two sides of the same coin. International Monetary Fund.

Betcherman, G. (2012). Labor market institutions: a review of the literature. Policy Research Working Paper, No. 6276. Washington, D.C.: World Bank.

Blanchard, O.J., F. Jaumotte and P. Loungani (2014). Labor market policies and IMF advice in advanced economies during the Great Recession. *IZA Journal of Labor Policy,* vol. 3, No. 1, pp. 1–23.

Duval, R., and P. Loungani (2021). Designing labor market institutions in emerging market and developing economies: a review of evidence and IMF policy advice. *Comparative Economic Studies,* vol. 63, No. 1, pp. 31–83.

Furceri, D., P. Loungani, and J.D. Ostry (2019). The aggregate and distributional effects of financial globalization: Evidence from macro and sectoral data. *Journal of Money, Credit and Banking,* vol. 51, pp. 163–198.

Furceri, D., P. Loungani, and A. Zdzienicka (2018). The effects of monetary policy shocks on inequality. *Journal of International Money and Finance,* vol. 85, pp. 168–186.

Hsieh, C.T., and others (2019). The allocation of talent and U.S. economic growth. *Econometrica,* vol. 87, No. 5, pp. 1439–1474.

Independent Evaluation Office (IEO) (2021). *Growth and Adjustment in IMF-Supported Programs.* International Monetary Fund.

Koedijk, K., P. Loungani and, P. Monnin (2018). Monetary policy, macroprudential regulation and inequality: an introduction to the special section. *Journal of International Money and Finance,* vol. 85, pp. 163–167.

Ostry, J.D., P. Loungani, and A. Berg (2019). *Confronting Inequality: How Societies Can Choose Inclusive Growth.* Columbia University Press.

United Nations, Economic and Social Commission for Asia and the Pacific (ESCAP) (2022). *Economic and Social Survey of Asia and the Pacific.*

Book review

FISCAL AND MONETARY POLICIES IN DEVELOPING COUNTRIES: STATE, CITIZENSHIP AND TRANSFORMATION

By Rashed Al Mahmud Titumir, Routledge, December 24, 2021, ISBN:9781032063461, 302 pages, Price: $128 (Hardcover), $39.16 (eBook)

Rashed Al Mahmud Titumir's book, *Fiscal and Monetary Policies in Developing Countries: State, Citizenship and Transformation,* is a testimony on the role of fiscal and monetary policies in state-building in developing countries. An economist from an advanced economy may be perplexed by the argument that fiscal and monetary policies contribute to state-building, because conventional thinking limits the role of fiscal and monetary policies in state-building. The book has provided food for thought for those who are intrigued by the role of fiscal and monetary policies in state-building in developing countries.

Fiscal policy can play an unwavering role in promoting economic growth, diversifying the economy, enhancing productivity, reducing poverty, improving living standards and reducing inequality in income, wealth and social status. Tax policy, public expenditure policy and public enterprises policy are pillars of fiscal policy that contribute to state-building in developing countries.

The role of monetary policy is crucial in state-building, by making a robust financial system and financial reform policy, growth-promoting interest rate and credit policy. Monetary policy contributes to stabilizing the economy through influencing money supply/credit, interest rate and exchange rate. Additionally, monetary policy tools can contribute to financial inclusion and expansion of citizens' access to credit and financial services in the formal financial sector in developing countries.

Conflicting objectives vs. complementarity of fiscal and monetary policies

Both fiscal and monetary policies face trade-offs, but together they complement each other. Developing countries face a tricky situation in the choice of fiscal and monetary policies. Politicians and policymakers have to reconcile conflicting objectives in a broader context that influences fiscal and monetary policies. Higher and faster economic growth and the equitable distribution of income are the crucial conflicting objectives in the fiscal policy regime. Similarly, economic growth, price stability and foreign exchange rate stability are conflicting priorities in the monetary policy regime.

The role of fiscal policy shot to prominence twice in recent years – first after the 2008 financial crisis and second during the COVID-19 pandemic – which challenged the neoclassical counter-revolution since the 1970s. The pandemic fractured pre-existing structural rigidities in developing and developed economies, and the author observed that this necessitated "a rethinking of fiscal and monetary policies—the main vehicles for relief, recovery, and reconstruction" (p. 269).

The author also says, "Keynes and post-Keynesians failed to incorporate politics and political processes into their analysis. Since politicians seek to benefit themselves rather than the whole nation or national economy through fiscal and monetary policies, this theory argues that it creates a worse economic performance than occurs under a free market" (p. 54).

The author emphasizes the existence of both formal and informal institutions in the political and economic sphere. Informal institutions drive the political settlement developed with the networks of political power in the economy in developing countries. He writes, "Political settlements are a significant determinant of the direction of fiscal and monetary policies, distorting the linkages between factors of production and labor vis-à-vis capital returns in the circular flow" (p. 61).

The choice between fiscal and monetary policies must be based not only on economic but also on social and political considerations. Both sets of policies impinge on effective demand; they are likely to produce significantly different effects on a community level. Policymakers need rigorous empirical studies on the distributional consequences of fiscal and monetary policy instruments (p. 118).

There is a consensus among economists that macroeconomic policies generally serve the ruling class's interests in developing countries. Thus fiscal and monetary policies should be taken less as economic policies but more as tools for a social contract and political settlements.

The author claims that his book contributes to a road map for transformation and sustainable fiscal and monetary policies catering to a citizen-state relationship. The author also captures the idiosyncrasies of state-building, the state-citizen relationship, equality, equity, fairness and welfare, economic growth, jobs creation, price stability, formal and informal institutions, and political settlement in developing countries.

The points of contention

The reader can find several trivializing issues in the book.

First, many studies suggest that only 50 to 60 per cent of the population in developing countries have access to financial services. According to the World Bank, 31 per cent of the population globally in 2021 still did not have access to formal financial services. The book could have included the necessary discussion on how economic growth, distribution and state-building can be achieved with the help of monetary policy in developing countries.

Second, the author criticizes Thomas Piketty's *r>g* mathematical formula for economic inequality. Piketty views that income inequality results from the situation when returns on capital *r* exceed the economic growth rate *g*. However, readers will find no convincing explanation of why economic inequality has increased in developing countries despite their low economic growth, low total factor productivity, low returns on capital and progressive taxation.

Despite the decolonization of developing countries, the author claims that the colonial legacy of an extractive fiscal policy has continued. However, Nepal, a least developed country which was never colonized by any Western power, has the most extractive fiscal policy among developing countries, reflected in a high tax-GDP ratio. The author's generalization of colonial legacy as a reason for extractive fiscal policy in developing countries does not hold in the case of Nepal. The question to ask is: should Nepal be considered an exception rather than the norm?

Former editor-in-chief of *Foreign Policy* magazine, Moisés Naím, writes, "Inequality will continue to rise in societies where 'c > h'. Here, 'c' stands for the degree to which corrupt politicians and public employees, along with their private-sector cronies, break laws for personal gain, and 'h' represents the degree to which honest politicians and public employees uphold fair governing practices."

The author discusses corruption as an event of tax evasion. However, the biggest threat to state-building in developing countries is fiscal and monetary policy corruption. Corruption is the leading cause of sluggish economic growth and growing income and wealth inequality and one of the primary sources of social unrest in developing countries.

The book is a good read on the role of fiscal and monetary policies in state-building for scholars, students, policymakers and politicians.

NOTE ON CONTRIBUTORS

Bhim Bhurtel, Nepal Open University, Columnist, *Asia Times.*

REFERENCES

Naím, Moisés (2014). The problem with piketty's inequality formula: in focusing on capital earnings, the economist overlooked a critical factor – corruption, *The Atlantic,* 28 May. Available at www.theatlantic.com/international/archive/2014/05/the-problem-with-pikettys-inequality-formula/371653/.